ACCLAIM FOR *WHERE YOU GO IS NOT WHO YOU'LL BE*

"Frank Bruni takes on the frenzy's underlying articles of faith, exposing as myths the beliefs that there are only 10 worthy colleges in America, that this is the most important decision of a child's life, and that those who don't get their ticket punched for the Harvard gravy train are doomed. And he does this with such finesse and such honest, accessible writing that he will have the gratitude of anxious parents everywhere. He should also be knee-deep in mash notes from every high school college counselor and most—though not all—deans of admission."

—*The Chicago Tribune*

"Deeply felt...Bruni tries to reeducate readers about what best really means."

—*The New York Times*

"A valuable and well-reported book...He makes concrete research come to life via heartfelt interviews with anxious parents and their children. Bruni is a writer's writer."

—*National Journal*

"Dispels the myth that elite colleges are a requirement for greatness."

—*Fortune*

"The supposition that intelligence can be measured, that success can be predicted and that the combination of the two creates happiness is rightly exploded in this sharply observed and deeply felt book. In deconstructing the college admissions process, Frank Bruni exposes the folly by which enfranchised people measure their own lives. He speaks with a voice of urgent sanity."

—Andrew Solomon, National Book Award–winning author of *Far from the Tree: Parents, Children, and the Search for Identity*

"Mr. Bruni will have earned our gratitude if even a few families heed his sensible advice and opt out of this rat race."

—*The Wall Street Journal*

"Excellent...The deeper message of *Where You Go Is Not Who You'll Be* is that who our children really are when they go matters a whole lot more than wherever it is they're going."

—*New York Times*, *Motherlode* blog

"Frank Bruni provides the perfect course correction for students *and* parents who get sucked into the college admissions frenzy. I should know. I was one of them."

—Katie Couric

"Written in a lively style but carrying a wallop, this is a book that family and educators cannot afford to overlook as they try to navigate the treacherous waters of college admissions."

—*Kirkus Reviews*

"With great energy and enthusiasm, *New York Times* columnist Bruni takes a pin to 'our society's warped obsession with elite colleges' and provides a commonsense check to the yearly 'admissions mania' of students competing for coveted slots at top schools."

—*Publishers Weekly*

"Parents naturally want the best for our children, and that's made us vulnerable to an exorbitant, anxiety-producing, soul-crushing college admissions process. Bruni not only challenges its premise but offers (desperately!) welcome relief, reassurance and comfort to those going through it. I will be giving this book to every single family I know with a high schooler!"

—Peggy Orenstein, author of *Cinderella Ate My Daughter*

"A mind-opening book. I'm pretty sure it's going to change my life. It's already changed the way I think."

—Pamela Druckerman, author of *Bringing Up Bébé*

"Here's a book that belongs on the coffee table of every family preparing to enter the college admissions war. Its message is clear: Lay down your arms and reframe your ideas about success and failure, winners and losers, and the American Dream!"

—*Spirituality & Practice*

"For students, parents, teachers and everyone else suffering during the college admissions process, Frank Bruni offers an outstanding resource. WHERE YOU GO IS NOT WHO YOU'LL BE is a thought-provoking look at how the system works—and a fresh, reassuring reminder of what really matters in the college experience."

—Gretchen Rubin, author of *The Happiness Project*

"His clear, well-researched book should be required reading for everyone caught up in the college-admissions game."

—William Deresiewicz, author of *Excellent Sheep*

"Your worth is not determined by the university you went to. Or, in other words, WHERE YOU GO IS NOT WHO YOU'LL BE. Hallelujah. That's the exact mantra every student and parent must heed as they navigate the stressful college admissions process. I'm doing it for the fourth time and this excellent writer's new book could not have come at a better time for me. As Frank Bruni brilliantly demonstrates, your worth is your worth and it's yours to make wherever you go."

—Maria Shriver

"For families caught up in college-application madness, this book provides a much-needed tonic. For the rest of us, it's an inspiring call for a wiser, saner approach to American higher education." —Paul Tough, author of *How Children Succeed*

"For any adolescent sweating college admissions—and perhaps more critically, for any parent sweating college admissions—this book is required reading…Bruni amasses evidence that lives up to his title, showing readers that there are thousands of paths to success in this world…and that the fetish we've made of marquee-name colleges is as practically misguided as it is psychologically destructive. The result is a beta-blocker and eye-opener all rolled into one."

—Jennifer Senior, author of *All Joy and No Fun*

Where You Go Is Not Who You'll Be

An Antidote to the College Admissions Mania

FRANK BRUNI

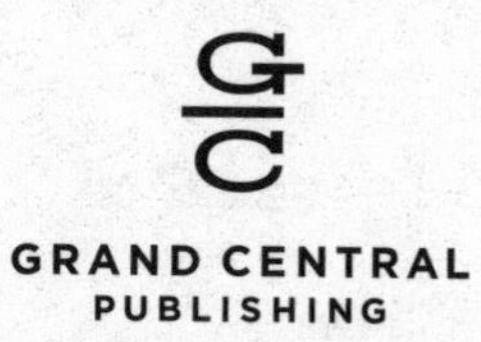

NEW YORK BOSTON

Grand Central Publishing
Hachette Book Group
1290 Avenue of the Americas
New York, NY 10104

www.HachetteBookGroup.com

Printed in the United States of America

LSC-C

Originally published in hardcover by Hachette Book Group
First trade edition: March 2016

10 9 8 7 6 5

Grand Central Publishing is a division of Hachette Book Group, Inc.
The Grand Central Publishing name and logo is a trademark of Hachette Book Group, Inc.

The Hachette Speakers Bureau provides a wide range of authors for speaking events. To find out more, go to www.hachettespeakersbureau.com or call (866) 376-6591.

The publisher is not responsible for websites (or their content) that are not owned by the publisher.

Library of Congress Cataloging-in-Publication Data

Bruni, Frank.
Where you go is not who you'll be : an antidote to the college admissions mania / Frank Bruni.
pages cm
ISBN 978-1-4555-3270-4 (hardback) — ISBN 978-1-4789-5621-1 (audio download) — ISBN 978-1-4789-5923-6 (audiobook) 1. Universities and colleges—United States—Admission. 2. College choice-United States. I. Title.
LB2351.2.B78 2015
378.1'610973—dc23

2014049043

ISBN 978-1-4555-3268-1 (pbk.)

To all the high school kids in this country who are dreading the crossroads of college admissions and to all the young adults who felt ravaged by it. We owe you and the whole country a better, more constructive way.

Contents

Introduction

Peter Hart didn't try for Harvard, Princeton or any of the Ivies. That wasn't the kind of student he'd been at New Trier High School, which serves several affluent suburbs north of Chicago. Nearly all of its roughly one thousand graduating seniors each year go on to higher education, and nearly all of them know, from where they stand among their peers and from the forecasts of guidance counselors, what sort of college they can hope to attend. A friend of Peter's was ranked in the top five of their class; she set her sights on Yale—and ended up there. Peter was ranked somewhere around 300: not great but wholly respectable considering the caliber of students at New Trier. He aimed for the University of Michigan or maybe the special undergraduate business school at the University of Illinois.

Both rejected him.

He went to Indiana University instead, and arrived there feeling neither defeated nor exhilarated. He was simply determined to make the most of the place and to begin plotting a career and planning an adult life.

Right away he noticed a difference. At New Trier, a public school posh enough to pass for private, he'd always had a sense of himself as someone somewhat ordinary, at least in terms of his studies. He lacked his peers' swagger and ready-made eloquence. He wasn't especially quick to raise his hand, to offer an opinion, to seize a position of leadership. At Indiana, though, the students in his freshman dorm and in his freshman classes weren't as uniformly poised and showily gifted as the New Trier kids had been, and his self-image went through a transformation.

"I really felt like I was a competent person," he told me when I interviewed him in June 2014, shortly after he'd turned twenty-eight. "It was confidence-building." He thrived during that first year, getting a 3.95 grade point average, which earned him admission into an honors program for undergraduate business majors. And he thrived during the rest of his time at Indiana, drawing the attention of professors, becoming vice president of a business fraternity on campus, cobbling together the capital to start his own tiny real estate enterprise—he bought, fixed up and rented small houses to fellow students—and finagling a way, off-campus, to get interviews with several of the top-drawer consulting firms that trawled for recruits at the Ivies but often bypassed schools like Indiana. Upon graduation, he took a plum job in the Chicago office of the Boston Consulting Group, where he recognized one of the other new hires: the friend from New Trier who'd gone to Yale. Traveling a more gilded path, she'd arrived at the very same destination.

Peter worked for three years with the Boston Consulting Group and another two with a private equity firm in Manhattan. When I talked with him, he was between his first and second year at Harvard's graduate business school. Yes, he said, many of his Harvard classmates had undergraduate degrees fancier than his; no, he said, he didn't feel that his Indiana education put him at any disadvantage. Besides which, he and most of the others in the Harvard MBA program had been out of college for as long as they'd been in it. What they'd learned in the workplace since graduation had more bearing on their assurance and performance at Harvard than did anything picked up in any class, let alone the name of their alma mater.

The main, lasting relevance of Indiana, he told me, was the way it had turned him into a bolder, surer person, allowing him to discover and nurture a mettle that hadn't been teased out before. "I got to be the big fish in a small pond," he said. Now, if he wanted to, he could swim with the sharks.

Jenna Leahy, twenty-seven, went through the college admissions process two years after Peter did. She, too, was applying from a charmed school: in her case, Phillips Exeter Academy, which was less than a mile from her family's New Hampshire home and which she attended as a day student. She wasn't at the very top of her class but she had as many A's as B's. At Exeter, one of the most storied prep schools in America, that was nothing to sneeze at. She was also a captain of the cross-country team and active in so many campus organizations that when graduation day rolled around, she received one of the most coveted prizes, given to a student who'd brought special distinction to the academy.

Jenna had one conspicuous flaw: a score on the math portion of the SAT that was in the low 600s. Many selective colleges cared more than ever about making sure that each new freshman class had high SAT scores, because that was one of the criteria by which *U.S. News & World Report* ranked schools in its annual survey, the influence of which had risen exponentially since its dawn in the 1980s. In fact, the college on which Jenna set her sights, Claremont McKenna, cared so much that its dean of admissions would later be exposed for fabricating and inflating that statistic.

Jenna applied early to Claremont McKenna. And was turned down.

She was stunned. She couldn't quite believe it. And partly because of that, she didn't sink into a funk but moved quickly to tweak her dreams and widen her net, sending applications to Georgetown University, Emory University, the University of Virginia and Pomona College, which is one of Claremont McKenna's sister schools. She threw in a few more, to have some insurance, though she was relatively certain that she wouldn't need it.

In early spring the news came. Georgetown said no. Emory said no. No from Virginia. No from Pomona. She felt like some kind of magnet for rejection: Earlier that semester, her first serious boyfriend had broken up with her. He was a sophomore at Stanford, the sort of school she was now being told she simply wasn't good enough for. What *was* she good enough for? What in the world was going on? Many of her Exeter classmates were bound for the Ivies and their ilk, and they didn't seem to her any more capable than she. Was it because they were legacy cases, from families with more money than hers?

All she knew was that they had made the cut and she hadn't.

"I felt so worthless," she told me. "It was a very, very depressing time."

As she remembers it, she was left essentially with two

options. One was Scripps College: another of Claremont McKenna's sister schools, though not quite as desired as Pomona. The other was the University of South Carolina. It wanted her badly enough that it offered her a significant scholarship. "But that wasn't enough for me," she said. "I wanted a name. I wanted some prestige." That was the immediate legacy of the application process. She was determined to grab whatever bragging rights she could.

But there was another, better legacy, which came later. Once she got through the summer, crossed the country to Southern California, beheld how gorgeous the Scripps campus was and saw how well she fit in there, she realized not only that the most crushing chapter of her life was in the past but that it hadn't crushed her. Not even close. Actually, it had helped her separate the approval that others did or didn't give her from what she believed—no, *knew*—about herself.

One day she happened to sign up for a day trip from Scripps to Tijuana, Mexico, to help do some painting and other charitable work in an especially impoverished neighborhood. When she got there, she recalled, "I held a baby who could barely breathe, and the mother didn't have the money to take the baby to the doctor, and you could literally see the United States on the other side of the border. I was just blown away." The moment stayed with her, and during her sophomore year, she applied for a grant that would give her the funds necessary to live in Tijuana for the summer and work with indigent children there. She got it.

A pattern emerged. "I applied for things fearlessly," she said, "because I knew now that I was worth something even if I wasn't accepted." Rejection was arbitrary. Rejection was survivable.

She entered a contest to attend a special conference at the Carter Center in Georgia and to meet Jimmy Carter, and she was chosen. She put in a request to study abroad in Senegal and then in Paris, and was permitted to do both. After graduation she went to work for Teach For America and, toward the end of her time with the organization, she sought a special fellowship in school administration that was typically given only to educators with more experience. She nonetheless received it, and later got a grant to develop a new charter school in Phoenix, where she now lives. That school, serving children from low-income families, opened in August 2014. Jenna is its cofounder and its director of students and operations.

"I never would have had the strength, drive or fearlessness to take such a risk if I hadn't been rejected so intensely before," she told me. "There's a beauty to that kind of rejection, because it allows you to find the strength within."

Is Peter's example so remarkable? I don't think so. People bloom at various stages of life, and different individuals flourish in different climates. The hothouse of secondary school favors only some.

And Jenna's arc isn't unusual in the least. The specific details, the proper nouns: Those are hers and hers alone. But for every person whose contentment and fulfillment come from faithfully executing a predetermined script, there are at least ten if not a hundred who had to rearrange the pages and play a part they hadn't expected to, in a theater they hadn't envisioned. Life is defined by little snags and big setbacks; success is determined by the ability to distinguish between the two and rebound from either. And there's no single juncture, no one crossroads, on which everything hinges.

So why do so many Americans—anxious parents, addled children—treat the college admissions process as if it were precisely that?

This book was born during the annual height of that process, as another March ended and the chatter among many of the adults around me grew predictably heavy with the words *acceptance*, *rejection*, *safety school* and such. Their children had been waiting three months or longer to find out whether the applications they'd submitted to their dream schools would do the trick. The notices would come in any day. The suspense was at its peak.

I was familiar with it from the previous March and the March before that, because to live among Americans affluent enough to give their kids a certain kind of grounding and gilding is to recognize a particular rhythm to the year and specific mile markers on the calendar. November 1 is the deadline for many early-admission applications, January 1 for a number of general-admission applications. In the days just before April 1, the schools' decisions dribble out, and I'll watch the parents in my orbit exult like they rarely exult or reel like they seldom reel. The intensity of these reactions always stops me short, because it attaches a make-or-break importance to a finite circle of exalted institutions—and to private colleges and universities over public ones—that isn't supported by the evidence, by countless stories like Peter's and Jenna's, by the careers and the examples all around me, by common sense. A sort of mania has taken hold, and its grip seems to grow tighter and tighter.

I'm describing the psychology of a minority of American families; the majority of them are focused on making sure that their kids simply attend a decent college—any decent college—

and on finding a way to help them pay for it. (Note: In this book I'll often use "college" as a catchall term, and interchangeably with "university," but only in reference to the undergraduate portion and years of an institution, like the University of Michigan or Stanford, that also has graduate schools and doctoral programs.) When I asked Alice Kleeman, the college adviser at Menlo-Atherton High School in the Bay Area of California, about the most significant changes in the admissions landscape over the twenty years that she has inhabited it, the lust for elite schools and the fixation on them was only the third dynamic she mentioned. The first? "More students are unable to attend their college of first choice because of money," she said, alluding to the country's economic doldrums over the last decade and the high cost of higher education. Second, she brought up what she saw as the positive development of colleges being willing to admit and extend financial aid to undocumented immigrants. Her answers were crucial reminders that an obsession with the Ivies and other colleges of their perceived caliber is far more privilege than curse.

But the number of parents and students who succumb to it is by no means small, and that's clear in the escalation of applications to elite schools and in the dizzying expansion and expense of college admissions coaching. There's a whole industry devoted to prepping and packaging students, to festooning them with all the right ribbons and all the prettiest bows. For too many parents and their children, getting into a highly selective school isn't just another challenge, just another goal. A yes or no from Amherst or Dartmouth or Duke or Northwestern is seen as the conclusive measure of a young person's worth, a binding verdict on the life that he or she has led up until that point, an incontestable harbinger of the successes or disappointments to come. Winner or loser: This is when the judgment is made. This is the great, brutal culling.

What madness. And what nonsense.

For one thing, the admissions game is too flawed and too rigged to be given so much credit. For another, the nature of a student's college experience—the work that he or she puts into it, the skills that he or she picks up, the self-examination that's undertaken, the resourcefulness that's honed—matters more than the name of the institution attended. In fact students at institutions with less hallowed names sometimes demand more of those places and of themselves, convinced that they have ground to make up, a disadvantage to compensate for. Or, freed somewhat from a focus on the packaging of their education, they get to the meat of it. In any case, there's only so much living and learning that take place inside a lecture hall, a science lab or a dormitory. Education is indeed everything, but it happens across a spectrum of settings and in infinite ways. It starts well before college. It continues long after college. College has no monopoly on the ingredients for professional success or for a life well lived.

I know many wildly accomplished people who attended Ivy League schools and other highly selective private colleges and benefited in precisely the ways that alumni of these institutions are supposed to. I know more who attended public universities and schools without major reputations, and in this book I'll introduce some of them, describing their paths, letting them reflect on their achievements and putting college in a saner, healthier, more accurate perspective. I even know a fair number of distinguished overachievers who never graduated from college. I wouldn't recommend that last route, but my reasons aren't solely practical. They're intellectual, philosophical, spiritual. College is a singular opportunity to rummage through and luxuriate in ideas, to give your brain a vigorous workout and your soul a thorough investigation, to realize how very large the world is and to contemplate your desired place in it. And that's being lost in the admissions mania, which sends the message that college is a sanctum to be breached—a border to be crossed—rather than a land to be inhabited and tilled for all that it's worth.

This mania has many roots, a few of which I'll look at in the pages to come. But it can't be divorced from a chapter of American life and a corrosion of American discourse in which not just Chevrolet and Cartier but everyday people worry about their "brands," and in which everything imaginable is subdivided into microclimates of privilege and validation. At the amusement park, you can do general admission or a special pass or an even fancier package that puts you instantly at the front of every line. At the Equinox fitness chain, trainers are designated by numbers—Tiers 1, 2 and 3—that signal their experience and hourly rate, and there are deluxe hideaways within certain Equinox clubs, which use eye-scanning technology to figure out who belongs. In the plane, it's no longer just first class and coach. For a surcharge, there's extra legroom. For frequent fliers, there are exit-row seats, early boarding and first dibs on the overhead bins. You ascend and cling to a designated stratum with designated perks: gold, silver, platinum, diamond. In the United States circa 2015, it's not just shoes, handbags and SUVs that signal your status and how enviable you are. It's a whole lot else, and colleges have climbed higher and higher up the list—against all reason, and with needlessly hurtful consequences.

"The demand for elite institutions is through the roof,"

Anthony Carnevale sighed to me one day. Carnevale is the director of Georgetown University's Center on Education and the Workforce, which studies their relationship and interplay, and I've gone to him repeatedly when working on columns for the *New York Times* about higher education. He's informed. He's wise. And he's flummoxed and deeply frustrated by the premium that so many families place on the supposed luster of a first-choice college and by the breathlessness with which kids approach the admissions process.

"Life is something that happens slowly, and whether or not they go to their first choice isn't that important," he noted. "It's not the difference between Yale and jail. It's the difference between Yale and the University of Wisconsin or some other school where they can get an excellent education.

"They should be thinking more about what they're going to *do* with their lives," he continued. "And what college is supposed to do is to allow you to live more fully in your time." It's supposed to prime you for the next chapter of learning, and for the chapter beyond that. It's supposed to put you in touch with yourself, so that you know more about your strengths, weaknesses and values and can use that information as your mooring and compass in a tumultuous, unpredictable world. It's supposed to set you on your way, and if you expect it to be a guarantee forevermore of smooth sailing, then you've got trouble infinitely greater than any rejection notice.

In March 2014, just before Matt Levin was due to start hearing from the schools to which he'd applied, his parents, Craig and Diana, handed him a letter. They didn't care whether he read it right away, but they wanted him to know that it had been written before they found out how he fared. It was their response to the outsize yearning and dread that they saw in him and in so many of the college-bound kids at Cold Spring Harbor High School, in a Long Island suburb of New York City. It was their bid for some sanity.

Matt, like many of his peers, was shooting for the Ivies: in his case, Yale, Princeton or Brown. He had laid the groundwork. He had punched all the necessary holes. Good SAT scores? After studying with a private tutor, which was pro forma for kids in his upper-middle-class community, he had scored close to the median for students at the Ivies in his sights. Sports? He was on Cold Spring Harbor's varsity baseball team, toggling between the positions of second baseman and shortstop. Music? He played alto sax in several of Cold Spring Harbor's bands. Academics? He was the recipient of a special prize for junior-year students with the highest grade point averages, and he was a member of pretty much every honor society at the school. Character? He had logged more than one hundred hours of community service.

For Yale, Princeton and Brown, that wasn't enough. Matt's top three choices all turned him down.

His mother, Diana, told me that on the day he got that news, "He shut me out for the first time in seventeen years. He barely looked at me. Said, 'Don't talk to me and don't touch me.' Then he disappeared to take a shower and literally drowned his sorrows for the next forty-five minutes." He kept to himself all that evening as he tried to summon the energy to study for a physics test. He went to bed after midnight—still mute, still withdrawn.

The next morning he rallied and left the house wearing a sweatshirt with the name of the school that had been his fourth choice and had accepted him: Lehigh University. By then he had read his parents' letter, more than once. That they felt compelled to write it says as much about our society's warped obsession with elite colleges as it does about the Levins' warmth, wisdom and generosity. I share the following parts of it because the message in them is one that many kids in addition to their son need to hear:

Dear Matt,

On the night before you receive your first college response, we wanted to let you know that we could not be any prouder of you than we are today. Whether or not you get accepted does not determine how proud we are of everything you have accomplished and the wonderful person you have become. That will not change based on what admissions officers decide about your future. We will celebrate with joy wherever you get accepted—and the happier you are with those responses, the happier we will be. But your worth as a person, a student and our son is not diminished or influenced in the least by what these colleges have decided.

If it does not go your way, you'll take a different route to get where you want. There is not a single college in this country that would not be lucky to have you, and you are capable of succeeding at any of them.

We love you as deep as the ocean, as high as the sky, all the way around the world and back again—and to wherever you are headed.

Mom and Dad

ONE

THE UNSUNG ALMA MATERS

"My wife really wanted to go to the University of Virginia and didn't get in. I really wanted to go to Georgetown and didn't get in. So we both ended up at Delaware. It was a place where all of us felt that if we worked hard, we could do well. I never felt like the school wasn't going to give me the tools to be successful."

—Chris Christie, the governor of New Jersey and a 1984 graduate of the University of Delaware

There's a widespread conviction, spoken and unspoken, that the road to riches is trimmed in Ivy and the reins of power held by those who've donned Harvard's crimson, Yale's blue and Princeton's orange, not just on their chests but in their souls.

No one told that to the Fortune 500.

They're the American corporations with the highest gross revenues. The list is revised yearly. As I wrote this paragraph in the summer of 2014, the top 10 were, in order, Wal-Mart, Exxon Mobil, Chevron, Berkshire Hathaway, Apple, Phillips

66, General Motors, Ford Motor, General Electric and Valero Energy. And this was the list, in the same order, of schools where their chief executives got their undergraduate degrees: the University of Arkansas; the University of Texas; the University of California, Davis; the University of Nebraska; Auburn; Texas A&M; the General Motors Institute (now called Kettering University); the University of Kansas; Dartmouth College and the University of Missouri–St. Louis. Just one Ivy League school showed up.

The chief executive of Wal-Mart, Doug McMillon, went on from the University of Arkansas to get a master's in business administration. That was at the University of Tulsa. Likewise, Joe Gorder, the chief executive of Valero, didn't end his education with his undergraduate degree, from the University of Missouri–St. Louis. He, too, acquired an MBA—from Our Lady of the Lake University.

When I looked just a few notches farther down the list of the Fortune 500 chief executives and took in the top 30, I spied the University of Central Oklahoma, the University of Pittsburgh, the University of Minnesota, Fordham and Penn State—along with Cornell, Princeton, Brown, Northwestern and Tufts. It was a profoundly diverse collection, reflecting the myriad routes to a corner office.

Among the American-born chief executives of the top 100 corporations on the list, about thirty went to college in the Ivy League or at a dozen or so schools, from MIT to Bowdoin, with similarly selective admissions practices. A handful did their undergraduate work at the most widely and traditionally revered public schools—the University of Texas, for example, and the University of Michigan. But forty or so went to public schools of considerably less luster, at least in the eyes of many college-bound kids and their parents; never finished school; or were educated outside the United States. The remaining quarter went to a mix of selective and less selective private colleges and to schools that exist in narrow niches or are overtly religious in nature.

In other words there was no pattern. None at all. But in so many of our conversations about success and so many of the portraits that those of us in the media paint of accomplished individuals, we insist on divining one. And we often go with the obvious, equating achievement later in life with time spent earlier in rarefied enclaves. It's a cleaner narrative than saying that anything goes. It's a more potent mythology: There are the Round Table's gleaming knights, chosen young and charmed forevermore, and then there are the vassals who make do on the other side of the moat.

The discussion about the fortune-kissed denizens of 1600 Pennsylvania Avenue is a case in point. We've heard repeatedly in recent years that elite schools have a stranglehold on the White House, because the last four presidents are draped in Ivy. Barack Obama got his undergraduate degree from Columbia, his law degree from Harvard. George W. Bush went from Yale to Harvard Business School. Bill Clinton: Georgetown and then Yale Law. George H. W. Bush: a bachelor's from Yale.

But that's only a fraction of the fuller story, whose moral is not the magic that happened the moment these men were accepted by the most exclusive clubhouses of higher education. For starters, Obama didn't *begin* college in the Ivy League. Where he headed right after high school was to Occidental College in Los Angeles. Columbia came later, via a transfer, proving that the initial culling isn't the last word.

As for the Bushes, they were both legacy cases at Yale. Prescott Bush, a United States senator, had studied there before them, paving the way for his son and grandson. For the two Georges, getting into Yale was less a seal of approval and a springboard to greatness than an inevitability, and their life trajectories arguably had more to do with their bloodlines—with networks independent of Yale—than with anything that the Yale admissions committee thrilled to or with anything they gleaned in a lecture hall on the New Haven campus. I don't say that as an insult, nor am I belittling their talents. I'm just describing how the world works.

But let's look beyond the Bushes, Clinton and Obama. Let's expand the ring of political heavyweights, first by reaching further back in history. Ronald Reagan? He attended Eureka College, a tiny school in Illinois that, in 2015, was ranked only 29th among "Regional Colleges (Midwest)" on the infernal *U.S. News & World Report* survey. Jimmy Carter? He moved around during his undergraduate and graduate years, landing not just at the U.S. Naval Academy but also at Georgia Southwestern College and Georgia Tech. Richard Nixon got his bachelor's from Whittier College in Southern California. Lyndon Baines Johnson got his from Southwest Texas State Teachers College.

And if we consider running mates and politicians who didn't make it all the way to the White House but got as far as their party's presidential nomination, the collection of colleges is similarly diverse. Vice President Joe Biden went to the University of Delaware (and then to Syracuse University's law school). Paul Ryan, the Republican vice presidential nominee in 2012, went to Miami University of Ohio. John Edwards, the Democratic vice presidential nominee in 2004, got his undergraduate degree from North Carolina State University and his law degree from the University of North Carolina at Chapel Hill.

I hesitate to mention anything about the education of Dan Quayle, the country's vice president from 1989 to 1993, given that he became known in no small part for his inability to spell the word *potato*. (He gave it a bonus vowel, dangling an *e* on the end.) But he *was* a mere heartbeat away from the presidency, and he traveled to that position by way of DePauw University in Indiana and law school at Indiana University. Biden's schooling in Delaware, Edwards's in North Carolina, Quayle's in Indiana and Carter's in Georgia illuminate something important: If a person is making a career that's closely tied to a particular geographic area, a school in and of that area may be more relevant and helpful than a highly selective institution elsewhere. And Biden, Edwards, Quayle and Carter all made such careers. The first three won election to the U.S. Senate from the states in which they had studied. Carter's stepping-stone to the White House was the governor's office in Atlanta.

Among the 100 men and women in the United States Senate in mid-2014, fewer than 30 got their college degrees in the Ivy League or in the slightly larger circle of schools widely deemed Ivy-caliber. Nearly 50 of them went to public and private colleges well below the top 25 in the sorts of conventional rankings to which so many Americans pay so much heed. And among the fifty governors in the same time period, the picture was similar. A quarter of them went to the most selective private and public colleges. Almost as many went to private colleges that don't cause applicants' hearts to go pitter-patter, and more than a third went to public schools that aren't remarkably selective.

Nikki Haley, a South Carolina Republican, is in the latter group. When she assumed office in January 2011, she was just thirty-eight years old, not to mention a woman and an ethnic minority (she has Indian ancestry) in charge of a conservative southern state. Her college degree is from Clemson University, whose regard in South Carolina far eclipses its national reputation, and she exemplifies politicians whose higher educations deepened their roots in—and their claims on—the states they'd eventually lead or represent. She told me that if you're going to make your career in South Carolina, there's no better badge than Clemson's. I suspect that someone in Alabama might make the same boast of Auburn's impact there and someone in Dallas would testify to Southern Methodist University's sway over that city. Geography plays such a key part in which college provides the best professional launch.

Haley told me that in South Carolina, "If you look at the graduates of Clemson, the network we have is absolutely amazing. It immediately takes away barriers, immediately allows transactions to take place that wouldn't normally happen. If you come to South Carolina and you went to a school out of state, you lose that entire network. And it's a huge resume booster if you're running for office to say that you're from one of the state's schools."

Even more important, she said, Clemson gave her an entirely new footing in the world. She grew up in a tiny South Carolina town where almost no one else had her family's skin color or looked like them. She needed to feel less isolated, and she needed exposure to all sorts of arts and sports and vocations that didn't exist in her community, but she also needed some sense of continuity and familiarity: a transition she could handle. Clemson, a big university in her home state, threaded that needle. "I was a small-town girl and it had this small-town feel but it was big enough that you could grow," she said. She started out majoring in textile management; switched to accounting; worked on the side as a chiropractor's assistant to help pay for school; graduated into a job for a waste management company and didn't enter politics for several years. When I spoke with her, the eldest of her two children had just begun to think seriously about colleges, but not about the Ivy League or the Northeast. "She wants to look at Clemson," Haley said.

Let's stay with politicians and politics a bit longer and examine the men and women who, in the fall of 2015, were most frequently discussed as potential candidates for the presidency in 2016. The field included many contenders without fancy undergraduate diplomas. Yes, the leader of the pack on the Democratic side was Hillary Clinton, who got her bachelor's degree at Wellesley and then went to law school at Yale, where her partnership with Bill was forged. But former Maryland governor Martin O'Malley, trying to make some headway and hoping to surge if she teetered, did his undergraduate work at Catholic University and then got his law degree from the University of Maryland. Elizabeth Warren, U.S. senator from Massachusetts, who remained a fantasy candidate for Democrats in the throes of Clinton Fatigue, was once on the faculty of Harvard but went to college at the University of Houston and law school at Rutgers. New York governor Andrew Cuomo, another of the "what if?" possibilities in the event of a Clinton collapse, did his undergraduate work at Fordham, followed by the Albany Law School. And then there was Biden, lurking on the race's edges, sending mixed signals, weighing how much damage Clinton had done to herself in the early stages of the race for the Democratic nomination, and measuring the intensity of his own desires. As mentioned, his alma maters were Delaware and Syracuse.

On the crowded Republican side, Governor Chris Christie of New Jersey also went to the University of Delaware, and then got his law degree at Seton Hall; Mike Huckabee, the former Arkansas governor, went to Ouachita Baptist University in Arkadelphia, Arkansas, then to the Southwestern Baptist Theological Seminary; John Kasich, the Ohio governor, to Ohio State University; Rick Perry, the former Texas governor, to Texas A&M University; Rand Paul, the Kentucky senator, to Baylor University, which he left before actually graduating to move on to medical school at Duke; and Scott Walker, the Wisconsin governor, to Marquette University, from which he never graduated. Before getting his bachelor's degree from the University of Florida, Marco Rubio first attended Tarkio College in Missouri for one year and then, briefly, a community college in Florida. He later studied law at the University of Miami. And while it's tempting to leave Donald Trump out of this analysis altogether—he defies the laws of gravity, be they political, educational or other—he, too, spread his undergraduate education across multiple schools, spending two years at Fordham in New York City before transferring to the Wharton business school at the University of Pennsylvania, from which he got his degree.

That gave Trump some Ivy and, indeed, there were Ivies and might-as-well-be-Ivies in the backgrounds of the sprawling cast of Republican contenders. Bobby Jindal, the

Louisiana governor, got his bachelor's from Brown, and Ted Cruz, the Texas senator, went to Princeton as an undergraduate and then Harvard as a law student. Carly Fiorina was a Stanford graduate and Ben Carson a graduate of Yale and then, for medical school, the University of Michigan. But those highly ranked institutions were easily outnumbered by ones considered less elite.

And the ones considered less elite also drew less attention, less commentary, reflecting our society's prejudices and its selective editing of the college truth. Take the discussion of Jeb Bush, one of the most prominent Republican aspirants. Even though he was routinely characterized as a policy wonk and as the brainier Bush (vis-à-vis his older brother George W.), his alma mater, the University of Texas, often went unmentioned, as if it contradicted his intellectual chops or was beside the point. In contrast, George W.'s stints at Yale as an undergraduate and at Harvard for business school were mainstays of the profiles of him when he ran for the presidency. The implication was that they vouched for an intelligence that wasn't always conspicuous in his public speaking and explained his rise to political power.

Most profiles of Cruz threw a spotlight on his alma maters, the way early profiles of Obama harped on Harvard Law. Many profiles of Christie left out Delaware and Seton Hall. One that didn't, in the *National Review*, felt the need to characterize them as "respectable but middling schools." And this was in a *flattering* story that was praising the New Jersey governor as a victor in "a war for fiscal sanity." It certainly didn't note that Christie and Biden, who were then two of the most prominent figures on the national political landscape, *both* went to Delaware, and it didn't wonder about the dawn of a new power school. Good luck finding a magazine, newspaper or television report that did.

I asked Christie if he'd noticed, as I had, a greater tendency to mention the Ivy League pedigrees of some politicians than to note the Ivy-less pedigrees of others, and what he made of it.

"I think there's a bias toward thinking that if they went to Princeton, Harvard or Yale, then that's a significant fact," he said. "But if they went to Rutgers or the University of Delaware or a school like that, it's less significant. It's the bias that we all feel that somehow the education at those places is better.

"It's interesting," he added, "because our oldest son goes to Princeton, and I remember when he was applying, he said, 'If I get in, do you want me to go?' I said, 'Sure.' He said, 'But you went to Delaware and turned out okay.' I said, 'You're absolutely right, but I had to work a lot harder.' That's the difference. There's this assumption that if you went to Princeton, you're smarter than the next guy."

Was the assumption a fair one? "I don't think it is," Christie said. "There are a lot of things that happen when you're fifteen and seventeen that affect your ability to get into a school like that." Those last years of high school are just one short stretch of a life with many passages before it and many to come, plenty of ups and plenty of downs, and intelligence is only part of what enables you, at that time, to walk through certain doors.

Christie, who graduated from high school in 1980, said that he'd applied to a mix of public and private schools, including Georgetown, his first choice, which rejected him. He went to Delaware primarily because it "offered me a good amount of scholarship and grant money," he said. "My family was not affluent at all, and it made a huge difference.

"The second reason was, I went down there and visited—it's strange the way you make decisions when you're seventeen or eighteen—and everybody seemed happy and everybody seemed to be enjoying themselves," he added. "The campus was nice and it was relatively close to home. It wasn't a whole lot more complicated than that."

When I asked him if, once he'd arrived on campus for good, Delaware felt like the right decision, his answer wasn't about his dorm or initial group of friends or classes he'd signed up for or any of that, and it underscored that in college as in everything else, messy, unplanned stuff intrudes. He was immediately grateful for Delaware, he said, because it was close to his New Jersey home and he winded up wanting and needing to return there frequently during his freshman year, just before which his mother had been diagnosed with breast cancer.

He's grateful still. He met his wife, Mary Pat, there. He majored in political science, with a minor in history, and whether it was a function of Delaware or of his personality, professors were readily accessible and several became lifelong friends, including one who volunteered to work the phone banks when Christie first ran for governor in 2009. And there were attributes of a state university that aren't shared in full by most elite private schools. "What I got out of being at a place like Delaware was a real diversity in terms of the economic and social strata of the people who went there. I met lots of different people who had lots of different life experiences." Although that's especially beneficial for a politician, it's obviously useful in most other jobs as well.

"I look back at those four years so fondly," he said. "I had an amazingly good time and great experience. There's nothing I would change." Through his four children, the second oldest of whom is a freshman at Notre Dame, he has noticed an awareness and veneration of elite schools that's much more pronounced than in the past; it was especially intense, he said, at the Delbarton School, in Morristown, New Jersey, from which his son Andrew, the one at Princeton, graduated in 2012. In Andrew's class at Delbarton, ten kids headed off to Princeton, more than went to any other college, and another sixteen went elsewhere in the Ivy League. Only one went to Delaware. I know this because the school breaks it all down for students and parents on its website, listing several years' worth of information about how Delbarton graduates fared.

Referring to both himself and his wife, Christie said, "The thing that really disturbed us was the extraordinary pressure that some parents were putting on their kids from the seventh or eighth grade. That's something that we don't quite yet know what effect it's going to have on kids over the long haul. My fear is that these kids are always going to be evaluating their self-worth in terms of whether they hit the next rung society has placed in front of them at exactly the time that society has placed it. And that's dangerous, because you're going to slip and fall in your life."

Christie said that he went to Seton Hall after Delaware because he didn't have the grades for one of the most prestigious law schools and felt that if he wasn't going to be in the top tier, he should be in New Jersey, where he planned to practice law and pursue his career. It was interesting to hear him mention academic shortcomings, because whatever else you make of Christie—whether you find him bold or bullying, a refreshing truth-teller or an egomaniacal schemer—he's an unusually nimble thinker, with a striking verbal dexterity. Once, at a charter school fund-raiser, I heard him deliver a half-hour keynote speech without a teleprompter or any notes, and every sentence, every paragraph, was impeccable. There's no equivalence between straight A's in school and sharp professional tools, and that's one of the many reasons to question the obsession with colleges that admit only students with the highest GPAs.

More than a few of the political masterminds behind recent presidents and presidential campaigns honed their intellects at schools of relatively modest repute. Donna Brazile, whose stewardship of Al Gore's 2000 race made her the first African American to manage a major presidential bid, graduated from Louisiana State University. Maggie Williams, who managed Hillary Clinton's 2008 race, graduated from Trinity Washington University, a small Catholic women's college. Karl Rove, a longtime aide to George W. Bush who was sometimes referred to as "Bush's brain," zigzagged from the University of Utah to the University of Maryland to George Mason University. He never got a diploma.

Steve Schmidt, the senior strategist for John McCain's ill-fated 2008 presidential campaign, went to—here it comes again!—the University of Delaware, which is *also* the alma mater of David Plouffe, who managed Obama's triumphant, history-making presidential campaign that same year. In 2012, the job of managing Obama's campaign fell to Jim Messina. He's a graduate of the University of Montana.

Both Schmidt and Plouffe left Delaware without diplomas. Neither had accrued enough credits to graduate. But when they returned to the campus in the spring of 2009 for a joint discussion of the 2008 campaign, the university president asked to see them and said, in Schmidt's recollection: "Guys, you're killing us, you've got to finish this." Delaware wanted to count them as honest-to-goodness graduates, so the president laid out for each of them what they had to do. Plouffe said he needed to do a nutrition, a human development and a math course. Schmidt just needed a math course: the one that Plouffe needed as well. They were assigned the same math professor, Kay Biondi, who was supposed to monitor and help them online.

"She was picked to deal with us psychologically, with our math phobia," Schmidt said with a laugh. He said that he sometimes conversed with her on Saturday mornings, from a bar near the ski slopes in Vermont, with a Bloody Mary in his hand. And he sometimes called Plouffe, his former adversary, to commiserate about being students again all these years later.

"Good memories," Plouffe told me in an email, maybe sarcastically, maybe not. He added that he and Schmidt "went from vicious adversaries to good friends." Plouffe quickly finished his courses and got his diploma in 2010. Schmidt dallied, getting his in 2013.

Schmidt said that while many of the policy advisers in campaigns and government went to elite colleges, "I don't think there's a tremendous amount of people at the top level of running campaigns who have Ivy League degrees." I asked if he had any theories about why. "I think part of the reason is that campaign politics is a rough business, a tough business emotionally," he said. "I think it carries a fair degree of common sense and a blending of emotional intelligence and IQ intelligence, which isn't necessarily a virtue of the people coming out of the most elite universities if you were to make generalizations and stereotypes."

In May 2014, the sociologist D. Michael Lindsay published the results of something he called the Platinum Study, which involved interviews with 550 American leaders, including more than 250 chief executives of corporations, more than 100 leaders of major nonprofit groups, a few former presidents and many government officials. Lindsay's aims were to see where they came from, how they reached their destinations and how they thought and behaved once they arrived.

"I fully expected that we would see that a large percentage of people had gone to highly selective schools both for secondary and higher education," he told me. He learned differently, as he spells out in the book that grew out of the study, *View from the Top: An Inside Look at How People in Power See and Shape the World*. He writes that "although we often assume that the most direct path to national influence goes through major academic universities (such as Ivy League schools), nearly two-thirds of the leaders I interviewed attended schools that are not considered elite institutions."

The reputations of the colleges that they attended, he discovered, seemed to matter much less than the reputations of the graduate schools that they moved on to, and they weren't shut out of these graduate schools on the basis of where they'd applied from. "Nearly two-thirds of the leaders who received graduate degrees went to a top 10 graduate school in their field," Lindsay writes.

But the belief in the primacy of a person's undergraduate pedigree is stubborn in many quarters, as I've learned when I've used my column in the *New York Times* to challenge that thinking and to argue that education is so much more than brand. "Oh yeah?" one reader wrote to me. "Tell me where you and your colleagues went to college. I bet it was the Ivy League."

In many cases, yes. In just as many, no. My own undergraduate degree is from the University of North Carolina, and there's a story about how I ended up there that I'll tell later. When I became an op-ed columnist for the *Times* in June 2011, I joined a group of accomplished writers that included Maureen Dowd, who got her bachelor's from Catholic University, and Gail Collins, who got hers from Marquette. Nicholas Kristof and Ross Douthat indeed went to Harvard and David Brooks to the University of Chicago. But Joe Nocera is an alumnus of Boston University, Charles Blow of Grambling State. Tom Friedman spent his first years in college at the University of Minnesota, after which he transferred to Brandeis.

Because I've reported extensively on candidates, campaigns and public office holders, the newspaper's leading political correspondents are among my close friends. They come from a spectrum of colleges. You won't find a saucier or more sophisticated chronicler of the nation's capital than Jennifer Steinhauer, who was previously the newspaper's Los Angeles bureau chief. She went to college at the School of Visual Arts in Manhattan. You won't find a wiser political analyst than Adam Nagourney, who has had a major hand in covering five presidential races for the *Times*. He went to the State University of New York (SUNY) at Purchase. Carl Hulse, perhaps the *Times*'s most trusted interpreter of Congress, studied at Illinois State University.

Jim Rutenberg, who was the newspaper's chief political correspondent during the 2012 presidential race and then moved to a prized writing slot on the *Times*'s Sunday magazine, attended New York University back when it was significantly less selective, but never actually got his diploma. He had financial and family challenges that sidelined him, but he wasn't, in the end, set back by that, because he had and has something better than any degree: a cunning, a drive and a grace in dealing with other people that are shared, to varying extents, by all of the journalists I just mentioned. Their careers weren't built on the names of their colleges. They were built on carefully honed skills, ferocious work ethics and good attitudes.

The *Times* is no aberration. After the winners of the Pulitzer Prizes in journalism were announced in 2014, I looked to see where they'd gone to college. The American schools on that list were the University of Richmond, Syracuse University, Boston College, the University of South Carolina, Middlebury College, the University of Michigan, the University of Minnesota, Boston University and Stanford. I rewound a year, to the Pulitzers in journalism for 2013. I found Northwestern, the University of St. Thomas, the University of Georgia, Boston University, the University of Colorado Boulder, Yale, Indiana University, the University of Chicago, Gannon University and the University of Minnesota.

And I rewound once more. The 2012 Pulitzer winners did their undergraduate work at Colby College, the University of Maryland, Villanova, Bowling Green State University, Purdue, Penn State, Cornell, Columbia, Pomona, Yale, the Rhode Island School of Photography, Lewis & Clark College and the State University of New York at Binghamton. The journalist who went to that last school is my friend and *Times* colleague David Kocieniewski. He won for explanatory reporting.

In the spring of 2014, he and I each taught a seminar as visiting faculty members at Princeton. He reveled in the irony of that. About three decades earlier, Princeton had rejected him. So had Harvard. Brown, too. SUNY Binghamton was one of his fallbacks, and he told me that because its students fancied themselves freer spirits than most, "They used to call themselves the Brown of public universities, though I've never heard anyone at Brown call it the SUNY Binghamton of the Ivies."

He said that going there was a mercy of sorts, as he would have had trouble affording a private college. But even with the in-state tuition break he got, he had to work his way through school, and for the first two years, he put in fifteen hours a week as a janitor. It was one of many unglamorous gigs over the years, including a stint in his early twenties as the driver of a Mister Softee ice cream truck in Buffalo. "Ah, the summer of Softee," he said. "It's the worst job ever. You work every sunny day. You're off when it rains. And you have no idea how many impotence jokes there are until you've driven a Mister Softee truck."

Journalism, of course, isn't representative. (Then again, no profession is.) So I cast my gaze in an unrelated direction, toward the world of science, and examined the alma maters of the 102 men and women, most of them in their thirties and forties, who had been invited to the White House as recipients of the 2014 Presidential Early Career Award for Scientists and Engineers (PECASE). I couldn't track down the college information for eight of the 102 winners; among the rest, 72 did their undergraduate work in the United States, and the list of schools they attended is by no means dominated by the likes of Stanford and the Massachusetts Institute of Technology, though both appeared on it more than once.

But then so did Rutgers, the University of Arizona and North Carolina State. Public schools, including those three, represented just under half of the list. When you also took into account private and niche schools well outside the Ivy League—and I don't mean Stanford, MIT, Wellesley and Smith, but institutions like Adelphi University, Linfield College and Augustana College—nearly two-thirds of the list was covered. The dubious importance of precisely where a driven, able person goes to college was underscored by something else. When I was hunting down the educational pedigrees of these distinguished scientists and engineers, it was usually easy to find the names of the schools where they'd done their graduate work. Their employers were sure to put that in their online profiles. It was less easy to identify the colleges they'd attended, which often weren't even mentioned. Those four years were clearly seen as the staging area, not the actual operation; as the throat clearing, not the aria. College wasn't considered the most rigorous or targeted work that these scientists and engineers had done, nor was it the place from which they'd been plucked for their enduring employment. With each year that they had moved beyond it, its relevance to who they were and how they'd been schooled waned.

The diversity of colleges at which PECASE recipients had studied was not unlike what I encountered when I researched recent winners of MacArthur Foundation "genius grants." The undergraduate alma maters of the two dozen geniuses anointed in 2013 included SUNY Purchase, SUNY Albany, Louisiana State, Villanova, DePaul and the University of California, Santa Barbara. And the alma maters of the twenty-one geniuses in 2014 included the University of Kansas, the University of Cincinnati, Coker College, the University of

Illinois, Columbus State University and the University of Maryland. My analysis of the winners in 2009 through 2014 showed that more than half of MacArthur's geniuses got their undergraduate educations at public and private schools that aren't typically placed in the highest echelon.

My interactions with the MacArthur Foundation's administrators, who helped round up the relevant information for me, prompted them to look back at the alma maters of all the geniuses, whom they refer to as "Fellows," to date. They sent me an analysis written by Cecilia A. Conrad, the vice president of the MacArthur Fellows Program. It also appeared in the *Huffington Post*.

"While the largest number of Fellows from a single institution graduated from Harvard," Conrad wrote, "others attended less selective institutions. One in five Fellows graduated from institutions with acceptance rates of over 50 percent. Fifteen graduated from either historically black colleges and universities or tribal colleges and 44 from women's colleges. Forty graduated from religiously affiliated institutions. Several Fellows, such as organic chemist Phil Baran, began their studies at community colleges. The 918 MacArthur Fellowship recipients attended 315 diverse post-secondary institutions."

The administrators additionally sent me a list of those 315 institutions. The names of many lesser-known colleges and universities quickly and easily caught my eye. They included not just Western Michigan University but also Western Illinois University, and not just Western Illinois University but also Southern Illinois University and Illinois Wesleyan University. Among the institutions beginning with *B*, Brown, Bryn Mawr and Brandeis were predictably present. But so were Bluffton University, Black Hills State University, Beaver College (since renamed Arcadia University), Butler University and Bowling Green. San Francisco State University and San Diego State University had produced two Fellows apiece.

The analysis from the MacArthur Foundation went on to note a possibly important trait of institutions that had produced a disproportionate share of Fellows. It wasn't selectiveness. "Our data provide one clue as to the educational environments most conducive for creative minds to develop: the relatively high number of Fellows who graduated from liberal arts colleges," wrote Conrad. "Liberal arts colleges are distinctively American institutions, typically small, that focus on undergraduate education. Less than two percent of U.S. college graduates graduated from a liberal arts college, but 14 percent of MacArthur Fellows did. Liberal arts colleges are a diverse group of institutions. Some are highly selective; others are not. The category includes women's colleges like Barnard College, which has produced ten MacArthur Fellows... The category also includes church-affiliated colleges like Siena College in Albany, New York, where writer William Kennedy graduated, and historically black colleges like Morehouse College in Atlanta, Georgia, where physician and scientist Donald Hopkins graduated."

Of course all of the sample sets I just referred to generally reflect people who have been out of college for more—in most cases, much more—than a decade. They don't say much about the fates of relatively recent graduates. But some hints of how these recent graduates are faring—and some validations of the idea that schools other than the most selective ones produce plenty of grant-worthy and grant-winning scholars—

can be found by looking at the annual list of Fulbright recipients and where they studied. This list combines students who've just received their bachelor's degrees and those who are in or finishing master's programs, and identifies those students in terms of their current or most recent school, so it's a slightly flawed referendum on the undergraduate years in and of themselves. But it's a useful, revealing yardstick nonetheless.

The Fulbright list, like the *U.S. News* rankings, separates large national universities and smaller liberal arts colleges, and during the 2014–2015 academic year, Harvard led national universities in terms of the number of its students—thirty-three—who won Fulbrights. But the University of Michigan, with twenty-eight winners, and the University of California, Berkeley, with twenty-two, placed ahead of each of the other seven Ivy League schools, and in Berkeley's case, about one in four applicants got the award, while in Harvard's case, it was about one in five. Of course Michigan and Berkeley are among the most selective public universities, but Rutgers isn't, and its nineteen winners placed it tenth in terms of universities that minted the most winners. The University of Minnesota, Twin Cities, with sixteen winners, was tied with Georgetown for thirteenth. Arizona State University, with fifteen winners, was fifteenth, and more than one in four of its applicants had succeeded. Ohio State University, with fourteen winners, was sixteenth, and the eight-way tie for seventeenth included the main branch of the University of Illinois, Penn State, the University of Pittsburgh and the main branch of the University of Massachusetts, each with thirteen winners. They placed ahead of such highly selective dream schools as Columbia, Johns Hopkins and Emory.

Only twenty-one liberal arts colleges had more than five Fulbright winners, and while that list included such exclusive institutions as Amherst, Middlebury and Williams, it also included less frequently and lavishly celebrated colleges. There was Occidental, whose thirteen winners put it in a tie for third. There were the College of the Holy Cross, Lewis & Clark College and Wheaton College, each with nine winners. And there was St. Olaf College, with six. St. Olaf accepts more than 50 percent of its applicants, Lewis & Clark more than 65 percent of its and Wheaton nearly 70 percent of its.

I checked in with the administrators of the Rhodes Scholarships, awarded to graduating seniors, to ask where the thirty-two American winners from the Class of 2015 had gone to college. They sent me the list. It was heavy, very heavy, with Ivy League and Ivy-like schools: Yale, Brown, MIT, Princeton, Harvard. But it was by no means owned entirely by them, and Elliot Gerson, the American secretary of the Rhodes Trust, explained to me that a disproportionate number of students from the most storied, selective colleges apply for the Rhodes, because they're more likely to be aware of it and to see it as well within their sights. So the results are deceiving and not simply a reflection of some Rhodes-enticing fairy dust that Ivy League schools sprinkle on their charges.

"Harvard had two winners, yes," Gerson told me, referring to Rhodes scholars selected in 2015. "But that's only twice as many winners as the University of Wisconsin–Eau Claire." There was a winner apiece from the University of Alabama, the University of Maryland, the Chattanooga branch of the University of Tennessee and Santa Clara University. There was one from Wabash College, whose acceptance rate is 70 percent. There was another from the

University of Puget Sound, whose acceptance rate is almost 80 percent.

Schools that showed up among the Rhodes winners from 2014 and 2013 included Mississippi State University, Montana State University, the University of Oklahoma, Luther College and the College of Idaho. That isn't, or shouldn't be, surprising: It stands to reason that each of the many hundreds of universities and four-year colleges in the United States would strike Rhodes gold from time and time, and that the students cycling through any one of them over time would include some superstars. But what's equally evident, and too seldom articulated, is that talented, motivated students can and do thrive in environments that aren't notably exclusive. And those environments are often edited out of their biographies, a dynamic that's apparent in news coverage of politicians, as I mentioned earlier, and that was pointed out by a brilliant, hilarious post by Peter Osterlund on a website named the 60second Recap.

The post responded to the "30 Under 30" list of promising young Americans that *Forbes* magazine has begun to put out every year. The *Forbes* list actually names thirty people in each of fifteen categories—law, media, tech, finance, etc.—so it encompasses 450 honorees in all. Osterlund's post happened to deconstruct the group of honorees for 2013. And it poked fun at Ivy mythologizing, observing that *Forbes* made sure to mention "Harvard, Stanford, Princeton, Princeton, Princeton" in the profiles of 30 Under 30 honorees who had graduated from those schools. *Forbes* simply omitted information about alma maters in profiles of nominees who hadn't.

"Well," Osterlund wrote, "we dug." And the discoveries? "*Forbes* tells us of one 30 Under 30 honoree's experiences as an undergraduate at Duke, but doesn't mention the Arizona State University undergraduate degrees carried by three of its young stars." In terms of the number of a school's graduates on the *Forbes* list, ASU actually beat out Duke, the post determined. "And it beats Dartmouth. And Cornell. And Johns Hopkins. And... you get the idea.

"We found that most *Forbes* 30 Under 30 honorees attended, well, ordinary colleges—in some cases, obscure places, in other cases, state schools like the University of Where-They-Just-So-Happened-To-Live-At-The-Time." For instance Isaac Kinde, who was an honoree in the category of science and health care, did his undergraduate work at the University of Maryland, Baltimore County (UMBC), which accepts more than 60 percent of its applicants. *Forbes* didn't identify that school. It did, however, make clear that Isaac was doing a combined MD and PhD program at Johns Hopkins.

I reached out to Isaac, now thirty-two, to learn more about how he ended up at UMBC. Our conversation was a reminder that there are many families and communities in which the mania over college admissions is an exotic and unthinkable luxury. They're either unable or loath to participate in it. And they don't necessarily suffer for taking a pass.

Isaac grew up near San Bernardino, California, and went to a parochial school where the college chatter wasn't all that constant or intense, he said. He was a standout who knew that he wanted a career in the sciences, almost certainly in medicine, and felt that he should probably not stray too far geographically from his home and his parents. So he applied to several schools in the University of California system and to Stanford. And got in everywhere.

He also applied to UMBC, specifically to its Meyerhoff

Scholars Program, not because he'd learned about it through extensive research but because a family friend had happened to mention it. It gives free rides to minority students with promise in the fields of science, technology and engineering. To get the scholarship, Isaac had to travel east one weekend for a series of interviews, and during that trip he got to see the UMBC campus and meet some of the Meyerhoff students and administrators. "What I remember is the immediate feeling of comfort that both my father and I had," he said. But the Meyerhoff promised more than just comfort: It was a tightly knit community within UMBC that existed for, and was dedicated to, the nurturing and advancement of its scholars. It was a ready-made support system, a guaranteed network. He felt that it would help him stay focused on his work and avoid the many distractions of college life. "I hadn't realized it was out there, but as soon as I was exposed to it, I thought, 'This makes sense. This seems right. Now that I see it, I want it.'"

The education he ended up getting at UMBC, he told me, was sufficiently excellent to give him his pick of many top medical schools and to provide him with the foundation he needed for success at Hopkins, where his research over the last ten years, which is how long it takes to get both an MD and the doctorate he chose, has focused on improving DNA sequencing in a way that may help detect certain cancers. But he said that he did have one big regret about UMBC. "It would have been nice to have a football team," he said. "I would have liked that. Now I don't feel as connected to college football as many of my colleagues are. That would be my only thing. Would I change anything else in hindsight? Absolutely not.

"I thought that it was a unique place to be," he said. "I

never have been the kind of person to care about the reputation of a particular program or school, in terms of, 'Is it Top Five?' I just think that that preoccupation is a little misguided." What matters, he said, is what you do in the classroom and in the laboratory, not the school banner that flutters over you, not the school colors in which you're dressed.

"I think you can get what you need out of college at most colleges," Isaac said. "The biggest thing that varies from college to college is the location and the price." For him the price at UMBC was right. So was the price at the University of California, Los Angeles, a more widely respected school that had also offered him a large scholarship. But UCLA, which he visited and liked, wasn't likely to give him the personal attention and have the investment in his future that the Meyerhoff did, or at least that was his strong sense of things. That was what his careful survey of his options and his gut both told him. Plus the Meyerhoff, on the other side of the country from where he'd grown up, was sure to be a different kind of adventure, and an expansion of his world. He went with the greater, longer journey.

Four years after he made that decision, his younger brother, Benyam, followed suit, also going to UMBC on a Meyerhoff. And Benyam, twenty-eight, is now doing a combined MD and PhD program of his own—at Harvard.

UMBC appeared in a pointedly jokey "15 Over 50" honor roll on Osterlund's *Forbes* takedown, which catalogued and lionized fifteen alma maters of 30 Under 30 designees that accept more than 50 percent of applicants, proving that more exclusive schools don't enjoy any monopoly on present talent and future glory. The other fourteen schools on the 15 Over 50 included the American River College, Westminster College (that's in Utah, not Britain) and Santa Fe College (that's in Florida, not New Mexico). American River and Santa Fe take 100 percent of their applicants. You knock; the door swings wide.

The 60second Recap didn't follow up in 2014 and examine the next batch of honorees. So I reviewed it, and again found no shortage of graduates of schools that aren't especially selective. There were several alumni of Penn State. One, Josh Blackman, was a law professor who had written a book about the constitutional challenge to Obamacare and had founded FantasySCOTUS, a popular Supreme Court online fantasy league and prediction market.

Another, Carryn McLaughlin, was a vice president at J.P. Morgan in charge of managing a $2.7 billion portfolio for real estate moguls and their families. McLaughlin appeared in the finance category, as did graduates of the City University of New York and of the University of Miami. I learned that by digging into just a small patch of the 30 Under 30.

It was clear that with the 2014 list, I could ask the same question that Osterlund had asked at the end of his analysis of the 2013 honorees. "Take a look and you tell us," he wrote. "Does a prestigious college make you successful in life? Or do you do that for yourself?"

TWO

THROWING DARTS

"When I went to college thirty or forty years ago, I said to my dad, 'What's the Ivy League?' And he said, 'That's just a bunch of snooty girls, you don't want to go there.' Today he would say, 'We absolutely must visit the Ivy League.' It's become a whole different thing."

—Jennifer Delahunty, former dean of admissions at Kenyon College and a 1980 graduate of the University of Arizona

Determined to get into one of the dozen or so most selective institutions of higher learning in America? No problem—as long as you're the winner of a national science contest, the winner of a national singing competition, a Bolshoi-ready dancer, a Carnegie-caliber harpsichordist, a chess prodigy, a surfing legend, a defensive lineman who led his region in tackles, a striker who scored a record number of goals in her soccer league, a published author and I don't mean blogger, a precocious chef and I do mean molecular gastronomy, a stoic political refugee from a country that we really loathe, a heroic political scion from a country that we really love, a Roosevelt of proper vintage, a Rockefeller of sufficient relevance, or Malia or Sasha Obama. If none of those descriptions fit and you don't have perfect scores on every standardized test since the second grade, your visions of Stanford would more correctly be termed hallucinations.

Of course I'm exaggerating, but not by all that much. And I'm singling out Stanford on purpose: In the spring of 2014, it established a new extreme in exclusiveness, offering admission to a lower share of supplicants than any school ever had. For the class of 2018, Stanford received 42,167 applications. It took roughly 5.1 percent of them. That's about one aspirant of every twenty, and those twenty weren't slackers, stumblebums, unhinged gamblers or delusional narcissists. At least not most of them. They were, generally speaking, accomplished secondary school students for whom Stanford wasn't and shouldn't have been a completely ludicrous wish.

In the spring of 2015, Stanford bested itself, as a story in the *Stanford Daily* in late March instantly announced. "Out of 42,487 applicants—the largest pool in University history—1,402 high school seniors received letters of acceptance to Stanford's Class of 2019, in addition to the 742 early action students accepted in December," the story spelled out. "At 5.05 percent, this year's undergraduate admissions rate is the lowest in Stanford's history, only slightly lower than last year's rate of 5.07 percent. The decrease in admissions rate follows the trend of increasing selectivity in recent years. The university admitted 5.7 percent of applicants in 2013 and 6.6 percent in 2012."

Days later, the *Harvard Crimson* followed suit with a story that began with this sentence: "A record-low 5.3 percent of applicants were offered admission to Harvard College's Class of 2019, when the University announced on Tuesday that it had accepted 1,990 of 37,305 applicants." Meanwhile there was this from the *Daily Princetonian*: "The University has offered admission to 1,908 students, or 6.99 percent, of the 27,290 applicants for the Class of 2019. This makes it the most selective admission year the University has seen to date." And Columbia University released figures showing that its acceptance rate had also fallen to a record low—of about 6.1 percent. That was down from 6.94 percent the prior year, according to the school.

The arithmetic was nowhere near as merciless for previous generations. It's important to emphasize that, to keep in mind that a kid today angling for acceptance to the kind of super-elite school that a parent attended is not trying to replicate that accomplishment but, in fact, to one-up it. Unless the child is applying to the exact *same* school that a parent attended (and, better yet, that a parent recently gave copious sums of money to), his or her challenge is significantly greater. At Yale, roughly 20 percent of applicants were offered admission back in the late 1980s. A quarter century later, in 2015, about 6.5 percent were.

That trajectory is mirrored at dozens of the most desired American colleges. At Northwestern University in Evanston, Illinois, for example, the acceptance rate fell from over 40 percent a quarter century ago to about 13 percent in 2014. And the sharpest declines in acceptance rates at these schools have occurred for the most part over the last fifteen years and especially the last ten, according to data from Noodle, a company that compiles education statistics that are meant to guide both consumers and policy makers. Researchers at Noodle took an ambitious look back at the last thirty years of admissions information from schools that *U.S. News* routinely ranked in its top 100, and Noodle shared those results with me. They show that between 1984 and 1994, many of these schools' acceptance rates were unchanged or even went *up* slightly. But those rates began to drop between 1994 and 2004. And since 2004, they've declined sharply. The acceptance rate at Tufts University went down only seven percentage points, from 34 to 27, between 1984 and 2004, but it has since gone down another ten. Bowdoin's 2004 rate was roughly the same as its 1984 one—about 24 percent—but it's now closer to 15. Amherst's held relatively steady at about 21 percent for the two decades leading up to 2004, but over the last decade, it's plummeted to below 15.

And while major public universities haven't reached nearly that degree of selectiveness, they, too, have become much more difficult to get into. The University of Michigan's rate fell from 56 percent in 1984 to 32 percent in 2014, and that's a combined figure for in-state students, who get the bulk of the spots in each class, and out-of-state students, who compete for fewer slots and face odds much worse than one in three. The University of California, Berkeley's rate fell over the same period from 48 percent to 17 (again, for in-state and out-of-state students combined).

The declining rates across the board have continued well past what anyone once thought possible. As the *New York Times* noted in a front-page story in April 2014 that was headlined "Best, Brightest and Rejected," "In 2003, Harvard and Princeton drew exclamations of dismay (from prospective applicants), envy (from other colleges) and satisfaction (from those they accepted) when they became the first top universities to have their acceptance rates dip below 10 percent. Since then, at least a dozen have gone below that threshold." And there are at least another dozen with acceptance rates not much higher than 10 percent.

What's happened at these schools is straightforward: The number of slots for incoming students either hasn't expanded significantly or hasn't risen nearly as much as the number of young people applying for them, and that surge in applications reflects a confluence of developments. One is that more and more students from outside the United States have been applying. More and more of them have been gaining acceptance, too, and that means fewer spots at some of the most fiercely competitive schools for American kids. I talked to many college admission consultants—the kind who charge lofty fees to advise families on packaging high school students to the liking of the gods of admission—and while I was primarily curious about the stratagems deployed, the consultants kept mentioning something else: the steady rise over the last five years in clients from Europe and Asia.

David Leonhardt, a colleague of mine at the *Times*, frequently analyzes data from different sources to get an accurate picture of college students and the college experience today, and in the spring of 2014, just as Stanford hit its milestone of selectivity, he reported that at elite colleges, international applicants now represented nearly 10 percent of the student bodies, and that at five of those schools, the number of slots available to American teenagers had dropped by more than 20 percent from 1994 to 2012. (The five were Carleton College, Dartmouth, Harvard, Yale and Boston College.)

"Colleges have globalized," Leonhardt wrote, suggesting two motivations for a more international student body: It diversifies campuses in a way that's consistent with the borderless nature of business today, and students from overseas tend to come from affluent families who can pay full freight.

But it's not just globalization that has plumped up the numbers of applicants to highly selective schools. More American kids are trying to get in as well. The Internet has made it easier for all kinds of students in all kinds of places to research and home in on schools that they might not have become as easily excited about before, and the ease and relative economy of long-distance travel mean that many students no longer feel as bound by geography to schools nearest them. For the most coveted colleges, this has meant many more comers. And while these schools are still attended predominantly by children of privilege—according to one widely cited estimate, roughly 75 percent of the students at the two hundred most highly rated colleges come from families in the top quartile of income in the United States—the funnel from top-drawer prep schools to the Ivy League doesn't function the way it did once upon a time, and there is a broader and more diverse network of secondary schools channeling students toward elite institutions. This is good. This is also an engine of increasingly cutthroat competition, which the schools themselves take great pains to encourage.

Somewhere along the way, a school's selectiveness—measured in large part by its acceptance rate—became synonymous with its worth. Acceptance rates are prominently featured in the profiles of schools that appear in various reference books and surveys, including the raptly monitored one by *U.S. News & World Report*, whose annual rankings of American colleges factor in those rates slightly. Colleges know that many prospective applicants equate a lower acceptance rate with a more coveted, special and brag-worthy experience, and these colleges endeavor to bring their rates down by ratcheting up the number of young people who apply. They bang the drums like never before. From the organization that administers the SAT, they buy the names of students who have scored above a certain mark and are at least remotely plausible, persuadable applicants, then they send those students pamphlets and literature that grow glossier and more alluring—*that leafy quadrangle! those gleaming microscopes!*—by the year. The college admissions office is no longer a mere screening committee. It's a ruthlessly efficient purveyor of Ivory Tower porn.

"Colleges really go overboard," Ted O'Neill, the dean of admissions at the University of Chicago for several decades until 2009, told me, explaining that a surfeit of applications "became a way to promote your college, and the admissions office became, in effect, a public-relations arm of the university." Bruce Poch, a former dean of admissions at Pomona College, said that to an extent unheard-of decades ago, emissaries from colleges will fan out across the country, extolling the magic of their schools and exhorting students to come aboard even as those very exhortations lengthen the odds against any one student getting in. The emissaries are ginning up desire in order to frustrate it, instilling hope only to quash it. In other words, their come-on is successful if it sows more failure.

And those come-ons can be as breathless as any telemarketer's pitch. An email that Rensselaer Polytechnic Institute sent unbidden to one high school senior invited him "to apply with **Candidate's Choice** status!" (The boldface letters and the exclamation point are Rensselaer's, not mine.) "Exclusively for select students, the **Candidate's Choice Application** is unique to Rensselaer, and is available online now," the email said, after telling its recipient that "a talented student like you deserves a college experience that is committed to developing the great minds of tomorrow."

"The marketing is unbelievable, just unbelievable," marveled Kay Rothman, the director of college counseling at the NYC Lab School, in Manhattan. "There are places like Tulane that will send everyone a 'VIP' application." She told me that she routinely has to disabuse impressionable students of the notion that they've won some prized lottery or been given some inside track.

"Colleges are actively saddling themselves with a whole group of applicants about whom they know little and who, in turn, know little about them," Lauren Gersick, the associate director of college counseling at the Urban School of San Francisco, told me. "You have a whole bunch of people fumbling along and freaking out."

Admissions officers even pay travel expenses to fly college placement counselors from high-profile secondary schools to their campuses and to give them a painstakingly choreographed pitch, so that these counselors might go back to the students they advise and promote the colleges that just treated them to such a polished song and dance.

"We did it at Pomona," said Poch, who left there in 2010. He now works in college guidance at Chadwick, a tony private school in the Los Angeles area that educates children from kindergarten through twelfth grade, and he noted: "The staff at Chadwick has been flown around." When the American economy turned sharply downward around 2008, the flying let up a bit, but it has since come back with a vengeance.

Gersick told me that from the fall of 2013 through the summer of 2014, she was flown to the College of Charleston; to the University of Southern California; to Smith College, in Northampton, Massachusetts; and to the College of the Atlantic, in Bar Harbor, Maine. It was her first year on the job.

All that traveling reflected the increasingly intense pressure being put on college admissions and enrollment officials to boost numbers. As Eric Hoover wrote in the *Chronicle of Higher Education* in late 2014, "Like football coaches, those in charge of bringing in students occupy hot seats watched by restless crowds. Presidents and trustees ask them tough questions: How do we get more applications?" Hoover's story went on to note that over recent years, "Dozens of enrollment and admissions leaders have lost their jobs. Others, worn down, have quit." He mentioned in particular the departure from Colby College of Terry Cowdrey, its vice president and dean of admissions and financial aid, in July 2014, right after the arrival of Colby's new president, David A. Greene. The word in higher-education circles was that Cowdrey had found some of the new application goals unwise and unrealistic. I reached out to her without luck, so I can't say with certainty what her thinking was.

I can tell you, though, that in the spring of 2015, following the first Colby admissions season that she hadn't steered, the college aggressively circulated a trumpets-blaring announcement of how spectacularly well it had fared, remarking that "a total of 7,591 applications were submitted for Colby's Class of 2019—a 47-percent increase over last year's 5,148." That's one swift, sharp spike, the kind that happens only because an already-selective school makes it a priority. And the increase begs the question: Were all of those new applicants truly in the running for admission to Colby, or were some of them just helping the college pad its numbers?

There's yet another factor in the surge of applications: the sheer ease of applying in the digital age. Students aren't dealing with paperwork per se and envelopes and stamps, the way someone like me did back in the early 1980s, which might as well be the Mesozoic era in terms of how much has changed. They aren't typing each application individually. They have the word-processing wonders of cut-and-paste, and beyond that they have the Common Application, a single electronic form that they can submit, along with specific supplements requested by particular schools, to most if not all of the colleges in their sights.

While the Common Application made its debut in 1975, decades went by before it took firm hold, and its currency and prevalence have increased with particular speed recently. During the 2008–2009 academic year, nearly 414,000 college-bound students used it. That number almost doubled over the next five years, and during the 2013–2014 academic year, about 813,000 students used the Common Application, according to the organization that drafts and promotes it. Its popularity with applicants tracks its popularity with colleges themselves, 517 of which accepted it during the 2013–2014 academic year. Scott Anderson, the senior director for policy for the Common Application, told me that for the 2014–2015 academic year, 550 colleges were on board. The number has since grown larger still.

The Common Application, or "Common App," renders it relatively painless for students to add another two or three or six schools to the list of ones that they're primarily interested in. So individual kids are applying to more schools than ever before—and individual schools are in turn seeing unprecedented numbers of applicants. A quarter century ago, only one in ten college-bound students applied to seven or more colleges. Now, close to one in three do. According to Naviance, an online tool that allows high school students to keep track of applications, 16.5 percent of the seniors using the service in 2014 said that they intended to apply to eleven to twenty colleges. Many of the college placement counselors, students and parents with whom I spoke told me that it's not at all unusual, in communities where a fee of $35 to $90 per application isn't considered prohibitive, for someone to apply to at least twelve schools and as many as twenty and for the thinking to be, "If I throw enough darts at the board, maybe one will hit the bull's-eye."

"I applied to fourteen schools," said Katherine Gross, an eighteen-year-old from Newton, Massachusetts, who began her freshman year at Johns Hopkins University in the fall of 2014. "I had friends who applied to twenty. I'm completely serious."

I had no doubt, and a *New York Times* story by Ariel Kaminer in November 2014 wholly supported her claim, introducing me and other readers to Alexa Verola, a senior at Mahwah High School in northern New Jersey. As Kaminer wrote, Verola took stock of her academic interests and possible career objectives and "drew up a list of some colleges where she would be happy majoring in anthropology and added more that would be good for photography or sound design: 18 in all. Then she applied to every last one of them. Eighteen is a lot, but good colleges are so hard to get into these days, Ms. Verola reasoned, and there will always be students with better board scores or higher grades. So after those 18 applications were in—most of them way ahead of schedule—she looked over the list and decided to add 11 more." I'll do the math for you. That's twenty-nine—yes, twenty-nine—schools.

Kaminer's story mentioned another student who, concerned about finding a spot in a music conservatory program, applied to fifty-six colleges. And the story cited a spokeswoman for Naviance who said that "one current user's 'colleges I'm applying to' tab already included 60 institutions. Last year the record was 86."

Kids have become accustomed to applying to schools almost reflexively, without any real attachment to many of them, and schools have become invested in the sheer number of applications they receive, regardless of the seriousness of the applicants. When Swarthmore College noticed a 16 percent drop in applications in 2014, it investigated the reason, and concluded that its requirement of two five-hundred-word essays in addition to the standard one had turned away students. That finding was consistent with the experiences of several other schools that have seen applications rise or fall markedly based on essay requirements. So Swarthmore, whose acceptance rate rose to 17 percent from 14 percent, is substituting the two supplemental essays with only one, of just 250 words. It could have decided to stay the course, on the theory that applicants going the extra mile were applicants with a passion for Swarthmore. It didn't.

The acceptance rates at individual schools don't tell a complete story or at least a sufficiently nuanced one, not the way John Katzman figures it. He's the chief executive and founder of Noodle; previously, he founded the *Princeton Review*, which evaluates and provides information about colleges. And he has a dissenting take on the admissions hysteria, which he sees as just that: hysteria.

"The process is much *less* selective today," he told me, adding that any contention to the contrary is "smoke and mirrors."

But he wasn't looking at Stanford, or for that matter at any given school in the Ivy League. He was looking at a bigger picture, by which I mean a broader group of colleges and universities that may not be ranked in the top 10 but are ranked in, say, the top 100 and regarded as superior. He noted that while the Ivy League perhaps hasn't seen any remarkable expansion in the number of undergraduates it can accommodate, many of these other schools—for example, the University of Michigan, Boston University and the University of California, Berkeley—have indeed grown significantly over the last thirty years. And during that time, many large schools like New York University and the University of Southern California have upgraded themselves enough to join the ranks of colleges generally considered elite. Katzman said that those two trends together mean that it's statistically easier today than it was thirty years ago for an American high school senior who seeks admission to one of the 100 or even 50 most highly regarded colleges to gain it.

Then he made a crucial clarification: He was talking about the odds of getting into *one or another* of those schools, not of getting into *the* one, two or four that your heart was set on. He was saying that if you apply widely within the universe of selective colleges, you're in better shape than you were decades ago to find a school that takes you, because that's the mathematical reality of the overall number of available slots for Americans your age who are applying to college.

"So why is everybody getting so worked up?" he asked.

There are several reasons. One is that the ratio of available slots per college-bound Americans doesn't take into account the intensity with which a greater cross section of those Americans are pursuing those slots: a fervor that translates into perfect, painstakingly constructed high school resumes and, in turn, a surfeit of overachieving students in the hunt. At some schools, the admissions bar has been lifted higher than it was before. Additionally, those of us in the media find the hunt so transfixing that we accord it ever more coverage, which further raises the anxiety levels of college-focused families, who get drawn further into the admissions mania, generating behaviors and statistics that justify another crop of news stories. With education as with politics, we're drawn to competition and mad for winners. As Katzman noted in a column that he wrote for the *Washington Post* in September 2014, "The *New York Times* wrote more about Harvard last year than about all community colleges combined."

And rightly or wrongly, sanely or insanely, most students aren't merely interested in going to *a* top school; they have strong preferences within that category. For more and more of them, those preferences are the top 20 or even the top 10 schools, where gaining admission is certainly more difficult than in the past.

The difficulty isn't even fully captured by those breathtakingly low acceptance rates, which don't represent the odds confronting a random candidate who's only generically outstanding. (How's that for an oxymoron?) No, that candidate faces even worse odds, because there are other applicants who belong to one of several preferred groups and thus have a leg up. Princeton may be taking about 7 percent of all comers, but it's taking significantly more than 7 percent of so-called legacies, or kids with a parent or other relative who attended the school, and it's taking significantly more than 7 percent of star athletes. So it's taking significantly less than 7 percent of brainy klutzes whose ancestors went to public colleges.

In 2011 Michael Hurwitz, who was then a doctoral candidate at Harvard University's Graduate School of Education, published the results of his research into just how much of an edge legacies enjoyed. He looked at more than 130,000 students who'd applied in the 2006–2007 academic year to be admitted as freshmen to one or more of thirty highly selective colleges. And he found that among students with seemingly equivalent grades, test scores and other qualifications, legacies had a 23.3 percent better chance of admission than nonlegacies.

If students were "primary legacies," meaning that a parent rather than an aunt or a grandparent had gone to the college in question, they had a 45.1 percent better chance. Put another way, if a given applicant who wasn't a legacy of any kind had a 15 percent chance of getting into a given school, a roughly identical applicant who was a primary legacy had a 60 percent chance. That's a profound difference, one that shocked many people when Hurwitz laid it out and one that students who are applying to top schools *without* any family connection should keep in mind. These schools may talk expansively about, and with a genuine belief in, diversity. These schools may advertise, and on some level desire, student bodies of exhilarating eclecticism. But these schools are unequivocally prioritizing alumni's progeny, who will be represented in abundance on campus. And that's because these schools are businesses as well as laboratories of learning—and maybe businesses *before* laboratories of learning—and children of alumni are equivalent to loyalty club members.

You can see that in Hurwitz's research or you can see it in a Pulitzer Prize–winning series of stories that the journalist Daniel Golden wrote for the *Wall Street Journal* eight years earlier, in 2003. Chronicling case after case in which some of the most revered colleges lowered their standards for affluent applicants, including legacies, he documented the power of social privilege, and of money in particular, in the admissions contest. He then updated and expanded that reporting for a 2006 book, *The Price of Admission*, whose subtitle pointedly summarizes his conclusions and makes clear that an advantage given to some applicants means a disadvantage endured by others. It reads: "How America's Ruling Class Buys Its Way into Elite Colleges—and Who Gets Left Outside the Gates."

In *The Price of Admission*, Golden writes that Duke University "accepted at least one hundred nonalumni children each year due to family wealth or connections." In these cases, the university wasn't rewarding past donors but panning for future ones. Golden also looks at the fate of Harrison Frist, who applied during the 2001–2002 academic year for early admission to Princeton University in the fall of 2002. "Admissions officers were taken aback: His grades and test scores fell far below university standards," writes Golden, who got someone on the inside to spill the beans. "On Princeton's 1 (best) to 5 (worst) academic scale for applicants, he was rated a 5. On its parallel nonacademic scale, he was a 3 or 4, signifying extracurricular leadership in his school but not talent of a state or national scope."

No matter. Harrison Frist was the son of Bill Frist, a Princeton alumnus who was then an important United States senator, representing Tennessee. And the Frist family, perhaps foreseeing the day when Harrison might need a boost, had pledged $25 million of their vast wealth to renovate and repurpose a former physics building at Princeton. It was also rechristened—as the Frist Campus Center.

Princeton opened its arms wide to Harrison Frist. It also did something else during that early-admissions cycle that Golden found especially fascinating. It admitted four classmates of Frist's from St. Albans, an exclusive private school near Washington, D.C., who had also applied; who possessed much better academic records than Frist did; and whose rejections would have made Frist's acceptance look even odder, perhaps generating chatter that Princeton didn't want. Golden writes that in the years just before and after, applicants from St. Albans hadn't enjoyed this magnitude of success with Princeton, which, he suggests, was trying to camouflage the favoritism it was showing Frist.

That favoritism endures. It flourishes. Over recent years, Harvard has acknowledged that children of alumni constitute 12 to 13 percent of a typical class. That percentage presumably ticks up a bit higher for all legacies, not just primary ones. Harvard has also acknowledged that the acceptance rate for primary legacies is in the vicinity of 30 percent—or roughly five times what it is for the overall applicant pool.

A post that appeared on the website of the *Nation* in 2011 asserted that the situation at Yale wasn't much different. According to the magazine, 13.5 percent of the freshmen arriving at Yale in the fall of 2011 had a parent who'd gone there as an undergraduate or a graduate student. And so it goes throughout the Ivy League. A few years ago, Cornell conceded that children of alumni accounted for about 15 percent of its student body.

So it's good to be a legacy. But it may be better still to be an athlete who is superior enough, or plays a sport that's obscure enough, to be of instant and sure use to a school. Cornell may not have a football team on a par with Auburn's, and swimming at Georgetown may not be anything like swimming at the University of Florida, but both Cornell and Georgetown care about a broad, rich palette of activity on campus. Both schools also care about a winner's aura, in all arenas. And both schools have alumni who participated in those sports, enjoy following them or both. Their feelings about their alma maters—and the size and frequency of their financial contributions—can be influenced by the teams' performances, so the schools want the teams to perform well. Athletics, in other words, affect the business. And there are no athletics without the right athletes.

In the spring of 2014, I taught a journalism class at Princeton and lived there for four days a week, mingling not only with the sixteen seniors, juniors and sophomores in my seminar but also with other students. And I was surprised by how often I brushed up against kids for whom sports had in some way been their entrance ramp to the school. One student I came to know told me that she had ended up at Princeton because just as she was entering her senior year of prep school, Princeton's coach for women's crew had identified her as a potentially valuable rower. Learning that she was also an excellent student, the coach ardently wooed her, and Princeton's admissions committee gratefully accepted her.

Another student came from the kind of neighborhood and private school in Manhattan that harbor an infinity of Ivy League aspirants and potentially lengthen the odds of admission: All those children of doctors, lawyers and Wall Street titans blur, and accepting too many of them runs counter to a diverse campus. But this student was an ace fencer. Princeton has a fencing team. And ace fencers aren't a dime a dozen.

Athletes are so prized and sports accorded such precedence that college coaches begin courting high school kids as early as the ninth grade and, soon thereafter, making them promises of admission if they keep their GPA above a 3.5 and get an SAT score that's not *too* far below the median for the given college's student body. I'm talking about coaches everywhere, not just at the huge Southern and Midwestern state schools whose football games are televised and whose basketball teams go to the NCAA semifinals. I'm talking about coaches at most of the colleges whose pride is rooted in academics, and I'm talking about sports in addition to football and basketball. For example, lacrosse and ice hockey coaches are especially aggressive about recruiting. They have fewer players to pick among, because not every secondary school fields teams in those sports.

But it's not just athletes and legacies who get preferential treatment. In *The Price of Admission*, Golden estimates that at elite schools, minorities make up 10 to 15 percent of students; recruited athletes, 10 to 25 percent; legacies, 10 to 25 percent; children of people who are likely to become generous donors, 2 to 5 percent; children of celebrities and politicians, 1 to 2 percent; and children of faculty, 1 to 3 percent. If you take the middle figure in each of those ranges, you're looking at as many as 55 percent of students who were probably given special consideration at admissions. I hedge because an applicant can be both a minority and a legacy, or both a legacy and an athlete, and so on. And I hasten to note that some legacies would have gained admission without that designation, and that athletic accomplishment is indeed accomplishment, something that often reflects discipline and character and warrants no less respect than academic glory.

Fifty-five percent, though, could also be a *conservative* guess. I'm using the middles of Golden's ranges, not the tops, and his breakdown doesn't take into account applicants who aren't legacies and aren't faculty children but are connected in some other way or have used their and their families' social networks to pave an inside track. Maybe they have a relative who knows a trustee of the university. Maybe they have a neighbor who knows the university president. Maybe their best friend's parent or Mom's fellow partner at the law firm or Dad's colleague at the hospital is a hugely influential graduate of the college. Someone somewhere can make a call or write a letter that will be heard above the din.

"I see that a lot," said Joie Jager-Hyman, the founder and president of College Prep 360, a Brooklyn-based firm that provides private tutoring and college admissions guidance. She told me that when a family swears to her that they have a connection that's going to make the difference at their child's top choice, they're right more often than they're wrong. "They'll say, 'Don't worry, don't worry,' and I'll say, 'Okay, but let's do six or seven safety schools,' and then the kid gets in," she said.

There's no straightforward, unbiased assessment of worth being made. For one thing, such an assessment is impossible, because worth is wholly subjective. For another, a given school may be using its applicant pool to microcast its student body. It may want some kids but not too many who dabble in amateur filmmaking, an oboe player for an orchestra that's been hankering for one, somebody from Idaho and somebody from Alaska, a few Farsi and Hindi speakers to complement all those kids fluent in Spanish and Mandarin. The wish list changes from school to school and year to year.

"Maybe they need a volleyball player, they need a squash player, they need someone who's worked with orphans but not five people like that," said Tim Levin, the founder and chief executive of Bespoke Education, a tutoring and counseling service that's based in New York but has offices and clients around the country and world. "You can take cooking classes, become a great high school chef. And then Yale will turn you down because they took three chefs in that class and they don't want a fourth."

Is the institution concerned about dwindling student interest in, and support of, a particular department? If so and the department is philosophy or art history, a kid who has demonstrated a strong interest in studying that subject has an edge—maybe without even knowing or having planned it. And after all is said and done, admissions officers are in some cases playing a hunch, exercising a whim—whatever. "I think the admission committees are thoughtful, but they're human and they're fickle and they're often reading these applications at ten p.m. at night," said Gersick. "What's their mood when they're reading? Who knows what's going to happen?"

And who knows how carefully or accurately they're even taking in the information an applicant gives them? Who knows what assumptions they're making? I've spoken with enough admissions officers and done enough reading and research to know that those officers approach their work earnestly and diligently, but that doesn't mean that they have anything close to a full, true understanding of the aspirants before them, and this fact was vividly demonstrated by a story in *BuzzFeed* in March 2015 by Molly Hensley-Clancy, a fairly recent Yale graduate who'd managed to get a look at her admissions file and at all of the notes and judgments that the readers of her application to Yale had made. Here is some of what Hensley-Clancy learned:

> *I was a student at a large inner-city public school in Minneapolis. My high school was under-resourced, with high percentages of poor, minority, and immigrant students. It had a robust program for Native American students and a program to support teenage mothers.*
>
> *But I am none of those things. I'm white and grew up middle class. Both of my parents graduated from college—from Princeton, to be exact. I attended a selective magnet program, a mostly white bubble within my school.*
>
> *And yet, there in my files, I found a note from [an] admissions officer: "She'd be a good admit for us from the Minneapolis Public Schools." The other officer's essay about me was even more explicit: "I'm in her corner," she wrote, "and would like to take one from the Minneapolis Public Schools."*
>
> *Yale, apparently, wanted—even needed—a student to represent not just my high school but my entire 35,000-student school district, which is just 33% white, where 65% of students fall under federal poverty measures, and where almost a third of students are English-*

language learners. The admissions officers knew, I think, that it would look unfortunate to overlook a public school system as large as Minneapolis.

So they picked me, the white daughter of two Ivy League graduates.

The flaws and quirks in the system are myriad, as are the efforts to game it, perhaps successfully. Take the dynamic of "demonstrated interest," to use an admissions-office catchphrase. It refers to an applicant's apparent seriousness about the school to which he or she is applying. Over the last decade, more colleges have attempted to measure this, deploying increasingly sophisticated means, in the hope of identifying those students who are truly likely to come (and aren't treating the institution as a so-called "safety school"). Colleges that succeed in figuring this out improve their "yield," or the percentage of accepted applicants who wind up enrolling. A higher yield makes a school look more desirable and can even, in small ways, improve its bond rating.

Admissions officers are "not only looking at whether the student has visited campus, been to a program they've run, or signed up to be on the school's mailing list on their website," said Liz Hirsch, one of the two directors of college counseling at the Park School of Baltimore, when I spoke with her in the summer of 2015. "What we're hearing—and this is all somewhat unsubstantiated—is that colleges are looking at how deeply kids click into their websites, how long they've been looking at things, whether they've opened emails they were sent."

Tina Forbush, the other director of college counseling at the Park School, chimed in: "I've talked to multiple schools that have said that they're starting to do that or that they're thinking of doing that."

That's quite likely, because the technology exists, and so do the eager service providers. During a phone conversation I had in September 2015 with W. Kent Barnds, who is in charge of admissions at Augustana College, in Rock Island, Illinois, he said, "I heard a term this week as I spoke to a vendor that I'd never heard before: *digital tattooing*. They can take my data pool of students and attach a digital tattoo to a student so that when I send outgoing correspondence or an electronic newsletter, through this process of digital tattooing, they can tell me to a person which of the students in my prospect pool clicked on which story. These are all students who have already opted into my recruitment program. This takes it a step beyond Google analytics.

"I don't know that I can afford the technology," he continued, "but I really like the idea of that." Already, he said, Augustana was keeping an eye out for, and noting, whether prospective applicants used social media—Twitter, Facebook, Instagram—to discuss and praise the college, their visits to it and their interactions with it. These mentions were appreciated yardsticks of enthusiasm.

While such monitoring is perhaps inevitable, it's also worrisome, because certain applicants may have the knowledge, incentive and time to make sure they signal "demonstrated interest," even if it's a total fiction, while others don't. "It creates a tremendous inequity and it encourages a tremendous amount of game playing," said Forbush. "A sophisticated counselor can tell a kid about demonstrated interest. But if you're a kid who doesn't have a lot of college counseling, you don't know about this." In many instances, she added,

"It ends up being just another part of the strategizing and not anything real."

Her observations, the *BuzzFeed* story, Daniel Golden's analyses and everything else I've described above make abundantly clear how particular, capricious and biased the admissions process can be. Equally clear is this: If you're a parent who's pushing your kids relentlessly and narrowly toward one of the most prized schools in the country and you think that you're doing them a favor, you're not. You're in all probability setting them up for heartbreak, and you're imparting a questionable set of values that I'll talk about later in this book.

And if you're a kid becoming desperately attached to a handful of those schools, you need to pull back and think about how quixotic your quest is, recognizing the roles that patronage and pure luck play. You're going to get into a college that's more than able to provide a superb education to anyone who insists on one and who takes firm charge of his or her time there. But your chances of getting into *the* school of your dreams are slim. Your control over the outcome is very, very limited, and that outcome says nothing definitive about your talent or potential. To lose sight of that is to buy into, and essentially endorse, a game that's spun wildly out of control.

THREE

OBSESSIVES AT THE GATE

"What is merit anymore? There are a million ways that people get into college that may not seem fair or right."

—Tara Dowling, who counseled students at the Choate Rosemary Hall school

If you maintain even a shred of doubt about how nutty this has all become, peek inside the office of an Ivy League professor I know and eavesdrop on a recent conversation he recounted to me.

He's being visited by some relatives. He knows them a bit—enough to make time to greet them—but not all that well. There are three of them: mother, father, daughter. And the daughter is getting ready to apply to college, though "getting ready" is a woefully inadequate phrase. It implies something relatively casual, something that she's just turning her attention to, rather than the full-on siege that has been under way for years as she, like many of her frantic and frazzled peers, aims for ever better board scores, ever dizzier heights of accomplishment, ever richer fodder for her applications. She and her parents know how fierce the competition is. The professor can see that in their faces, which communicate more than mere nervousness, more than garden-variety hope. What these three tremulous pilgrims seem to be feeling is closer to desperation.

They're in his office and on this campus not just or even mainly to acquaint themselves with the school. They're here to genuflect and prostrate themselves before it. To grovel. To preen. They're trying to recruit the professor to their cause, to impress him with their pitch, so that after they leave, he'll perhaps pick up the phone or peck out an email and tell someone in the admissions office that he just met the most fabulous girl. That the school could really use someone like her. That she's a keeper.

So she and her parents tell the professor about her grades. They tell him about her tests. They tell him about her extracurricular activities. And as the girls' parents wonder if they've exhausted the treasure chest of her charms, they realize that there's yet one more bauble they haven't retrieved, one more gem they haven't flaunted.

"Tell him," they say to their daughter, "about how you're president of your school's survivors-of-bulimia group."

I would have doubted that story if, around the time that he told it to me, I wasn't hearing so many similar tales about kids so keyed up about getting into colleges with low acceptance rates that they'd examined every facet of their personalities and scoured every byway of their biographies for admissions bait, willing to repurpose any and all oddities, humiliations, hardships.

When I met with Michael Motto, a former admissions officer at Yale who screened applicants there from 2001 to 2003 and then again from 2007 to 2008, he recalled leafing through an application from a young woman whose grades, test scores and all else were hugely impressive. He was poised to recommend her to the wider committee.

Then he got to her essay. As he remembers it, she mentioned a French teacher she greatly admired. She described their one-on-one conversation at the end of a school day. And then, this detail: During their talk, when an urge to go to the bathroom could no longer be denied, she decided not to interrupt the teacher or exit the room. She simply urinated on herself.

"Her point was that she was not going to pull herself away from an intellectually stimulating conversation just to meet a physical need," Motto told me, shaking his head. He called the college guidance counselor at her school to express his bafflement with the girl's choice of subject matter and to make sure the school knew about it, in case it reflected some self-sabotaging instinct or emotional trouble. The counselor knew about the essay, had also been baffled by it and wasn't sure what it all meant.

The girl was rejected at Yale, and so was a boy whose essay Motto also mentioned to me as an example of how disturbingly eager kids seem to be to stand out or curry sympathy in any way possible. "He wrote about his genitalia, and how he was under-endowed," Motto said. "He was going for something about masculinity and manhood, and how he had to get over certain things."

I ran those anecdotes by Marilee Jones, who was the dean of admissions at MIT from 1997 to 2007. They didn't shock her. "Kids would talk about the 911 calls because their father was beating their mother up," she told me. "Or anorexia. Or terrible, wrenching things about siblings with problems." She recalled at least one essay describing the author's struggle with the form of self-mutilation known as "delicate cutting." "And there are some things where I just feel like: Don't write that," Jones said. "Please. Don't expose yourselves."

Yearning and scheming have long been a part of applying to colleges, but they've turned into something darker. There's a swell of panic, a surrender of principle, a spreading cynicism and a disturbing gallows humor in stories I heard from students, parents, counselors, consultants and admissions officers, and in stories I read about:

- A kid who isn't gay writes an essay about the difficulty of coming out to his Asian-American family and community, then brags to classmates about his cunning subterfuge.
- A couple become the primary funders of an African orphanage so that it can be named after their kids, who then visit it a few times, do some token work and talk and write about their munificence during the college application process.
- A mother storms into the home of another mother in her affluent northeastern suburb in a fit of accusatory rage, blaming her own daughter's rejection from MIT on the fact that the other woman's daughter applied and got in without having any real intention of going there.
- A boy at a northeastern prep school studies the directory of students in his class, circling the pictures of the ones he thinks he'll be competing against for admission to Stanford and Harvard. He wants to keep an eye on them.
- A group of students at a private school in Manhattan start a sort of fantasy league for odds and predictions about where different kids will be accepted or rejected.

- A group of students gathered in the library at a public school in an affluent suburb of New York note that the high-achieving kids in the Model United Nations club are away on a trip and joke that it would be a blessing if the bus crashed, because it would free up room in the "cum laude" society, reserved for the top 10 percent of the class.
- A mother in Westchester County screeches at an SAT tutor because her son's scores rose only 200 points, from the mid-1500s to the mid-1700s (out of a possible 2400), between the first time he took the test, in March of his junior year of high school, and the second time, in May. She decides that he must take it again in two weeks, in June, and puts him on a grueling ten-day schedule of additional preparation, including three full practice exams of more than three hours each.
- A parent trying to get his child off the "wait list" for Union College calls the director of admissions and yells, "I can't believe this happened! This is a horrible thing!" The parent calls again minutes later to apologize. Then the parent calls a third time: "I know you don't like me. I'm being a complete pest."

Motto recalled that an applicant eager to get off the wait list at Yale once sent him a box full of cookies arranged so that they spelled out Motto's name. (The applicant didn't ultimately get in.) Motto moved on from Yale and, a few years ago, founded Apply High, a Manhattan-based business guiding students through the college admissions process. It gave him a new vantage point on the determination and deviousness of people intent on the most exclusive schools.

He told me about a client whose parents thrust themselves

into the crafting of his applications—if an outside coach was going to augment their son's efforts, why not Mom and Dad, too?—and came up with an idea for what they felt was the perfect college essay. It had struggle, suspense and a happy ending, describing their son as the product of "an exceptionally difficult pregnancy, with many ups and downs, trips to the hospital, various doctor visits," Motto said.

"The parents drafted a sketch of the essay and thought it was terrific," he told me. Then they showed it to their son, "and he pointed out that everything mentioned happened before he was born." He ended up choosing a topic that spoke to his *post*-utero life as a math lover who found a way to use those skills to help patients at a physical rehabilitation center.

Another student called Motto at eleven thirty at night because she'd changed a few punctuation marks in a letter to a college admissions office, and Motto had already looked at and endorsed the prior version of the letter. She told him that she couldn't get to sleep until he'd examined her revisions and assured her that they were okay.

"It wasn't even an essay," Motto said. "It was a piece of correspondence."

The mother of a student in Europe who was between his junior and senior years of high school called Motto in a frantic state. She had just read somewhere that college admissions offices looked for kids who had spent their summers in enriching ways, ideally doing charity work, and her son was due to be on vacation with the rest of the family in August.

"Should we ditch our plans," she asked Motto, "and have him build dirt roads?"

Motto reminded her that she lived in a well-paved European capital. "Where would these dirt roads be?" he said.

"India?" she suggested. "Africa?" She hadn't worked it out. But if Yale might be impressed by an image of her son with a small spade, large shovel, rake or jackhammer in his chafed hands, she was poised to find a third-world setting that would produce that sweaty and ennobling tableau.

This magnitude of hysteria certainly isn't the norm. Nor are the rich, addled clients of Motto and other private consultants whose work centers around the supercharged environments of New York and other cities with concentrations of powerful, self-consciously influential people who are convinced that they can rig the system in their children's favor and are determined to. But they and their antics are extreme manifestations of a broader anxiety that permeates a bigger, more economically diverse world of families gearing up for college admissions. And they open a window onto an industrialization of the college admission process that extends well beyond the wealthiest Americans.

New York is undoubtedly ground zero of the great race, which begins for some kids when they're mere toddlers. Susan Bodnar, a Manhattan psychologist, told me that about fifteen years ago, she took her son, Ronen, then three, to an interview of sorts at Hollingworth Preschool, which all the parents in her Upper West Side neighborhood told her was a must, the start of a track that led straight to the Ivies. Currently its website boasts of "a hybrid program, influenced by a range of educational theories and approaches, as well as progressive beliefs in pedagogy."

Bodnar remembers arriving there, looking around at the other kids and getting the sense that they'd already somehow been prepped for what was happening, which was that a school administrator was walking around and asking them, one by one, to tell her stories related to the castles they were building or the figurines they were holding. "The three-year-olds were talking about the knight and the princess and all that," she said. "My son had a plastic frog in his hand, and she said, 'What's your frog doing?' And he said, 'Hopping.' And that was the end of his story.

"It was over," Bodnar said. "He didn't get in. His frog was only hopping. It had to be involved in a drama or a narrative, and his frog was only hopping. He was three."

Before Anthony Marx began his eight-year chapter as the president of Amherst College in 2003, he lived in New York. His children were then very young, and when his son was ready to start school, he told me, "I went to a parent orientation for admissions into Hunter [College Elementary School] kindergarten. I walked into that room and you could cut the adrenaline with a knife. You could physically feel it: 'Look at all these people we have to kill to get our six-year-old into Hunter.'"

Small wonder that in 2009, a former investment banker who had done her undergraduate work at MIT before getting an MBA at Columbia started the Aristotle Circle, which provides, for up to $450 an hour, guidance and test preparation for kids vying for admission to selective grammar schools, kindergartens and even preschools. The Aristotle Circle—the name is worth repeating—belongs to a growing business in tutoring for tykes, and in 2012 the *Times* reported a noticeable increase in the scores of four-year-olds and five-year-olds trying to qualify for spots in space-limited programs for gifted children in New York City's public schools. These programs were able to accommodate less than a sixth of the students whose test scores made them eligible, and the *Times* floated the unanswerable question of whether the hand of private tutoring was being seen.

A subsequent story in the *Times* provided an even better example of how early and enormously parents can get worked up about the scholastic track that their children are on. It examined the "implicit belief that a premier prekindergarten program guarantees an early leg up in a nearly 14-year battle to gain admission to the country's most competitive colleges." Note the use of the word *battle*. Note the battle's estimated duration: *nearly fourteen years*. The *Times* then did a lengthy, deadpan, utterly earnest analysis of various paths, public versus private, from the crib to the fearful, white-knuckle crossroads of college admissions, providing the pros and cons of expenditures of hundreds of thousands of dollars. Over the course of this analysis, the reader learned that the acceptance rate for the kindergarten at the Trinity School in Manhattan is 2.4 percent for kids without some family connection to the school, that half of Trinity's graduating high school class in a given year are students who've been there *since kindergarten*, and that a full year of full-day nursery school at Horace Mann in Manhattan costs roughly the same as any other grade at Horace Mann, Trinity, Riverdale, Fieldston and other members of a New York City group that calls itself the "Ivy Preparatory School League." That price tag is more than forty thousand dollars.

And many parents pay for private tutoring on top of that, especially as college looms closer. Tim Levin, the Bespoke Education founder, said that while some families contract with his firm for only SAT preparation and spend perhaps $5,000 on that, others contract for different tutors in multiple subject areas and for mentors who help kids prioritize their time and complete their homework. These families may wind up spending $30,000 a year.

When I interviewed Michele Hernández, a longtime college admissions consultant, in June 2014, she was charging in the vicinity of $50,000 to families who signed their kids up in the eighth or ninth grade for ongoing guidance through the college application process four or three years later. She would get them ready for it by advising them on which courses to take, which summer programs to enter, and how to prioritize or reconfigure their extracurricular activities. Or families could pay $14,000 to enroll a kid in the Application Boot Camp that she staged every summer. For each of several sessions of the camp, twenty-five to thirty kids between their junior and senior years would be tucked away for four days in a hotel to work with a team of about eight editors on what Hernández told me are as many as ten drafts each of three to five different essays. The fee they paid didn't include travel to the camp, which was held in Cambridge, Massachusetts, or the hotel bill, breakfasts and dinners. It did include lunch and a range of guidance in addition to essay editing.

The very name of IvyWise, a college consulting firm in Manhattan, telegraphs the promise it's making, the reward it's dangling in front of salivating parents. Its founder, Katherine Cohen, whose diplomas come from Brown and Yale, sells a "platinum package" of twenty-four guidance sessions and an hour of weekly phone time during the junior and senior years of high school, for a price of about $30,000. Most years she cannot accommodate the number of people who want to go the platinum route. "I've got to clone myself," she told *New*

York magazine, whose profile of her was like that of a movie star, replete with flattering appraisals of her furniture, clothes and even body.

But the type of professional who came to mind as I read about Cohen and spoke with people like Motto and Hernández wasn't an actor. It was the beauty-queen whisperer who studies the swimsuits and strides of past victors to make sure that current contenders have the most eye-pleasing jiggle, the most ear-tickling giggle. Just do your hair the right way and murmur "world peace" whenever possible and the crown could be yours. College consultants insist that they try to steer the parents and kids who come through their doors away from any belief in a surefire script and toward a healthier investigation of colleges that merely match their interests and goals, but that's not exactly what their come-ons communicate.

"Let us help you rise above the rest!" said Hernández College Consulting's home page in late 2014, when I rummaged around there, clicking on a special section titled "Ivy League Stats." I then flitted over to the homepage of Apply High, which read: "It's harder than ever to get into the top universities. Let Apply High give you a competitive edge." The homepage for Jager-Hyman's College Prep 360, to its credit, talked instead about filling educational gaps and positioning kids for the most rewarding college experiences possible, but when I clicked on "About Us," I was led to a page rife with testimonials like one in which the parent of a former client said that there was "no way my son would have gotten into Yale Early Action without Joie. She encouraged him and helped through every step of the way." It was signed by a "proud mother," a phrase that struck me as odd, coming as it did from someone who'd just attributed the difference between acceptance and rejection to a hired gun.

You can find even more exhaustive and elaborate coaching outside New York, but you have to go to China. Tara Dowling did, and what she saw floored her. Dowling has worked in college guidance for more than three decades and, when I spoke with her in late 2014, was the associate director of college counseling at Choate Rosemary Hall, a renowned private boarding school in Connecticut. But from 2010 to 2012, she was involved in a venture to create an Americanized high school program for Chinese kids that would lead to a virtual diploma recognizable to admissions offices in the United States. It ultimately didn't take root, but Dowling got a glimpse of how Chinese students applying to American colleges approach the process.

"They hire someone to create a profile and, if they can get away with it, take tests for them," she said. "Nobody submits an essay that isn't sanitized or ghostwritten. There are these crazy agents who make people believe that they can guarantee them admission. Virtually no transcripts seen in the U.S. are authentic, because they don't have transcripts like we do, so they have to Americanize what they have. It doesn't mean there aren't brilliant, amazing kids. But they're so different that most of them have to submit something doctored just to fit into the American system."

And some of them, she told me, do get into the elite schools that they're set on. I asked her if that enraged or disillusioned her. Her answer was surprising, revealing and, I think, quite wise. "I think it's unfortunate when people cheat their way into anything," she said. "But that includes American kids."

* * *

Just how well does all the fluffing work? People who are familiar with the admissions process and aren't financially invested in believing that you can buy a meaningful advantage say that the screeners of applications have grown savvy to, and cynical about, all the flamboyant charity work; all the leadership positions in self-started organizations with memberships of three; all the summers spent learning Swahili; all the soul-baring essays about family melodramas as fulcrums for personal growth.

But it's impossible to know. And it's hard not to wonder if a statistic that I mentioned before—that roughly 75 percent of the students at the two hundred most highly rated colleges come from families in the top quartile of income in the United States—isn't influenced somewhat by all the high-priced prepping and primping. At the least, a kid whose parents can afford elementary and secondary schools with more expansive and rigorous programs has a better-than-average shot at the kinds of grades, Advanced Placement (AP) classes, extracurricular activities and SAT and ACT scores that are the very foundation of a potentially successful application to one of the most selective colleges. There's in fact a proven correlation between high SAT scores and high family income, and this surely reflects the sustained investment being made in a fortunate subset of kids. It also suggests that admission to an Ivy is in many cases a badge of privilege as much as of any intrinsic or earned mettle.

And while the Application Boot Camp and the "platinum package" are used by a small minority of the wealthiest families, some form of help in addition to the input of high school guidance counselors may not be all that rare. In 2009, a national survey of more than 1,250 high school seniors who scored in the top third of all students on the SAT or the ACT found that 26 percent of them had used the services of a paid college placement consultant.

Mark Sklarow, the chief executive of the Independent Educational Consultants Association, told me that he thinks that number is high, or at least was at the time. His own estimates as of July 2014 were that 25 percent of kids bound for private four-year colleges and 10 to 15 percent bound for public universities paid for at least some outside advice, and he said that the number of advisers grows continuously and has gone up with particular speed of late. A decade ago, he said, there were maybe 1,500 professionals working full-time as independent college consultants, meaning that they weren't paid by, or affiliated with, any school that gave students their services for free. In 2009, he said, there were perhaps 2,500, and by 2014, about 7,500: a tripling of the ranks in just five years.

Meanwhile, the test prep industry—special camps, special classes, targeted publications—is a multibillion-dollar behemoth, underscoring its insinuation into the lives of kids across a fairly broad economic spectrum. With differing intensities and strategies on different rungs of the economic ladder, kids are trying to boost their odds of admission, and there's no way it doesn't queer the process somewhat, favoring certain aspirants over others. Do the kids getting into their top-choice schools have greater potential? Or do they just have a better understanding of the system and how to work it?

An obsession with its workings is pervasive, and is evident in Internet traffic and in the volume of books that promise help. The College Confidential website, which is devoted to the admissions process, attracts tens of millions of unique visitors annually. It has its own insider shorthand, its own insider vocabulary. Often visitors, saving themselves keystrokes, don't bother to spell out Harvard, Yale and Princeton, which are simply "HYP." "HYPS" signals the inclusion of Stanford as well and "HYPSM" the addition of MIT. And "chance me" is the command for a popular game that visitors play; one of them describes his or her transcript and which school he or she dreams of attending, then others weigh in with predictions. The College Confidential chatter revolves largely around admissions odds and admissions tips.

As for books, well, Hernández is the author of *A Is for Admission: The Insider's Guide to Getting into the Ivy League and Other Top Colleges*. Jager-Hyman wrote *Fat Envelope Frenzy: One Year, Five Promising Students, and the Pursuit of the Ivy League Prize*, followed a few years later by *B+ Grades, A+ College Application*.

The creative titles of these overlapping manuals suggest how many are out there and how carefully and energetically each must try to distinguish itself from the others. You can choose among *Going Geek: What Every Smart Kid (and Every Smart Parent) Should Know About College Admissions*, *Crazy U: One Dad's Crash Course in Getting His Kid into College*, *How to Be a High School Superstar: A Revolutionary Plan to Get into College by Standing Out* and *How to Make Colleges Want You: Insider Secrets for Tipping the Admissions Odds in Your Favor*, to name just a few.

For writing tips, there are *Escape Essay Hell! A Step-by-Step Guide to Writing Narrative College Application Essays* and *Conquering the College Admissions Essay in 10 Steps* and *The Art of the College Essay* and *100 Successful College Application Essays* and *50 Successful Ivy League Application Essays* and *50 Successful Harvard Application Essays*. That's not to mention the pages upon pages of study guides for standardized tests. For the sake of college admissions, vast forests have died and whole continents could be denuded.

Shelves of books like that weren't around when Dick Parsons was finishing high school in the early 1960s, and he wouldn't have read them if they had been. He didn't sweat anything about the application process, not even the schools he set his sights on—all *three* of them. His approach was improvisatory, whimsical, accidental, leading him to Honolulu and the University of Hawaii. It wasn't exactly a likely destination for an African-American teen who was born in the Bedford-Stuyvesant section of Brooklyn, who grew up in South Ozone Park, Queens, and whose parents had both attended historically black colleges. And it isn't the alma mater you expect on the resume of a man who went on to become the chairman and chief executive of Time Warner, then the chairman of Citigroup. A trailblazer and a titan, Parsons was once rumored to succeed Michael Bloomberg as mayor of New York, and when President Obama took office, he put Parsons on an economic advisory team alongside Warren Buffett, Robert Rubin, Robert Reich and Google's Eric Schmidt. In 2014, he drew a messier appointment and was chosen as the interim chief executive of the Los Angeles Clippers basketball team, charged with cleaning up the mess made by Donald Sterling.

His own three children grew up in more affluent circumstances and in an environment where the competition to get into highly selective colleges was keen and out in the open. And sometimes, he told me, his wife would present him and his educational background to the anxious fellow parents around them as a reality check and calmative. "She would have people talk to me as a kind of confidence-building exercise: If this idiot can end up on the right side of the ledger, you can," Parsons said with a laugh.

Against the backdrop of the current obsession with college admissions, it's funny to be reminded of just how little thought many spectacularly successful people put into where they went to school—and of just how unremarkable that was in an earlier (and, admittedly, different) era. But it's also important. Instructive. And that's not because such heedlessness is worth emulating, a strategy superior to all the fretting that occurs now. No, a story like Parsons's simply puts the relevance and predictive power of a fancy diploma in context. And it underscores that many of the talents and strengths that wind up fueling someone's achievements don't necessarily emerge or play a part in the college application process, and aren't honed in the classrooms of exclusive schools.

Parsons did dream of the Ivy League—or, rather, of Princeton. Growing up, he knew he was supposed to aim for, and go to, college—his parents drilled that into him and his four siblings—and when he was in the seventh grade, his class took a trip to Princeton to see a football game.

"And I was gobsmacked," he said. "Those ivy-covered walls, the archways: It was what college was supposed to be. If you grow up in the Northeast, you have an ideal of college, and Princeton just looked like it." Its quadrangles had the right aura of authority, its spires the right air of enchantment.

So that was that. It was settled. "Whenever anybody would say, 'Where are you going?' I'd say, 'I'm going to Princeton,' as if it were a rite of passage," he recalled. He was certainly a fine student; he'd even skipped two grades. And he reliably aced standardized tests. But he could also be lazy and inattentive, and there were plenty of B's on his transcript. A few of the adults around him advised him not to pin all of his hopes on his Princeton application. His parents insisted that he apply to City College of New York as an insurance policy and more affordable alternative. He was sure he wouldn't need a fallback, but, even so, he was determined that CCNY not be his only one, as he was eager to travel farther from home. So he filed a third application to a place *very* far away: the University of Hawaii. It had popped into his head in part because a pretty high school classmate of his was from Hawaii.

"It was a lark," he said.

That is, until he didn't get into Princeton and had to pick either CCNY or Hawaii. He went for the Pacific and the palms, and began to cast it as a considered choice. "They had this very exciting astrophysics department," he said, explaining that it had something to do with mountaintop telescopes and a sky unsullied by pollution and excessive light. In his mind he dwelled on how wonderfully exotic his adventure would be.

When he headed west, it wasn't just to school but to an unprecedented kind of independence, a degree of self-reliance unlike anything he had experienced before. With five kids, his parents couldn't contribute much to his education and he didn't have a scholarship, so he had to pay for his tuition and living expenses himself and took a sequence of jobs, putting in enough hours at some to qualify as nearly full-time.

His first year, he worked at a biomedical research center, and while he had a title that smacked of seriousness and pleased him—"lab assistant"—he had duties less vaunted. "I washed test tubes," he said. He might as well have been dealing with dirty dishes in a restaurant kitchen.

Later he worked as an attendant in a parking garage, and for his last year he laid pipes for a local gas company. Along the way he played some school basketball and went to his classes, though he wasn't an intensely dedicated student. He started out as a physics major but found the coursework grueling and switched to history. Even so, he was six credits shy of what he needed for a diploma by the time graduation rolled around. He never bothered to get those credits or that diploma, because he'd aced yet another exam—the one for law school applicants—and Albany Law School was willing to enroll him despite his shortfall of credits. To help with his bills there, he worked part-time as a janitor.

Although his college days don't read like the prelude to professional greatness, he said that they actually were pivotal, as was the University of Hawaii. "I cannot remember a single thing I learned in college," Parsons told me. "But it worked for me because what I learned was that I could make it in this world." He had traveled five thousand miles from his home, and was able to circle back to Queens to visit his family only once a year, during the summer. He had been sixteen when he arrived in Honolulu. He didn't have local relatives, local connections, any kind of ready safety net. He was utterly on his own. And the magnitude of that dislocation had forced on him a maturity and poise that another, different college experience might not have.

"At the end of four years, I was still standing," he said. "Maybe wavering a bit, but still standing. I learned that surviving and prospering—with a small *p*—was something that I could do." Back in elementary and middle and high school, when he'd been skipping grades and prophesying Princeton and was blissfully unaware that the boldest plans have a way of being thwarted, he'd had arrogance. Now he had something less gaudy but infinitely more useful.

"Confidence," he said. "And for me, that was an essential part of the equation of success."

Parsons doesn't think that his particular trajectory would be right for everybody. No single trajectory is—and that includes one that takes a student to and through an exclusive, brand-name college. "You should try to find a school that fits you," he said. "You should ask yourself where are you going to develop those other important life skills.

"By the time I got out of law school," he added, "nobody asked me where I went to college. They didn't care. Everybody goes to college, and with the exception of maybe a few brands, you don't really know what that means, wherever they went." The source of an MBA or JD can have significant impact, he said, but even then, the degree is no substitute for abilities nurtured outside the classroom.

I asked him which abilities those were, what "important life skills" he'd been referring to. "The ability to relate to people," he said. "To be comfortable with risk. To manage ambiguity and to be resilient.

"Are you prepared to bet on yourself?" he asked. "Are you prepared to show up?" In going to Hawaii, he'd taken an enormous bet on himself. And maybe that set him up to take a sequence of additional bets—to reach high—as the years went by.

I would have chalked up the way that Parsons chose the University of Hawaii as some anomalously superficial oddity had I not spoken just a few days earlier with Bobbi Brown. She's the founder and chief creative officer of Bobbi Brown Cosmetics, one of those companies that divined an unoccupied niche and an untapped market in a business that seemed utterly saturated with competitors. And she's been hailed as a savvy entrepreneur because of that.

I reached out to her because I was intrigued by where she'd received her degree: Emerson College in Boston, which specializes not in business but in communications and the arts. And when I spoke with her, I learned that her adventures in college were even more surprising than that. Emerson was the third institution of higher learning that she attended. And while it was chosen in a thoughtful fashion, the first two weren't.

Brown grew up and went to a public high school in the mid-1970s in an affluent suburb of Chicago. Many of the kids around her were acutely concerned about where they'd be going to college, but she and the other girls in her crowd weren't. She graduated a semester early, and that wasn't because she was such a great student. It was because she'd dutifully finished all her requirements. She then enrolled for the spring semester at the University of Wisconsin Oshkosh. She had one and only one reason for doing that. Her boyfriend at the time was older than she was and was already a student there.

After that semester, she convinced him to pack up and move on with her, to a destination that she deemed more exciting, but it wasn't a highly selective school picked for its specific programs or academic boasts. "The only consideration in where I went was, honestly, where my friends were going," Brown told me. And that turned out to be the University of Arizona.

"We knew we could get in there, it wouldn't be a big deal,

it was far enough from Chicago, it was fun," she said, explaining that among her peers in that place at that time, you headed to school in Colorado if you wanted skiing and Arizona if you wanted sun. Her friends chose sun.

She completed only one year at the University of Arizona, after which she announced to her mother: "School's not for me." Her parents were supportive but insistent: A college education—some kind of college education—was a must. Her mother asked her what she was really passionate about. The honest answer: makeup. And rather than dismiss that as irrelevant, mother and daughter actually sought to incorporate it into a plan. Makeup was important in theater and movies, the world of which included professional makeup artists. So maybe Brown should look for a school that trained people for theater and movies.

Emerson qualified, though Brown told me that what really hooked her was her visit to the school. She spotted a bunch of people at an outdoor café, and instantly liked the look of it and them. She had a feeling.

At that time, she said, Emerson was aggressively wooing students and trying to establish itself as an institution uniquely responsive to their creative impulses, so they let her design a concentration that didn't exist. "I told them, 'I want to study makeup,'" she recalled. "I thought I wanted to do theater makeup. They had one makeup class. They said, 'You can work with the director of the school play, you can work with the TV department.'" So that's what she did: She journeyed through genres—theater, TV, film—that were a part of the curriculum, and in each, she focused as much as possible on foundation and powder, chins and cheekbones, shadow and light.

"I left with a bachelor of fine arts in makeup with a minor in photography, but what I really left with was the knowledge that it was all up to me," she said. Emerson had cast her as the captain of her fate, a role she continued to play from then on. "Everything in life—everything—is what you put into it. It's not just Harvard, Stanford or Yale that gets you a foot in the door. There are so many options for how you can live your life and make a career for yourself."

But there's one guideline she finds unfailingly reliable: If you can identify and stick with something you're genuinely passionate about, you're ahead of the game. "Often kids say they want to be a lawyer or go into marketing or go into business and make a lot of money," she said. "That's the wrong answer. You'll figure out how to make money *once* you figure out what you love to do."

Emerson turned out to be the right school for her but not because she'd had to beat out her peers for the privilege of studying there, just as that dynamic wasn't what made the University of Hawaii work, in its way, for Parsons. She and Parsons connected with their colleges in other fashions. They're hardly alone in that, or in wandering to those schools in ways that didn't include nighttime sweats, daytime tutors, four stabs at the SAT, essays that veritably bled on the page and a jittery conviction that absolutely everything was on the line.

FOUR

RANKINGS AND WRONGS

"I think U.S. News & World Report *will go down as one of the most destructive things that ever happened to higher education."*

—Adam Weinberg, the president of Denison University

What's troubling about the fixation on a small cluster of colleges to the exclusion of others isn't just the panic that it promotes in the people clamoring at the gates, the unwarranted feelings of failure that it creates in the kids who don't make it through and the pessimism that it suggests about America's fortunes. It's the number of rickety assumptions that it's built on, and chief among them is that rankings of schools—in particular, the rankings revised annually by *U.S. News & World Report*—have enormous meaning.

They don't. In the case of *U.S. News*, they're largely subjective. They're easily manipulated. They rely on metrics and optics of dubious relevance. They're about vestigial reputation and institutional wealth as much as any evidence that the children at a given school are getting an extraordinary education and graduating with a sturdy grip on the future and the society around them. They're an attention-getting, moneymaking enterprise for *U.S. News*, not an actual service to the college-bound. They don a somber gray suit of authority, but it's a hustler's threads.

And yet the *U.S. News* rankings maintain their quasi-biblical power, year after year, exploiting people's insecurities about their own judgments and indulging our love of tidy and digestible lists, preferably numbered ones with scores attached, in a digital world of so much random information. We use such lists and scores for cars, for dishwashers, for restaurants, for hotels. And, with four years and a king's ransom on the line, secondary school students and their parents use them for colleges, which have indeed become more and more like products, albeit expensive ones. The assumption is that the No. 5 school must somehow be better, and more likely to yield returns, than the No. 25 school, which in turn must be an infinitely safer bet and more enviable boast than anything below 50. And that belief is unshakable, surviving countless attempts to shake it.

"We might as well rail against Cheetos, soft drinks, lotteries, or articles about the Kardashians," wrote John Tierney in a spirited post for the *Atlantic*'s website in late 2013 that did a masterful job of capturing many observers' frustration with the rankings. "You can bash people over the head with information about how empty, useless, or bad-for-you some things are, yet lots of folks will still want to consume them. Each of us has some kind of tripe that sustains us. For many, it's the *U.S. News* college rankings." The paradox of pervasive contempt for them and yet widespread obeisance to them was underscored by the title of Tierney's post. "Your Annual Reminder to Ignore the *U.S. News & World Report* College Rankings," it read, with a subtitle that asserted that their "real purpose is to 'exacerbate the status anxiety' of prospective students and parents."

I refuse to accept that the bashing is fruitless. I'll proceed to bash, because I believe passionately that the college experience can't be reduced in this fashion, nor can an individual college's merits be evaluated by this formula. I also worry, despite all the bashing, that many parents and kids still don't understand how questionable the *U.S. News* approach is and how much contempt many of the people *in* higher education, including those whose schools benefit from the rankings, have for it.

Nearly all of the current and former educators I know cite the *U.S. News* rankings as a major culprit in the admissions mania, and nearly all of them disparage the criteria behind the rankings as fatally flawed. One of the most thoughtful laments that I've heard or seen came from Jeffrey Brenzel, who spent eight years, ending in 2013, as the dean of admissions at Yale, a school that routinely appears at or near the top of various rankings, including the ones by *U.S. News*. Brenzel posted it on Yale's website after he stepped down from that job. "Make no mistake," he wrote. "The publication of college rankings is a business enterprise that capitalizes on anxiety about college admissions."

He said that while choosing a college is indisputably more important than buying a household appliance, "College rankings systems all take a far *less* thorough and scientific approach than *Consumer Reports* does when testing vacuum cleaners. Another problem with rankings is that they allow the dominant player—*U.S. News & World Report*, a magazine that has actually gone defunct and exists now only as a purveyor of rankings—to exert undue influence."

He then relayed the story of a former Yale admissions colleague who went on to work as a college placement counselor at a high school. Time and again, she watched students jettison carefully constructed lists of colleges that might be right for them in favor of lists with a familiar cast of schools. "These new lists always seem to correlate with the rankings in *U.S. News*," Brenzel wrote. "Students tend to discard excellent and appropriate colleges ranked lower in *U.S. News* and to add 'stretch' schools that are unlikely to offer them admission.

"The simplicity and clarity that ranking systems seem to offer are not only misleading, but can also be harmful," he continued, adding, "Rankings tend to ignore the very criteria that may be most important to an applicant, such as specific academic offerings, intellectual and social climate, ease of access to faculty, international opportunities and placement rates for careers or for graduate and professional school."

International opportunities are not part of the *U.S. News* survey. Nor are job-placement rates (which, to be fair, would be awfully difficult to define and measure) or any assessment of the distinction that graduates of a given school go on to achieve. Do those graduates feel that the school gave them the grounding in the world and the launching into adulthood that it should have? The only part of the *U.S. News* scoring formula that comes close to getting at that is the percentage of alumni who give money to the school, and that's a fuzzy yardstick with an additional problem that I'll explain in a bit.

But the SAT or ACT scores of admitted students? These are important to *U.S. News*; in fact, their impact on a school's ranking has increased in recent years, to 8.125 percent for the rankings published in the fall of 2014. "It's like what Einstein said about measurements," said Hiram Chodosh, the president of Claremont McKenna College, when I asked him about *U.S. News*. "You measure what you can count easily, and then often fail to measure what really counts."

U.S. News rightly and smartly divides schools into a few categories, the two most prominent of which are "national universities"—which is where you find big state schools, the Ivies, and other doctorate-granting research institutions like the California Institute of Technology, Emory, Notre Dame, Carnegie Mellon and Howard—and "national liberal arts colleges," which is where you find smaller schools like Williams, Reed and Colorado College. Beyond that its decisions grow more and more debatable.

More than a fifth of the score that *U.S. News* assigns a school reflects what high school guidance counselors think of it and the regard in which presidents, provosts and admissions deans at other colleges hold it. But most of these people, when surveyed, aren't likely to be weighing in with deep and continuously updated knowledge of the entire higher-education landscape. They haven't been in the classrooms of the colleges they're grading. They've met only a few, if any, of most colleges' current students and recent graduates.

"I don't know how to rank Sewanee College," said Jennifer Delahunty, who was the longtime admissions dean at Kenyon College. She was thus one of three people at Kenyon, along with the president and the provost, who were annually mailed a form by *U.S. News* that asked them, in an absurdly superficial manner, to give each college on a list of more than one hundred a grade of distinguished, strong, good, adequate, marginal or "don't know" by checking the relevant box. The scoring is no more nuanced than that. And she was using Sewanee as a somewhat random example. "I have a good friend who's a dean there, so should I rank it high?" she said. "Should I just go through and make Kenyon excellent and everybody else good? Would that be the thing to do?"

In the end, she said, "I just throw it in the trash." Year after year. And she's pretty sure she's not the only one in academia who takes that approach.

Those who dutifully check the boxes and size up their peer institutions are often going by reputation. And because one of the principal engines of reputation is, well, the *U.S. News* rankings, there's a self-fulfilling prophecy at work. Schools are rated highly because they've been rated highly before.

"It's a teenage thing," Marilee Jones, the former admissions dean for MIT, told me. "We're a bunch of lemmings. There is no best. *There is no best.*"

Schools are also judged by how much they spend per student, and *U.S. News* insists that it's able to distinguish between money that goes to education and money that merely goes to upgrade the fitness facilities, beautify the communal spaces, multiply the amenities and add layers of nonacademic services—all of which are done not to educate students but to gild campuses in a way that boosts applications. But many education experts with whom I've spoken are doubtful that *U.S. News* can and does seperate definitively between the two kinds of expenditures, and there's spending that falls into gray areas.

In any case, dollars don't equal learning. Nor do they equal teaching, and yet the *U.S. News* scoring formula rewards schools that pay higher faculty salaries, as if professors getting bigger checks are somehow going to be giving better instruction.

"As I understood it, there's nothing in there, directly, about the quality of education," said Anthony Marx, the former Amherst president, referring to the *U.S. News* formula. His assessment wasn't sour grapes: Amherst has traditionally fared as well as Yale in the rankings. "Basically," he continued, "the driver is how much money does an institution have and therefore how much money does it spend. And how many kids can you turn away. The incentives of the rankings are to raise the price and fund-raise so as to spend more, and make it more crazy-selective, not for any measured educational outcome."

One of the most disturbing wrinkles of the *U.S. News* rankings is that they have a potentially adverse effect on keeping the cost of college down. Why would rankings-cognizant administrators, eager to see their schools rise on the list and attract more applicants, look for economies and limit tuition increases when *U.S. News* rewards schools that have a whole lot of money sloshing around but not those that are seemingly concerned with affordability?

U.S. News endorses selectiveness in several ways. A part of a school's score, albeit a tiny one, is determined by its acceptance rate, with lower being better. Other parts are determined by the SAT or ACT scores of the students it admits and by their class rank. All in all, the harder a school is to get into, the more worthy it's deemed. Why?

Sure, its selectiveness may confer some immediate professional advantage on some graduates, inasmuch as there are job recruiters, looking for a shortcut to outstanding students, who assume that the University of Pennsylvania or Northwestern has done the heavy-duty screening for them and that they can now limit their own canvass to those schools and others like them. And, yes, high scores and class ranks often connote smarts and a seriousness of purpose, which an ideal student body would be brimming with. But while a campus full of kids in the upper 3 percent of SAT scorers can boast about that and find an impressed audience at *U.S. News*, is it truly more attractive than, and superior to, a campus full of kids in the upper 15 percent?

"I have long believed that below a 30 percent acceptance rate, a class is not really getting better," wrote William M. Shain when he was the dean of admissions at Vanderbilt University. "Rather, test scores rise from the very high to the stratospheric, and more valedictorians are denied admission. To my knowledge, no one has ever documented that this brings any improvement in the quality of intellectual discourse on campus. Institutions do not change as rapidly as do guidebook ratings."

This assessment was made a decade ago, even before acceptance rates plummeted to their current levels, and it was echoed by Todd Martinez, a professor of chemistry at Stanford University. He told me that the sorts of distinctions being drawn between applicants to a school that's accepting only 5 or 10 or 20 percent of them are almost inherently meaningless and subjective. "All that human beings can do is triage—good, bad, mediocre," he said. "That's about the limit of our ability to divide things up. When it gets below thirty percent or twenty percent, it's just a lot of noise."

Selectiveness is hardly a straightforward proxy for desirability. It's in some cases a decision a school makes, principally by drumming up applications. It can be fudged, prettied up. Bruce Poch, the former admissions dean at Pomona, said that when *U.S. News* revises its rankings yearly, in part to take into account the fresh group of students who have arrived at a school, it looks only at freshmen who enter in the fall. As a result, he said, some schools, which he declined to name, will accept the sorts of lower-scoring students who won't impress *U.S. News* for enrollment in the spring semester, making them wait to come to campus, or will offer them a guaranteed place as transfers into the sophomore class.

Schools also throw around lucrative merit scholarships to woo the high scorers who elevate a student body's statistical profile, though they do this with more than just *U.S. News* in mind. Whatever the motive, this practice appears to be significantly more prevalent than it was decades earlier, and much of the money involved is going to kids who don't really need it instead of kids who sorely do. A 2008 study by the Institute for College Access & Success found that in the 2005–2006 academic year, 30 percent of the roughly $11 billion in financial aid that institutions of higher education provided was "non-need-based."

"It's odious, it's wrong, but at your peril, you don't participate," said Kenyon's Jennifer Delahunty. "I am so lucky. I am the envy of my peers. No trustee here ever said, 'Drive up those SAT scores.' But the truth of the matter is, I'm evaluated on those benchmarks. If our test scores drop, people are going to get very concerned."

Ted O'Neill, the former dean of admissions at the University of Chicago, said that schools monkey around with more than just how distinguished their student body appears. *U.S. News* smiles, understandably, on colleges with smaller class sizes, so administrators will try to schedule such seminars and tutorials "in the fall quarter, which is what *U.S. News* cares about," he said. *U.S. News* also smiles on alumni generosity—specifically, as I mentioned before, what percentage of a school's alumni is donating money—and this metric, too, is corruptible: Just launch a fund-raising campaign that stresses that full participation is paramount and that $1 is as appreciated as $100. "There's been a lot of pretty blatant manipulation of alumni giving numbers," O'Neill said.

His verdict on the *U.S. News* rankings wasn't any kinder than that of others who spoke with me about them. "They seem to imply a kind of scientific evaluation of quality," he said, "and they're really not talking about quality at all. That's an illusion. They're doing a profile of a college's power."

Those were mild, measured words in comparison with what the renowned political economist Robert Reich, who was the country's labor secretary during Bill Clinton's administration, wrote in a blistering attack on the *U.S. News* rankings in September 2015, after the latest installment was published. He complained that the rankings were "analogous to a restaurant guide that gives top ratings to the most expensive establishments that are backed and frequented by the wealthiest gourmands—and much lower rankings to restaurants with the best food at lower prices that attract the widest range of diners." He was making a point about diversity that I'll elaborate on later.

He noted that the method behind the rankings puts public universities at a serious disadvantage, although, he said, "The best public universities provide a higher-quality education, in my view, than many of the private elites.

"Full disclosure: I was educated in private elite universities—Dartmouth and Yale," he added. "And I taught for many years at Harvard. These venerable institutions rate at or near the top of the *U.S. News* rankings. For the past decade, though, I've been teaching at the University of California at Berkeley. One thing I've discovered: My Berkeley students are every bit as bright as the students I met or taught in the Ivies."

It is hard, maybe even impossible, to engage anyone in higher education about the college admissions frenzy, its causes and its negative consequences without *U.S. News* coming up. And, sure enough, Condoleezza Rice alluded to it relatively soon into my conversation with her.

She currently teaches at Stanford, where she served as provost just before her years in George W. Bush's administration, first as his national security adviser and then as his secretary of state. And she has no gripes with Stanford's standing: In the *U.S. News* rankings released in September 2015, it tied with Columbia and the University of Chicago for fourth place among national universities, behind Princeton, Harvard and Yale, in that order.

"I think Stanford is unbelievable," she said, her voice brimming with an enthusiasm that seemed genuine. "But there are other places that are also great to go: big state universities that have a different character; research universities; small liberal arts colleges; regional colleges that are very good and maybe there's a reason a particular student would be better off close to home." And one of her chief problems with the *U.S. News* rankings—and with the kind of attention accorded them—is the phenomenon that Yale's Jeffrey Brenzel mentioned in relation to the college placement counselor he knows: They unnecessarily shrink the pool of schools that kids consider. In constructing a hierarchy of colleges, they give short shrift to the multitude and diversity of them, and they imply that certain schools are better for everyone, when they may only be better for particular students with particular dispositions. "I think we end up limiting students' horizons too early," she said. Certainly few students would be prodded by the *U.S. News* rankings to attend Rice's alma mater, which placed 86th among national universities in the fall of 2015 and has come *up* in the world since she graduated from it. It's the University of Denver.

She went there because it was close to home and because her father worked there, which meant that she got a financial break on tuition. In 1968, John Rice had moved her and her mother from Alabama to Colorado to take a job as an assistant dean of admissions at the University of Denver, where he would subsequently rise to other, higher posts. He enrolled her at a private, Catholic all-girls school whose graduates were expected to go off to college, though she told me that few set their sights on the Ivy League or, for that matter, schools outside the state. The message she got from her parents was that she should attend either the University of Denver or Colorado College.

That's partly because she, like Dick Parsons, had zipped through school quickly and would be starting college younger than most other kids—in her case, at the age of fifteen. Her parents, understandably, didn't want her going too far away just yet. She lived at home for her first years at the University of Denver, and she initially majored in piano at the university's Lamont School of Music. She'd been studying the instrument since she was a little girl, and she'd often been hailed as a piano prodigy.

At the University of Denver, she learned that she wasn't. She was good, not great, or maybe great, but not quite great enough. And so, about midway through her time there, she went on the hunt for a new field of study. She flirted briefly with English, but it didn't feel quite right. Then she happened across something that did. As my *Times* colleague Elisabeth Bumiller writes in *Condoleezza Rice: An American Life*: "In the spring of 1973 Rice wandered into a course called 'Introduction to International Politics,' taught by Josef Korbel, a sixty-three-year-old Czech refugee who had founded Denver's Graduate School of International Studies and was a university elder statesman. In one of the great coincidences and complications of modern American diplomatic history, Korbel also happened to be the father of Madeleine Albright, who would become the only other woman secretary of state." (Bumiller's book preceded Hillary Clinton's appointment to the job.)

"For Rice, like Albright, Korbel would be one of the great influences of her life," Bumiller writes. "Until she met him, Rice had shown almost no interest in foreign policy...But when Rice heard Korbel speak to her class on Stalin, she 'fell in love'—the phrase she has used in virtually every interview she has given about this moment in her life."

During my conversation with Rice, years after all those other interviews, she was still marveling at the hand of happenstance in her academic trajectory, something that she emphasizes to the young men and women at Stanford who turn to her for guidance. "My students will come in and say, 'How do I do what you do?' which means they want to be secretary of state," she told me. "I say, 'So here's how you do it—you start as a failed piano major.' They're stunned. But what I'm trying to get them to see is that you have some time to recognize that special combination of what you love and what you're also good at. Taking the time to do that is very important." Rice noted that a college admissions process that focuses on selectiveness and heated competition doesn't properly stress that. If anything, it encourages methodical planning, blind conformity.

Rice also said that there's a transcendent importance—all too frequently overlooked—in how fully students throw themselves into the college experience and how much they demand and extract from whichever institutions they wind up at. Great educations aren't passive experiences; they're active ones. At the University of Denver, she got involved in student government and, for a short stint, with the student newspaper, though she quickly decided that journalism wasn't for her. For a while she ran the university's speakers bureau: a great way to meet and mingle with prominent visitors to the campus and a good motivation for keeping up on current events. She remembers an episode from her time in that job that made her feel as if she were in the middle of history (a place she'd later grow accustomed to inhabiting). Bob Woodward, one of the *Washington Post* writers who broke the Watergate story, was supposed to come to the campus for an appearance. Just beforehand, she recalled, "I got a panicked phone call that he had canceled. They said, 'Something's come up.' This was 1974. It was the tapes." She was referring to the public release, in the spring of 1974, of transcripts from audio recordings that President Nixon had made in the White House. "I had to hustle and get notices that Woodward had canceled and that ticket prices would be refunded," Rice told me. "You don't get that kind of organizational experience and skill just in your classes."

But with classes, too, "I was very aggressive," she said. "I was very assertive in getting to know faculty. I was always the first kid to make an appointment during office hours the first week of class. And then I'd go in knowing how I wanted to talk to faculty, how I wanted to use it.

"I tell students: If you're taking a class and you see a faculty member that you're interested in, read something the faculty member's written, then go see them. Faculty are vain. They'll love that. And then they'll remember you. No matter what university you're in, you'll find this across the board. I've had friends who've taught at San Diego State, at Hamilton College. Across the board, the student who shows initiative in a way that captures the imagination of that faculty member is going to get more time."

And, she added, "You will find faculty at almost every college who are vibrant and exciting. I found Josef Korbel at the University of Denver, and it changed my life." Although she got her master's in political science at Notre Dame, she returned to the University of Denver—and to Korbel—for her PhD. It was a decision that had nothing to do with rankings or with any hierarchy of esteem. It had to do only with a relationship that she'd forged, through her own initiative, and with a plan that made sense to and for her.

I asked Rice if her perch at Stanford affords her a perspective of how much hope and work many kids today invest in getting into a school of its altitude. She said she knows the score simply from listening to friends' children talk. (Rice herself isn't a parent.) She recalled a recent conversation with the son of someone she knows well. "I said to him, 'Are you going to look at Stanford? Where do you want to look?' And he said, 'Well, I'd never get in there.'

And then he could recite, for the last five years, who in his high school class *had* gotten in.

"Now that seems to me a little extreme," she said.

U.S. News isn't alone in the rankings racket. Over recent years, there's been an uptick in attention to the annual "College Salary Report" by PayScale, a website that lists schools in accordance with the "median mid-career salary" of their graduates. Budding plutocrats, take note: These are the institutions that will supposedly help you maximize your earning potential. Emphasis on *supposedly*.

For starters, PayScale doesn't randomly survey alumni across a broad spectrum of schools. It doesn't conduct a scientific poll along the lines of Pew, Gallup or Quinnipiac. Instead it requires visitors to its website, which is a resource for employers and employees who are trying to figure out the usual compensation for various positions in an array of fields, to fill out questionnaires that ask where they attended college and what they're making.

So PayScale is entirely reliant on the people who happen to come to it, and there's no way they're going to be a representative cross section of the population of college graduates. They're going to be people more concerned with matters of compensation, in professions where such matters are central. For some colleges, PayScale has thousands of completed surveys; for others, a statistically dubious fraction of that.

The surveys rely to some extent on respondents' honesty. And the results for a given school have more to do with which majors and career tracks are most popular there—and, thus, the kinds of students the school attracts—than with the quality of instruction or timbre of campus life. Accordingly, schools that specialize in engineering or send legions of students to Wall Street tend to fare well in PayScale's rankings.

Flawed as the information that PayScale rounds up is, it's what *Forbes* leans on for *its* annual rankings, which use earnings along with an array of other factors, including how positively students speak of their teachers on the entirely voluntary, entirely unscientific website RateMyProfessors.com. The PayScale information is also used by *Money* magazine, which joined the college rankings party in 2014. For its list of top colleges, *Money* combined graduates' earnings with the "quality" and "affordability" of the school.

The metrics that *Money* used for a school's quality—SAT scores, graduation rates—mirrored those employed by *U.S. News*, and were equally debatable. But in considering affordability, which *Money* determined based not only on tuition but also on the amount of aid available to students and how many years they were taking to complete school, the magazine in some sense improved on both *U.S. News* and PayScale. It also guaranteed findings that would be original and would thus garner some attention from the news media. On *Money*'s top 20 in 2015, Harvard, Princeton, Stanford and MIT made predictable appearances. But Babson College (No. 2), the Maine Maritime Academy (No. 8), Cooper Union (No. 9, in a tie), the University of California, Irvine (No. 13), Brigham Young University (No. 15, in a tie), Bentley University (also No. 15) and Texas A&M (No. 20) made unpredictable ones.

Part of what's so frustrating about the *Money*, *Forbes*, PayScale and *U.S. News* rankings is that there are all sorts of other lists and all manner of other measurements that get little attention and that, in some cases, communicate information that's relevant. Why not look, for example, at which schools have the most students who do at least some study abroad? These kids presumably come back to campus with stories and perspectives that will enrich the entire study body, and the popularity of studying abroad may well say something about an institution's signals to students and about their intellectual curiosity. *U.S. News* in fact compiles this data, which it doesn't use in its rankings.

But for what it's worth, the ten schools with the greatest percentage of students who had ventured outside the country for part of their studies, at least according to information released by *U.S. News* in the fall of 2014, were Goucher College, Soka University of America, Thomas More College of Liberal Arts, Centre College, Goshen College, Kalamazoo College, Pitzer College, Susquehanna University, Carleton College and Elon University. Along with those institutions, a dozen others sent a greater percentage of their students abroad than any Ivy League school did.

Global university assessments are done by several organizations, which tend to focus on the output of an institution's graduates, as measured by prizes, publications, patents. And there are schools in the United States that shine much brighter on these lists than they do in the eyes of American students fixated on certain brands. Among them: the University of California, San Diego; the University of California, San Francisco; the University of Wisconsin–Madison; the University of Washington and the University of Illinois.

These institutions don't soar in the *U.S. News* rankings in part because of their sheer size and the big gap between their highest-achieving students and their lowest-achieving ones. They're less exclusive. But what's clear in the global rankings is that at each of them, there's no shortage of top-notch scholars who find everything they're looking for and more. And if the people around those standouts aren't the survivors of a screening process as intimidating as Stanford's, is that really a minus? With exclusivity often comes sameness, and there's an argument that college shouldn't take you out of the real world but thrust you into it, exposing you to places unlike the ones you've already inhabited and people different from the ones who've surrounded you thus far. There's nothing in the formulas used by *U.S. News*, PayScale or most other organizations in the rankings racket that addresses that. And there's no way a formula really could, because a school that will be old hat to a student from one background will be eye-opening to a student from another.

The limited, dubious utility of rankings was summed up succinctly by the man who's been in charge of the *U.S. News* list for several decades now. His name is Bob Morse, and in September 2014 he gave an interview to the *Washington Post* in which he jovially acknowledged that his rankings are "like the 800-pound gorilla of higher education" and shared his own thoughts on the relevance of a college's reputation to a student's future.

"It's not where you went to school," he told the *Post*. "It's how hard you work." Morse got an undergraduate degree at the University of Cincinnati. His MBA is from Michigan State.

FIVE

BEYOND THE COMFORT ZONE

"Be as curious as you can. Put yourself in situations where you're not just yielding to what's familiar. I came out of college with a level of confidence and self-understanding that I don't think I could have possibly gotten from an East Coast school, where I would have been among the kind of people I grew up with and lived near."

—Howard Schultz, the chairman and chief executive of Starbucks and a 1975 graduate of Northern Michigan University

From the tenth through twelfth grades, I attended a private school, Loomis Chaffee, in the suburbs of Hartford, Connecticut. Before then my siblings and I had always gone to public schools, but my parents grew nervous, as college neared, about whether they were giving us the very best chance of admission to the most selective colleges. Loomis was supposed to help. Most of the students there belonged to families in the upper-middle class or above. Most set their sights on one of several dozen elite private colleges in the Northeast. And those colleges, despite earnest stabs at diversity, tended to have disproportionate numbers of kids much like the ones at my private school. What these students found at college was a bigger theater and more intense work but not an unfamiliar milieu. College was an upsizing and extension of secondary school.

It was initially going to be that way for me as well. The elite northeastern colleges were the ones mentioned most frequently and admiringly around my house. They were our quarry, and my parents were ecstatic when my older brother, Mark, went from Loomis to Amherst. They were equally thrilled when I applied successfully the following year for early admission to Yale. But before I had to commit to Yale, I was nominated for, and then received, something called a Morehead Scholarship. Financed by a foundation affiliated with the University of North Carolina at Chapel Hill, it sought (and still seeks) to lure students away from private colleges and to Chapel Hill by paying all of their expenses there, giving them access to special seminars and even funding summer internships and experiences like Outward Bound.

I'd had my heart set on Yale, partly because it had always been held up as the point of my hard work at Loomis. It was the return on the investment, the validation. My parents were in a comfortable enough financial position to pay, without grave hardship, the bill for tuition, room and board, which would have been about $60,000 over four years. (Adjusted for inflation, that would be about $140,000 today.) But they weren't so well-off that the figure was utterly negligible. They told me, repeatedly, to forget about the money. They insisted on it. But a part of me refused to. I didn't want to be a person who could forget that so easily.

I had never thought about applying to Carolina. But when I gave it a close examination, I realized what a strong reputation it enjoyed and how many excellent professors and departments it harbored. I also realized something else: It might well be a greater challenge for someone like me, given where it was and where I was coming from. I'd spent my childhood in upper-middle-class suburbs in New York and Connecticut and, if I discounted one trip to Virginia and maybe two to Florida, was wholly unfamiliar with the South. Chapel Hill took 85 percent of its student body from North Carolina, and that meant that the look, accent and vibe of the place would be nothing like Loomis's—or Yale's—and would be new to me. Chapel Hill threatened to make me uncomfortable, at least briefly and at the start. I worried about that and simultaneously came to believe that my worry was the best reason to go.

So I went. Was it the right call? Would I be a more knowledgeable, happier, better person today if I'd made the opposite one? There's no answer to that. The road not taken can never be anything more than a guess, a hypothetical. So there's nothing solid to judge the road taken against.

I can tell you that I have many regrets. They're about the classes I didn't take at Chapel Hill because I didn't want to overburden myself; the classes I didn't take because they conflicted with the soap opera *All My Children*; the classes I didn't take because I didn't want to get up before 8 a.m.; the lectures I skipped because friends could be counted on to share their notes; the study-abroad opportunities I didn't seize; the people I didn't push myself to meet; the people I wasn't open or sufficiently kind to; the romantic relationships I cut short because I couldn't respect anyone who respected me too readily; the number of fried-chicken biscuits I ate; the number of egg-and-cheese biscuits I ate; the bulimia I fell prey to for a while; the excess of time I spent in front of a mirror; the paucity of time I spent trying to improve my Italian; the frequency with which I indulged my newfound fondness for bourbon; and the fact that after getting my scuba-diving certification, I used it only once. I'd go back and change all of that. And I'd finish *Middlemarch*, *An American Tragedy* and *Beowulf*, all of which I faked having read. On second thought, I'd leave *Beowulf* be.

But Chapel Hill? I wouldn't take that back. It's where I happened to learn that you could put blue cheese on a burger, which for me was like a first kiss. The sky in autumn and spring was the gentlest, rarest, most perfect of blues. I needed that solace, because I did initially feel out of place, but I also learned that out-of-place was endurable and that a person can play neat tricks with it in his or her mind, converting the dross to gold. I fancied myself an iconoclast. I fancied myself quirky. I took advantage of those times when I retreated from it all by reading and reading and reading, though not always what I was assigned.

English was my major, and more than a few of the professors in that department were extraordinary. One, who specialized in twentieth-century English and American drama, allowed me into two of his graduate seminars, where I marinated in Samuel Beckett and Harold Pinter and Tom Stoppard and Edward Albee and Sam Shepard. The school newspaper was an ambitious one, and once I found my way there, I also found an enduring posse. There and elsewhere at the university, I was among people who took much less for granted than the kids at Loomis had. And it wasn't just because all of us were now a few years older, a few years less reckless and naive. It was because the in-state kids at Chapel Hill hadn't, as a group, come from backgrounds as economically privileged as my prep school peers.

My younger brother, Harry, ended up going to Dartmouth. My sister, Adelle, the youngest of us four, went to Princeton. Mark's, Harry's and Adelle's closest college friends had second homes on Caribbean islands or the slopes of North America's prettiest mountains and had enough of a financial safety net under them to do things like follow the Grateful Dead around all summer long. My closest college friends had part-time jobs off-campus to help pay for their tuition or to pick up some of the spending money that their parents couldn't lavish on them. It wasn't that Chapel Hill had much grit to it; if anything, it had too little. But it seemed to hover closer to the earth than my siblings' schools did. And it gave me a perspective that I appreciated then and appreciate even more now.

I did wind up taking a spin through the Ivy League, attending Columbia for nine months in the service of a master's degree in journalism. The Columbia name, I concede, was part of what lured me, and a teacher I had there connected me with my first full-time position, at the *New York Post*. But the *Post* hired me only after, and because of, a four-week tryout, the success of which had less to do with the classes I'd taken at Columbia than with the writing I'd done at the UNC newspaper and on the side. And none of the people who hired me for subsequent jobs ever asked about or mentioned Columbia—or, for that matter, Chapel Hill.

* * *

Among the young men and women I interviewed for this book were a few Yale alumni, including Rebecca Fabbro, who graduated in 2009. She headed to Yale from the wealthy New York City suburb of Edgemont, which shares a zip code with Scarsdale, and from a high school whose college counselor was savvy enough to press her to get some high-level physics and computer science on her transcript, telling her that girls with those leanings stood out.

Rebecca said that her one qualm with Yale was how many other students there were like her, in the sense that their passages to Yale had been smoothed by the advantages of growing up in an affluent or relatively affluent family. That qualm has grown stronger over time, partly because Rebecca spent two years after Yale working for Teach For America in a public school in Marks, Mississippi, once the starting point of the "mule train," a 1968 trek to Washington to protest the poverty in which so many black Americans were mired. Rebecca said that when one of her seventh graders learned that she'd gone to Yale, the student said, "Oh, are you rich?"

She told me about an email that she'd received from Yale's president in the fall of 2013 about the class of 2017, whose members were starting just then. It praised their variety of backgrounds, noting proudly that "over half attended public schools." That boast stuck with Rebecca, because the more she thought about it, the odder and less boast-worthy it seemed. "Given that most students in this country (nearly 90%) attend public schools, I was surprised that having more than 50% of a Yale class coming from a public institution was a mark of diversity to celebrate (especially since many of those students who attend public schools attended affluent ones like

Edgemont and Scarsdale)," she wrote to me in a long email shortly after we'd spoken.

As it happens, Yale had posted some information online about that very same incoming class, and I checked it, discovering that the percentage of public-school kids was 57.6. From the same post I learned that 13.8 percent of the class of 2017 had some kind of legacy connection to the university, a situation that hardly abets diversity.

Rebecca said that she'd dug into some literature that Yale had sent her over time and had also done some other research, and she'd learned that 52 percent of students at Yale receive some level of need-based aid, a figure in which the university takes pride. But, she wrote in her email, "It concerns me that 48% of students at Yale are not on need-based aid. Given that nearly all families who make between $0 and $200,000 a year qualify for financial aid and that 'many families who make more than $200,000 a year receive some need-based aid,' that means (unless I'm reading the stats wrong) that nearly half of all Yale students who accept Yale's offer of admission are coming from families who make more than $200,000 per year. So, around 50 percent of Yale students are from families in the top 5 percent in this country."

Her deconstruction reminded me of a column written by a Harvard alumnus, Evan Mandery, that the *Times* published in April 2014. He, too, was troubled by what he saw as insufficient socioeconomic diversity at elite schools. "To be a 1 percenter," Mandery wrote, "a family needs an annual income of approximately $390,000. When the *Harvard Crimson* surveyed this year's freshman class, 14 percent of respondents reported annual family income above $500,000. Another 15 percent came from families making more than $250,000 per year. Only 20 percent reported incomes less than $65,000. This is the amount below which Harvard will allow a student to go free of charge. It's also just above the national median family income. So, at least as many Harvard students come from families in the top 1 percent as the bottom 50 percent."

Rebecca's focus on figures like these wasn't motivated simply by questions of justice and fairness, though those concern her. She was wondering as well about the educational implications of a school so rife with children of wealth. "I have certainly learned more in more diverse environments than in others," she wrote.

"When I was making my college decision," she added, "I was concerned with prestige. Smart, successful people from my school went to places ranked highly by *U.S. News* and featured prominently in the *Times*'s wedding pages. I wanted to be like them. I also wanted to make my parents proud.

"But I had very little conception of the world outside the one in which I had grown up," she wrote. "And most students from the school I went to did not attend very socioeconomically diverse institutions."

They could have looked at a broader universe of schools. They also could have consulted rankings other than the ones by *U.S. News*. For instance, the magazine *Washington Monthly* does some of its own, which are devoted to the "contribution to the public good" that schools make, and these receive minimal attention. They try to gauge the promise of social mobility that schools offer, and they do this—imperfectly, I concede—by looking at the high percentages of poor kids admitted and how many of them are successfully ushered to diplomas. They also reward schools at which many kids do community service or go on to the Peace Corps or participate in ROTC.

By *those* measures, the top 10 national universities as of the fall of 2014 were, in order, UCSD, UC Riverside, UC Berkeley, Texas A&M, UCLA, Stanford, the University of Washington, the University of Texas at El Paso, Case Western Reserve University and Harvard. And the top 10 liberal arts colleges were Bryn Mawr, Carleton, Berea, Swarthmore, Harvey Mudd, Reed, Macalester, the New College of Florida, Williams and Oberlin. Needless to say, that lineup was a departure from the one showcased by *U.S. News.*

In the news media, I'm noticing more and more attention to the subject of how much colleges are (or aren't) doing to identify, recruit and retain students from poor and middle-class families. It's a clear and laudable outgrowth of the intensifying concern over income inequality in the United States. Along these lines, the *Times* crunched numbers and, in September 2014, published what it called a College Access Index, evaluating and ranking schools according to the percentage of students who qualified for federal Pell grants, which are reserved for low-income families, and the net price being paid by students whose families weren't affluent. The *Times* looked only at "top colleges," which it defined as those whose four-year graduation rate was at least 75 percent. The schools that scored highest on the index were, in order, Vassar, Grinnell, UNC Chapel Hill, Smith and, in a tie for fifth place, Amherst and, actually, Harvard.

Even more interesting were the discrepancies between schools. According to the index, Washington University in St. Louis had a remarkably less economically diverse student body than Pomona did, and Princeton lagged far behind Harvard and Columbia. Yale trailed Princeton. Wake Forest did poorly; so did George Washington University.

For the second College Access Index, released in September 2015, the *Times* tweaked its criteria, expanding the pool of schools to those with a *five-year* graduation rate of at least 75 percent. This change brought many more public institutions into the fray. The *Times* also factored in not just how many students with Pell grants were being admitted to various colleges but how many of those students were being shepherded successfully to graduation.

Seven of the top 10 schools in 2015 were public ones: *six* different branches of the University of California (in order, Irvine, Davis, Santa Barbara, San Diego, Los Angeles and Berkeley), along with the University of Florida. The only three private schools to make the top 10 were, in the eighth, ninth and tenth positions, Vassar, Amherst and Pomona. Celebrated private colleges whose lack of socioeconomic diversity landed them *below* the top *100* included George Washington University, NYU, Carnegie Mellon, Washington University and Oberlin. I wonder how many prospective college students see this kind of information. I wonder if more than a few even go looking for it. They should, and I say that not out of some politically correct, reflexively liberal concern for the concept of diversity, though diversity has a whole lot going for it. I say it because a diverse campus is going to be truer to the grand, messy chaos of life and less like the deceptive nook into which the circumstances of your birth tucked you.

Vassar's president, Catharine Bond Hill, explained her push to recruit and admit low-income students—and to have a student body varied in all kinds of other ways as well—in terms of not just what's best for the kids trying to climb the ladder but what's best for every student at the school and what honors the mission of education. "If our students are going to make successful contributions to the future well-being of our society, they need to understand how to deal with diversity, and college campuses are a perfect place—an important place—to learn that," she told me.

Students from affluent families who attend a truly diverse school may be more likely to "understand that the rest of the United States hasn't grown up in the same circumstances that they have, and they might think about whether that's a fair society," she said. Whatever they conclude, it's an essential question to mull. Even from a purely careerist viewpoint, she added, there's an argument for diversity on campus. "I think that just about anything you're going to go on to do for the rest of your life—be a lawyer, a doctor or a teacher—you're going to be dealing with people very different from the kids you've gone to high school with, and understanding that is going to make you more successful when you go forward."

Those people invariably widen your frame of reference. Maybe they test you, too. Perhaps they even knock you off your stride. If so, that's a good thing.

Howard Schultz saw it that way.

He didn't go to a school that he knew to be especially diverse, and he wasn't looking to make sure that poor kids were in the mix: He *was* one of those poor kids. But he went to a college that was a complete, abrupt departure from his high school and from everything he'd known until that point. It unsettled and disoriented him, at least at first. And that was perhaps its greatest blessing, he said.

"Here's this Jewish kid from Brooklyn who lands in the Upper Peninsula of Michigan," Schultz, the chairman, president, and chief executive of Starbucks, said, recalling his journey in the early 1970s to Northern Michigan University. "I was the only Jewish kid in my dorm. I remember hearing so often, 'I've never met anyone who's Jewish.'" His tone of voice as he recounted this for me wasn't bitter or astonished. It was amused, fond, even grateful. While he often jokes that he might have *really* amounted to something if he'd gone to an Ivy League school, he of course doesn't believe that. Northern Michigan, he said, served him well, and in ways that aren't easily measurable and don't translate into catalogue-ready copy.

Simply going to college was an event and thrill for him, because neither of his parents had been able to take their education that far. As he was growing up, his father suffered through a sequence of jobs that he didn't like much and that didn't pay well, at one point driving a truck that delivered and picked up diapers, the smell of which made every workday a misery. The family of five—Schultz has a sister and a brother—lived in the projects. Schultz remembers occasionally being told by his mother to answer the phone and to say that his parents weren't home, even though they were. They were trying to avoid a bill collector.

They wanted more for him and his two siblings, both younger. "My mother drilled in us that we were going to college, come hell or high water," he told me. College was the way out, the ladder up. But there wasn't much chatter at home or among his friends at Canarsie High School about *where* to go to college. Nor was he sure how to pay for it. So when a football recruiter who had come to one of Schultz's high school games and had seen him play quarterback asked him if he'd be interested in a scholarship to Northern Michigan, he said a relieved yes and moved enthusiastically in that direction. In Schultz's autobiography, *Pour Your Heart Into It*, he writes that his family's road trip during his last semester of high school to see the campus in Marquette, Michigan, was his first time out of New York State.

At Northern Michigan he majored in communications. He joined a fraternity. He didn't, in the end, play football, at least not for long: An injury prevented him from making the kind of contribution that he'd hoped to. The scholarship went away, and he had to take out loans and work part-time. He tended bar. He even on occasion sold his blood for money. He put enough energy into his studies to maintain a B average, but not enough to do any better than that. His graduation, he said, was one of the happiest moments of his mother's life—but she didn't attend the ceremony. The trip out would have cost more money than she and his father felt they could spend at the time.

In the end, he said, what mattered most about college was that he "came of age" there, getting a glimpse of a world far beyond Brooklyn and being forced to stand on his own two feet in it. In this sense he sounded a lot like Parsons—and he provided another reminder of how fundamentally different the college experience is for kids who can't count on Mom and Dad for frequent visits or generous handouts. That difference is often termed a disadvantage, a bit of nomenclature that should probably be revisited. It's a burden, no question. It's not something most parents would elect for their kids or most kids would volunteer for. But it winds up steeling some young people in ways that can actually prove advantageous. It's how their resolve is forged.

Schultz said that he drew particular strength from his success navigating terrain that was an adjustment, to say the least.

"I was in farmland," he said. "All the kids I was meeting were from the Midwest: Michigan, Ohio, Illinois." And he was as exotic to them as they were to him. "If you are part of a very diverse background of young adults, both inside and outside the classroom, I think the experience adds significant value to the kind of person you're going to be," he said. "I'm not saying that that doesn't exist at an elite school, but when you go to a state school that doesn't perhaps have the same patina or reputation, the opportunities to expose yourself to things outside the classroom provide a different kind of education."

As I listened to Schultz, I longed more and more for a robust, sustained national conversation about the ways in which all college students, and in particular those at exclusive institutions, navigate their years of higher education and what they demand from that chapter of life. And I yearned for that largely because college has the potential to confront and challenge some of the most troubling political and social aspects of contemporary life; to muster a preemptive strike against them; to be a staging ground for behaving in a different, healthier way.

We live in a country of sharpening divisions, pronounced tribalism, corrosive polarization. We live in the era of the Internet, which has had a counterintuitive impact: While it opens up an infinite universe of information for exploration, people use it to stand still, bookmarking the websites that cater to their existing hobbies (and established hobbyhorses) and customizing their social media feeds so that their judgments are constantly reinforced, their opinions forever affirmed.

And college is indeed a "perfect place," as Catharine Bond

Hill said, to push back at all of that, to rummage around in fresh outlooks, to bridge divides. For many students, it's not only an environment more populous than high school was; it's also one with more directions in which to turn. It gives them more agency over their calendars and allegiances. They can better construct their hours and days from scratch—and the clay hasn't yet dried on who they are.

But too many kids get to college and try to collapse it, to make it as comfortable and recognizable as possible. They replicate the friends and friendships they've previously enjoyed. They join groups that perpetuate their high school cliques. Concerned with establishing a "network," they seek out peers with aspirations identical to their own. In doing so, they frequently default to a clannishness that too easily becomes a lifelong habit.

If you spend any time on college campuses, you'll notice this. And you'll understand why one of my utopian fantasies is a student orientation period in which students are given these instructions, these exhortations: Open your laptops. Delete at least one of every four bookmarks. Replace it with something entirely different, even antithetical. Go to Twitter, Facebook, Instagram, Tumblr and such, and start following or connecting with publications, blogs and people whose views diverge from your own. Conduct your social lives along the same lines, mixing it up. Do not go only to the campus basketball games, or only to campus theatrical productions. Wander beyond the periphery of campus, and not to find equally enchanted realms—if you study abroad, don't choose the destination for its picturesqueness—but to see something else. Think about repaying your good fortune by mentoring kids in the area who aren't sure to get to college, or who don't have ready guidance for figuring it all out. In some American studies classes at Columbia University, this is a course requirement, and there are similar arrangements and programs at other schools. It's a trend that's worth tilling, a movement that should grow.

Now more than ever, college needs to be an expansive adventure, propelling students toward unplumbed territory and untested identities rather than indulging and flattering who they already are. And students, along with those of us who purport to have meaningful insights for them, need to insist on that.

SIX

FROM TEMPE TO WATERLOO

"I've had students who've had transformative experiences at schools that nobody's ever heard of."

—Alice Kleeman, the college counselor at Menlo-Atherton High School in California

With colleges as with so much else, we have an unfortunate tendency to indulge in stereotypes, and Arizona State University suffers from an especially negative one, which was captured by its description on the College Confidential website as "a party school and you will always be just a number there." That's what a student who identified herself only as AZseniorchick wrote not long ago. She also opined that Northern Arizona University was "for hippies and ugly people." What a shame that she didn't proceed, school by school and cactus by cactus, through the whole state. Her eye is as keen as her judgments are subtle.

Arizona State, better known as ASU, has long fought against a factory-like impression given by its size. With some 60,000 students enrolled at its main campus in Tempe and another 13,000 or so at nearby satellites, it's the largest single-administration university in the United States. (There are university *systems*, with different administrations for different branches, that are bigger.) It has also struggled against its location in "a place with bright sunshine and palm trees and beautiful weather," as Michael Crow, its president, described it in an on-camera interview for the 2014 documentary *Ivory Tower*, about higher education in America. There's a broad assumption that no one can really study when it's summertime almost all of the time. ASU's meteorological blessing is its reputational curse.

Ivory Tower includes footage of kids at ASU drinking and dancing. One of them shouts, "It's the party school! Come on, what are we doing right now?" Another exults, "It's paradise, baby! What's not to love?" There are also images of the annual "undie run" on the last day of classes, which looks like the kind of fitness regimen Hugh Hefner might prescribe, and there's an onscreen reminder of ASU's 2011 ranking by *Playboy* as the No. 3 party school in the nation. Over the last decade, it has toggled into, out of and around *Playboy*'s top 10.

The typical ASU student "comes to get drunk out of their minds and be in this sort of like vapid, hedonistic area," a senior identified as Brendan Arnold says in one scene in *Ivory Tower*. He's cut off by someone who approaches him and shouts something unintelligible. The impression is of beery bedlam in the desert. Bring Ray-Bans, Coppertone and Advil.

But that's not the ASU suggested by its multiple appearances on the *Forbes* 30 Under 30 list of young movers and shakers that I mentioned earlier in the book. And that's not the ASU that Wendy Zupac experienced.

Wendy, now twenty-eight, is the only child of two electrical engineers who immigrated to the United States from Serbia just before she was born. In their field, your actual skills and what you technically knew were more important than the source or even the fact of your diploma, and in Tempe, where they settled and raised Wendy, elite schools weren't mentioned as incessantly and anxiously as in the moneyed suburbs of New York, Boston, Washington and Los Angeles. Besides which, an elite college's yearly price tag of about fifty thousand dollars back when Wendy was in high school struck her parents, and her, as extravagant. Although Wendy was an A student who took many Advanced Placement classes and could have tried her luck with any number of colleges around the country, she wanted to go to ASU, where her in-state tuition would be around six thousand dollars a year and she could keep other expenses down by living at home.

"My plan was to go to a really good law school, and I felt I could get there through ASU," she said. "A lot of law schools will publish annual statistics of their incoming class, and one of the things that struck me was how the law schools I was looking at admitted kids from all kinds of undergraduate schools. I also knew that things like LSAT scores and undergraduate GPAs were important, and I knew I'd be focusing on that at any school I went to."

She worried somewhat about too many lectures in miniature auditoriums with hundreds of students, but she often found herself in seminars with fewer than twenty students, thanks in part to her admission into the Barrett honors college within ASU. Unbeknownst to kids who don't take a serious look at public universities, many of them have programs like

Barrett that enable the most academically accomplished students to take more advanced and adventurous courses. But Barrett wasn't the only reason Wendy encountered class sizes smaller than she'd expected. More than 40 percent of classes at ASU have fewer than 20 students; only 17 percent have 50 or more.

"If you were self-directed, you could do all kinds of things when you were there," Wendy said. "It was surprising how easy it was to find a group of people who were truly motivated, and professors responded really well to those students. I could walk into a professor's office at any time and they'd be happy to see me." She developed an especially close relationship with Jack Crittenden, who teaches political theory. He got his doctorate at Oxford, has won a National Endowment for the Humanities grant and has written three books that explore the confluence of politics and psychology, *Beyond Individualism*, *Democracy's Midwife* and *Wide as the World*. Wendy remembers taking at least four of his classes, including one or two at the graduate level.

She was also allowed into other graduate classes and into several classes at the law school. She took many more classes than she needed to and ended up completing three majors: political science, history and Spanish. The sun didn't distract or deter her. And she got into her first-choice law school, Yale, beginning there in the fall of 2009. She told me that she didn't find herself to be any less well prepared for Yale than kids who'd gone to smaller, more selective colleges. After her graduation from Yale in 2012, she clerked for a federal judge on the Ninth Circuit Court of Appeals in San Francisco, then took a job with a big, prestigious litigation firm in Washington, D.C. "I love it so far," she said.

A friend of hers from the honors college at ASU, Devin Mauney, twenty-nine, is clerking for a judge in the U.S. District Court for the District of Columbia. All four of his years at ASU were paid for by a Flinn scholarship, which is given to outstanding Arizona high school students who elect to stay in the state for college. Because of the Flinn, Devin did precisely that, though he'd been accepted at Yale and Brown, among other schools. He told me that while most of his peers endorsed his decision, one close friend thought it was cracked.

I asked Devin why.

"He just repeated the words *Yale* and *ASU* to me," Devin said. "He didn't have much more than that. It was mostly about prestige."

I asked Devin if he had any of his own misgivings or worries along those lines.

"My first semester of school, I certainly doubted my choice," he said. "I had set my sights on prestige in high school, and walking around school in my ASU shirt, I thought, 'What if I were at Yale?' And it seems silly now, because I'm happy with the way things worked out. And I wasn't unhappy then! And I didn't think I was getting a bad education. I was challenged. I had access to great opportunities and resources."

One aspect of his ASU education that he particularly appreciated was how permeable, even nonexistent, the barrier between the Tempe campus and the community around it was. The school wasn't just located in Tempe and in Arizona; it was entwined with them.

"I was involved in politics in Arizona during the entire time I was a student at ASU," he said. "I testified at the legislature a couple of times, one time about a bill aimed at limiting academic freedom. I ran a local campaign for a candidate running for county office. My friends who went to prestigious places weren't involved that way. These places that draw students from all over the country are islands."

He majored in economics, graduated in 2009 and, in the fall of 2010, began law school at Harvard. In terms of where his fellow Harvard students had done their undergraduate work, he said, "My class was extremely diverse: University of Georgia, *lots* of students from the UC system, lots of UT students, Michigan." I asked him whether he'd noticed much of a difference between them and classmates who'd gone to more selective schools. He said that it was difficult to generalize but that in a few cases, the alumni of elite institutions were less clear about why they were at Harvard and what they wanted from it. For them it was the next box in a series that they were dutifully checking over the course of their lives. They were also more likely to be from the Northeast, he said, and to have attended private schools before college.

ASU will never be a badge of exclusive honor, because its very composition, identity and mission work against that. It's *intended* to be accessible and to try to counter, and change, the fact that in the United States, according to one study from a few years ago, less than 10 percent of children from families in the bottom quartile of income are likely to get a college diploma by the age of twenty-four while more than 70 percent of children from families in the top quartile are. To that end, ASU basically admits any high school graduate in Arizona who maintains a B average or better in sixteen courses considered essential for college readiness. The average ASU student pays only about $3,800 a semester for tuition. And more than 40 percent of the school's students receive federal Pell grants, a form of tuition aid available only to lower-income families.

ASU sacrifices the kinds of attributes that impress prospective college students eager for a discerning club, and it throws in the towel on statistics that move the needle on rankings like those done by *U.S. News*. Its undergraduate acceptance rate is more than 80 percent, so it doesn't get points for selectivity. Its four-year graduation rate is just over 40 percent and its six-year graduation rate is just over 60 percent, both of which are similarly damning even though they're entirely understandable: Studies show a close correlation between low family income and the probability that a student who starts college doesn't complete it. And, as it happens, ASU has commendably nudged its graduation rates upward over the last few years.

"We live in a country where the number one predictor of college success is not intelligence or hard work—it is student zip code," Michael Crow, the president of ASU, wrote to me in a letter in the summer of 2014, during which we had several exchanges, by mail and in person and over the phone. When I brought up *U.S. News* rankings, which in the fall of 2015 put ASU in a tie for No. 129 among national universities, he said, "They hammer us because of our graduation rate, and we're not able to be viewed as a top institution because we don't have these rising admissions standards."

But the school's emphasis on access and inclusivity means that it's potentially doing much more than any elite college to improve the social mobility that's central to our country's narrative, that's at the core of America's self-image and that's imperiled in this era of increasing income inequality. Who wouldn't want to go to a university with such laudable values? And while the student population at ASU may not be a model of geographic diversity, it's an exemplar of socioeconomic and ethnic diversity.

"If you come to ASU, you'll have the whole cross section of our society," Crow told me. "And you'll have them at scale, not just two Native American kids but several thousand. We make that case, but you've got to be a very sophisticated seventeen-year-old to grasp all of that."

And ASU, like many universities of its size, has no shortage of distinguished professors and programs for students who summon the initiative to connect with them. As of the summer of 2014, the school's faculty included two Nobel laureates, ten members of the American Academy of Arts and Sciences, eleven members of the National Academy of Sciences, twenty-five Guggenheim Fellows and five Pulitzer Prize winners. Almost all began teaching there after 2002, an indication of the school's vigorous efforts to upgrade itself. But because of its party-school stereotype, you don't hear much about that.

In 2010, the *Wall Street Journal* did a survey of recruiters at 479 of the largest public and private companies, nonprofits and government agencies, asking them which schools they liked best and trusted most when they were looking for college graduates for entry-level jobs. ASU ranked fifth. But because of its party-school stereotype, you don't hear much about that, either. Or about its high rank among schools producing students who win Fulbright grants.

There are reasons to be envious, not suspicious, of ASU's size. "We don't limit what you can study," Crow said, noting that thousands of classes are offered annually. "The student has—I won't call it infinite—a menu of opportunity beyond any menu they can imagine." There are three hundred degree programs in fifteen colleges, "and in those micro-environments, you find your niche," he explained. For example, he said, "You can be in our opera program inside the school of music inside the Herberger Institute for Design and the Arts." And as Wendy Zupac and Devin Mauney attested, you can be completely satisfied with your education and what it leads to.

The difference between the negative image and the promising reality of ASU suggests just how perniciously superficial assumptions factor into the appraisal of schools and the esteem in which the general public, along with minimally informed applicants, holds them. Elite colleges don't have all the best teachers, students and facilities, though their endowments certainly help them attract or construct a disproportionate share. What elite colleges really have is a set of carefully maintained characteristics that are broadly accepted as synonyms for quality, along with a history of acclaim that it's easier for parents and children to buy into than to examine and question. What elite colleges have is a consensus, along with the benefit of the doubt.

Schools like ASU don't have that, and I've singled it out and dwelled on it for that reason, but also to illustrate just how ridiculously narrow the thinking about higher education can be, especially by parents and kids with enough resources and ambitions to be finicky about the schools they consider applying to. The same cast of colleges gets the same bounty of adulation year after predictable year, and students in certain geographic areas and socioeconomic groups draw up lists of target colleges that are comically redundant and sadly unimaginative.

* * *

I made prominent mention of ASU's Barrett honors college above and noted that many other state universities have programs like it. In fact, honors programs and honors *colleges*—which are essentially larger, more formal versions of honors programs, sometimes with extra resources and even designated buildings and residences—have been expanding rapidly over recent years, and they got a prominent bit of publicity during the spring 2015 admissions season, thanks to a high school senior from Tennessee named Ronald Nelson.

Every year, the media finds and fawns over the rare students offered admission to all eight Ivy League schools, and Nelson, from the Memphis area, was one of them. Newspaper stories marveled at him; MSNBC and other networks invited him on air. But his story had a fresh wrinkle. Nelson turned down Harvard, Yale, Princeton and the rest of them and chose instead to stay in the South, at the University of Alabama. Its lower price tag and the bounty of aid it gave him were two reasons. But he also cited another: He'd been invited to take classes at Alabama's honors college, which promised him an environment of especially dedicated, high-achieving students within a larger, more diverse community of more than 30,000 undergraduates.

That decision threw a spotlight on the rise of honors programs and colleges, which a growing number of public schools are starting, refining and assertively promoting. Students in turn are becoming more aware of them and giving them more consideration, but could pay them even greater heed—and should. Honors programs and colleges are ignored, for example, by far too many students who are fixated on the Ivy League, who may well find their hopes dashed by Ivy League admissions offices, who could benefit mightily from exposure to a state university's student body and who just might find that the financial equation at a state university's honors college works in their favor. Honors programs and honors colleges give students some of the virtues and perks of private schools without some of the drawbacks, such as exorbitant tuition and an enclave of extreme privilege.

The honors college at Alabama has been around only since 2003 and has grown steadily since then. It now includes more than 6,500 students. In a neighboring state, the University of Tennessee at Chattanooga recently put the finishing touches on its own ambitious honors college. There are dozens more honors colleges like these across the country, and they're helpfully described and authoritatively evaluated by a website and book that, surprisingly, fly somewhat under the radar even in an era when applicants and their parents are hungrier than ever for any college admissions resource that might help.

The book could use a title snappier and sexier than the one it has, *A Review of Fifty Public University Honors Programs*. It was first published in 2012 and updated in 2014. It's linked to publicuniversityhonors.com, which began in 2011 and, like the book, provides thorough appraisals of individual honors colleges and programs and intelligent thoughts on how they fit into the higher-education landscape.

There's a post, for example, that explores "College Value: Public Honors vs. Private Elites." Another, "Honors and Career Success," explains why a state university honors college or program might be the smartest of all options for some students. "Because of the broader student body at a public university, there's a lot more reach in terms of the type of people you're going to encounter," John Willingham, the author of the book and the architect of the website, told me when I spoke with him at length in the summer of 2015.

And it's likely that at a public university's honors college, there will be a smaller percentage of students from extremely wealthy families than at one of the most highly selective private schools. "They're not all elite," Willingham said, referring to honors college students, "though most are capable. There's a more egalitarian quality."

The honors colleges and programs to which he gives highest praise include the Barrett honors college, which is widely considered the gold standard; Schreyer Honors College at Penn State; the South Carolina Honors College at the University of South Carolina; and the honors program at the University of Kansas.

Generally speaking, honors programs and colleges give students who've distinguished themselves through their SAT scores, ACT scores or grade point averages access to, and dibs on, small classes filled with other honors students. In some instances, students are invited to step onto the honors track, based on the strength of their application to the wider university. In others, they must take it upon themselves to go through the extra paces and specific process of admission to an honors college.

There are a few reasons *not* to applaud these honors tracks. Some universities lavish disproportionate energy on them, eager for bragging rights and trying to draw students whose profiles may bolster the university's stature and rankings, and they use financial aid money that could go to needier cases for honors college recruits. (Then again, private colleges intent on moving up in the rankings similarly use merit aid to compete for top students.) Also, honors colleges in some ways replicate, within a public school, the kind of stratified, status-conscious dynamic at play in the hierarchy of private schools.

But as Willingham rightly noted, the honors college cocoon isn't as gilded as that of many of the most highly selective private colleges, which draw heavily from prep schools and affluent suburbs. And the honors college or honors program is part of a public university that's likely to have considerable socioeconomic diversity.

Jonathan Fink, a vice president at Portland State University who successfully pushed for its honors program to become a full-fledged honors college, told me, "The students that PSU draws are so different from the ones that my sister teaches at Mount Holyoke or that my other sister teaches at Sweet Briar." As a result, he said, PSU arguably illuminates "more about the real world, which is the world you'll ultimately be immersed in.

"It gets you exposed to reality more," he said, referring to the diversity that honors students at PSU encounter. "The role that a place like PSU plays is increasingly important as society becomes more economically split."

Fink's daughter graduated in 2014 from Barrett at ASU. Its dean, Mark Jacobs, previously taught at a small private college in the Northeast. Fink noted that Jacobs "often talks about having been at Swarthmore and wishing he could have had Penn State next door—at ASU, he more or less got that." Barrett combines the intimacy and academically distinguished student body of a Swarthmore with the scale, eclecticism and sprawling resources of a huge university. It's two experiences in one.

Perhaps most important, honors colleges provide a supportive, challenging haven to some gifted young men and women who don't make the cut at private schools with plunging acceptance rates or who aren't prepared, for financial and other reasons, to pursue higher education far from their homes.

Robert Fisher, for example. A factory worker's son who was the football captain and student body president at his high school in Clarksville, Tennessee, he applied to a variety of schools in the state, including Vanderbilt, which rejected him. He ended up at the University of Tennessee at Chattanooga, on its honors track, which was his gateway to special summer internships in Washington for talented African-American students and to a ten-day cultural seminar in London. The seminar, he told me, was his first time out of the country.

He graduated in the spring of 2015 and, in the fall of 2015, headed back to England. Remember my mention, in an earlier chapter, of a 2015 winner of a Rhodes Scholarship from UT–Chattanooga? That person was Fisher, and his destination in England was Oxford University.

Honors programs and colleges demonstrate that there's so much more out there, in terms of options, in terms of opportunities, than the narrow discussions and dreams of too many status-conscious, blinkered, unduly anxious teenagers take into account. There are big schools like ASU with pockets of moderately priced excellence less recognized than they should be. Texas A&M, for example, has a weekly business seminar unlike any other I've ever heard of. Every semester for about nine years now, it has been taught by Britt Harris, a wealthy financier who served as the chief executive of Bridgewater Associates when it was one of the world's largest hedge funds. He's not an academic, and the class, called Titans of

Investing, wasn't put together, and isn't conducted, in a conventional fashion.

Although it covers market history and economic theory, it concerns itself just as much with questions of leadership, and of wisdom: recognizing it, acquiring it, using it. To that end, the seventeen participants in the class—juniors, seniors and graduate students—read and discuss an eclectic mix of books specifically suggested by American business bigwigs, including Wall Street giants, several of whom interact with the students by fielding and assessing their written analyses of those classics. One week, the class might dive into *Moby-Dick* or de Tocqueville's *Democracy in America*. The next, it's on to a biography of Benjamin Franklin or Steve Jobs. Discussions are followed by long dinners promoting fellowship and sustained reflection, and the course's alumni aren't just encouraged, but pretty much required, to form an ongoing professional network.

A good friend of mine spent the fall semester of 2014 as a visiting professor at the University of Wyoming, with which she'd been wholly unfamiliar, and was blown away by the university's deep funds (thanks to the state's oil and gas wealth), the sophistication and training of its faculty, and the international diversity of its graduate students, most of whom interact extensively with undergraduates, sharing their worldviews. My friend was teaching in the Global & Area Studies Program, and when she went to a retreat sponsored by the program at the start of classes, she found herself tangled in a back-and-forth between a professional soldier from India who was taking a break to get a master's degree and a graduate student from Kenya; they were debating and discussing marriage practices in their respective cultures. Three visiting scholars from Shanghai at the retreat were still getting accustomed to Wyoming's chill and altitude. One of two female students engaged in a game of checkers was blond, blue-eyed and from Wisconsin; the other was from Tunisia and wore a headscarf. Nearby, a Californian just back from several years in Taiwan chatted with a Moroccan who was teaching in the school's Arabic program.

At the University of Wyoming my friend also met two professors, a married couple, with doctorates from Cambridge University and a herd of Wagyu cattle that they raised on their nearby ranch. She crossed paths with a sociologist from Sweden who'd begun her career as a detective with the Stockholm police department. And the class that my friend herself was teaching included a graduate student from Turkmenistan and another from Strasbourg, France.

"This is in Laramie, Wyoming!" my friend marveled—a city of about thirty-two thousand people in the least populous state in America. "Everyone I meet here is interesting. I hope these students understand how privileged they are." As she said that, I smiled. She'd invoked "privilege" in a way that it's too seldom used in conversations about college, but she'd done truer, fuller justice to the word.

There are also scores and scores of small institutions with distinctive strengths and one-of-a-kind wrinkles. But these colleges, like the University of Wyoming and ASU, are overshadowed and routinely overlooked as too many families chase the heralded brand, the envied address. They're looking for some imagined jackpot, and in their tunnel vision, they're not seeing any number of out-of-the-way opportunities and magical possibilities for four stimulating years that none of us ever get back.

* * *

Did you know that there's a New Jersey school with a behavioral psychology course that takes place largely among the land and sea mammals at the Six Flags Great Adventure amusement and safari park? It's Monmouth University, in West Long Branch, and a few years ago a psychology professor there, Lisa Dinella, took her own children to the park and realized that the trainers' testimonials about animal behavior had significant overlap with her campus lectures. So she devised a new class at Monmouth that includes weekly meetings with trainers at Six Flags and fieldwork with the animals. It has been offered twice over the last three years.

Did you know that there's a New York school with a dormitory of yurts? Yes, yurts, those cylindrical Mongolian tents. The school is St. Lawrence University, in the upstate town of Canton, and I'm stretching by using the word *dormitory*, but not by much. St. Lawrence offers a program every fall called the "Adirondack Semester," and it's for a small group of students who elect to live in a yurt village in Adirondack Park, about an hour's drive from the campus. There's a lake and a thick canopy of pine trees, but no wireless. No electricity. No Chipotle. The students learn survival skills and make their own meals, largely with provisions from a nearby farm. And as they adapt to the wilderness, they contemplate its meaning and man's stewardship of it through a menu of courses on such topics as environmental philosophy and nature writing.

At Denison, in Granville, Ohio, there's an academic concentration in bluegrass music, designed by a professor with an upstairs-downstairs history of fiddling. He performs frequently with the Columbus Symphony; he has also repeatedly won the Georgia State Fiddle Championship. DeSales

University, a Catholic school in Center Valley, Pennsylvania, has established an internship program with the Vatican that sends as many as six students to clerical and communications positions there every year.

St. Norbert College, in De Pere, Wisconsin, maintains a close relationship with the Green Bay Packers football team, including regular visits to the campus by players and internships with the Packers organization for students. Webster University, in St. Louis, emphasizes internationalism and has so many residential campuses in so many different countries, including Thailand and Ghana, that a student could study in a different place with a different language and culture almost every semester. It also had the top-ranked collegiate chess team in the United States in 2013, 2014 and 2015.

Oberlin College, in Oberlin, Ohio, is a veritable staging ground for doctorates and, since 1920, has had more graduates go on to earn PhDs than any other liberal arts college of its size. Speaking of which, the National Science Foundation ranks colleges by how high a percentage of their graduates go on to get PhDs in science in particular, and many of the top spots are claimed by small liberal arts colleges, including Reed (No. 4), Swarthmore (No. 5), Carleton (No. 6) and Grinnell (No. 7).

S. Georgia Nugent, who was the president of one such college, Kenyon, from 2003 to 2013, told me: "There would always be parents who would come with their prospective students and say, 'We love the college, but Billy really wants to major in science.' In fact, the small colleges are much more successful at producing STEM (science, technology, engineering and math) bachelor's graduates, and they're disproportionately successful at having those people go on to earn PhDs in the STEM fields."

Nugent's experience and perspective are interesting: She spent an earlier span of her career teaching at Cornell, at Brown and—for many years—at Princeton, where the jobs she held over time also included assistant to the president and associate provost. Kenyon exposed her to a more intimate academic environment, and she got an additional education into life well outside the Ivy League through her work at Kenyon and, since then, with the Council of Independent Colleges. It includes Kenyon, Denison, St. Lawrence and more than 600 other small and midsize independent liberal-arts colleges and universities that are, in almost all cases, less widely venerated than Princeton, Brown and Cornell. And she has come around to the firm conviction that for undergraduates, they're ideal environments: especially approachable, uniquely nurturing. She said that each has a much greater bounty of programs than its size might lead an outsider to expect. And she noted that the colleges as a group present an extraordinary spectrum of options, with distinctive colors for individuals who take the time to notice.

For instance Luther College, a school in Decorah, Iowa, that's affiliated with the Evangelical Lutheran Church of America, has proven to be a surprisingly sturdy cradle for winners of some of the most prestigious academic prizes. Although it has an endowment of only $116 million and just 2,500 students at a time, it has produced eight Rhodes scholars.

I could fill ten paragraphs this way. I could fill forty or four hundred or an entire book. Despite all the challenges facing higher education in America, from mounting student debt to grade inflation and erratic standards, our system is rightly the world's envy, and not just because our most revered universities remain on the cutting edge of research and attract talent from around the globe. We also have a plenitude and variety of settings for learning that are unrivaled. In light of that, the process of applying to college should and could be about ecstatically rummaging through those possibilities and feeling energized, even elated, by them. But for too many students, it's not, and financial constraints aren't the only reason. Failures of boldness and imagination by both students and parents bear some blame. The information is all out there. You just have to look.

Micheal McKinnon helps high school students do precisely that. He's a private college admissions consultant in the Chicago area, but unlike many of the high-priced transcript polishers I described earlier in the book, he doesn't emphasize the Ivy League—in fact, he tends to steer clear of it—and he does extensive pro bono work with children from relatively poor families. His particular focus is finding colleges that kids tend to overlook—maybe because these schools are in odd locations or have unremarkable public images—and colleges that are real values, in terms of what they charge or the amount of aid they can offer.

And there are many, many schools in this category. A conversation with McKinnon is an eye-opening, option-diversifying revelation. "I tend not to even work with people anymore who are going the elite-school route," he told me. "It's nothing but heartache. I'm serious. They do themselves more of a disservice. I'll give you a classic example."

He proceeded to tell me about a boy who'd been a client of his a little more than five years before. The boy was very bright but not at the top of his high school class, and McKinnon had guided him toward Central College in Pella, Iowa, a small liberal arts school with, in McKinnon's estimation, a track record of serving its students well. The boy thrived there and, upon graduation, was admitted to medical school at Duke. Meanwhile, a girl who had been the valedictorian of his high school class and had gone to college at Northwestern didn't blossom the way he did. She, too, set her sights on medical school, but had to apply two years in a row before finding a spot that she wanted, and even then it wasn't at an institution as esteemed as Duke.

McKinnon told me that there are all sorts of quasi-secret schools out there, or rather schools with attributes and promises that go unnoticed by too many students. He mentioned Utah State University. It's not exclusive—it accepts nearly all of its applicants—but for a high-achieving student who's looking for a real deal and is concerned primarily with immediate employment after graduation, it's a find. For one thing, it has enough money and enough interest in superior students that it's likely to "waive all tuition, whether you're in state or out of state," he said, adding: "The state of Utah has always had a highly educated workforce with a low cost of living, so corporations have continued to move there because of that. With more companies coming in, the state needs more highly trained, highly qualified individuals." Thus graduates of Utah State frequently find themselves snapped up quickly by local employers. He noted that the school also has strong scientific programs, reflected in its extensive collaboration with NASA and its central involvement in studying the behavior of wolves in Yellowstone National Park.

Central College, Utah State: I asked him what else he had up his sleeve. He told me to keep an eye on the University of the Incarnate Word in San Antonio, Texas. He also said that for the right kinds of students, three relatively small Midwestern schools—Hope College, in Holland, Michigan; Edgewood College, in Madison, Wisconsin; and Kalamazoo College, in Kalamazoo, Michigan—had much to recommend them. (You may recall that Kalamazoo was among those schools that, according to *U.S. News*, sent an unusually large percentage of students abroad for study.)

Our conversation was just another reminder that there have long been schools that dominate the discourse and schools left inexplicably outside of it. I've marveled for some time over the fact that when I was in secondary school and people all around me spoke incessantly about the options beyond graduation and what some of the better or more interesting ones were, I never once heard anyone mention St. John's College. And while I've lived at least briefly in more than a half dozen states and interviewed thousands of people across scores of professions, I don't think I've met anyone who went there, or at least told me that he or she did, or brought it up as a school worth fantasizing about or prodding one's children toward.

Yet it's a fascinating, fierce, one-of-a-kind institution. At its two campuses, in Annapolis, Maryland, and Santa Fe, New Mexico, each with fewer than five hundred students, the relentless focus is on Great Books and great thinkers and the Western canon: the Greek philosophers, the Bible, Milton, Shakespeare, Hobbes, Rousseau, the Declaration of Independence, Eliot, Twain. St. John's is about classic erudition, timeless discipline and rigorous thought. Students don't get formal grades but rather face-to-face oral appraisals, done on the basis of their participation in tiny classes and on their many written papers, which substitute for tests. In surveys, they say they adore the school and feel wholly satisfied.

Both the Annapolis and Santa Fe campuses have been mainstays on the list of Colleges That Change Lives, which originated with a 1996 book of that title that sought to showcase and exalt lesser-known schools outside the Ivy League. It embraced the idea that at a certain point of selectiveness, a college is corrupting its mission and skewing its identity in a manner that doesn't serve a true education. And it hinges on the belief that no one college, no matter how celebrated, is right for anyone and everyone who can gain admission there. A school, like a dress or a suit, has to have the contours and colors that work for the person choosing it. It has to fit.

When I spoke with guidance counselors, I often asked which colleges had proven to be spectacular experiences for the students sent off to them. I heard kind words about Stanford, about Brown, about Johns Hopkins. But I heard equally kind, if not kinder, words about the College of Wooster, in Wooster, Ohio, which requires students to do an ambitious independent study project in their senior year; about Butler University, in Indianapolis, whose theater program drew praise; about Indiana University, especially for music majors; about DePauw University, in Greencastle, Indiana, which has upgraded its campus significantly over recent years; about the University of Rochester, in upstate New York, which has strong science instruction.

Alice Kleeman, the Menlo-Atherton High School counselor, singled out Evergreen State College, in Olympia, Washington. It's somewhat famous as a progressive alternative to traditional schools, with narrative evaluations instead of grades, a pronounced attention to environmental issues and a student body of nonconformists. Kleeman said that when a boy from Menlo-Atherton who went there came back to visit her after his freshman year, "I almost didn't recognize him, because of the confidence that he'd gained, because he'd finally found a place where other students shared his interests and where people weren't judged in the same way they're judged in the college admissions process. He had friends. He stood up straighter. He had a whole new image of who he was, because he'd chosen a college that was a really great match for *him*. If you'd picked him up and dropped him into Harvard or Stanford, it just wouldn't have worked."

Each college-bound student has his or her own needs, and there are schools that are likely to meet them and schools that aren't. David Rusenko determined that Carnegie Mellon, which had accepted him, fell into the latter category. So he chose to go to Penn State instead.

He wanted the frat parties, the football games, the crowds. And that wasn't because he gravitated naturally to those. The opposite was true. But his goal was to change, to stretch, to become more, to become different. He'd had an unusual upbringing in an unusual world, and now was the time to round out the picture.

His parents, English teachers, had raised him abroad, first in France and then, from the time he was seven years old, in Casablanca, Morocco. They'd actually started an English-language high school there. It was tiny, an island in an exotic sea. He was one of its students. In his graduating class in 2002, there were all of eleven others.

"At Carnegie Mellon," he said, "kids would be supersmart, I'd learn a lot and there was a computer science angle."

All of which was good; computers were his strength and his interest. But he worried that he would emerge from Carnegie Mellon as "an unsociable nerd who wasn't going to have the people skills he needed to succeed.

"I was a quiet kid," he said, "and I figured it would be critical for me to pick up people skills. My thinking was that people skills, soft skills, play such a critical role if you're going to lead people. And it was always my desire to start a company."

So at Penn State he made it a point to stray from the classroom, to mingle, to get a taste of Greek life. And he indeed developed into a more outgoing, articulate, chattier guy. "Fraternities are a microcosm," he said. "You can learn a lot from them."

He benefited from his academic experiences, too. The school had just begun a special computer science major that focused not only on technology but on working in teams, giving presentations: the sorts of talents necessary for entrepreneurs who are trying to sell investors on their product and trying to rally employees toward a goal.

"The theory behind the program was to develop more well-rounded technologists," he said. "I probably gave more than sixty presentations over the years."

He benefited from Penn State in yet one more way, meeting and becoming friendly with two fellow students there who shared his ambitions. With them he developed Weebly, a service that guides people through the creation of websites. They started it in 2006. By 2009 it was profitable. And in 2014, it received a fresh infusion of $35 million from Sequoia, a venture capital firm that valued it at $455 million, according to Rusenko, thirty, who is its chief executive officer and now lives in the tech utopia of San Francisco.

Rusenko said that Penn State had served him well, that fancier schools don't necessarily leave people in better stead, and that I should talk with Sam Altman, the president of Y Combinator, which is arguably Silicon Valley's most famous and influential source of first-step seed money for tech start-ups. Y Combinator had given Weebly its initial funding and has done the same for nearly 750 other young companies, out of thousands more who have developed and pitched ideas. Altman, Rusenko said, would have a sense of whether the graduates of elite schools were especially good at proposing and developing successful ventures.

So I called him. Altman, also thirty, went to Stanford but never finished, because he and a classmate founded Y Combinator instead. He said that Stanford, by introducing the two of them, had blessed him, and he loved his time there, among what he described as "a density of smart people."

But, he added, "to my chagrin, Stanford has not had a really great track record." He meant that most of the proposals that Stanford students and grads had brought to Y Combinator didn't hold much promise and pan out. He noted that Y Combinator's biggest success, Airbnb, was started by graduates of the Rhode Island School of Design.

I asked him if any one school stood out as a source of students and graduates whose ideas sparkled and winded up doing Y Combinator proud.

"Yes," he said, identifying an institution that hadn't sired supernovas like Airbnb but that had an unusually good track record of exciting ideas worth funding. "The University of Waterloo." It's a public school in the Canadian province of Ontario with more than thirty thousand students.

"I try not to travel very much, but I'm going to spend three days there this fall just to meet more students," Altman said when we spoke in July 2014. "They train really great engineers. Waterloo came up enough times that I thought: 'I really have to go there.'" He has paid visits to schools before, of course, but none, ever, for three whole days.

The list he gave me of successful startups that could be traced to Waterloo was eight ventures long: Thalmic Labs, BufferBox, Pebble, PagerDuty, Vidyard, PiinPoint, Reebee and Instacart.

Altman told me that in his opinion, the importance of attending an elite school "is going down, not up," because there are avenues to entrepreneurial success that don't involve submitting a transcript and flaunting your academic bona fides to a graduate school or a corporation. "Now a lot of the best people are not taking those paths out of college," he said. "They're doing a startup or doing something else."

And they're judged, he said, by the existing work that they can point to, the examples they can show. "Did you contribute to an open-source project? Did you create a video that did well on YouTube? Now you can answer how good you are with the Internet. It's a showcase for people. You can read about them on Twitter. You can look at what they've built.

"Writers get book deals based on the quality of their blogs," he added. "Anyone can produce content. Anyone can make it available. And good work gets shared and then rises to the top. Before, there was no way for that to happen. Whoever had connections got their book published. Whoever had connections got their startup funded."

His vantage point is Silicon Valley, which isn't entirely representative. There are still plenty of freshly minted graduates hitting up companies for employment in a more old-fashioned way. But what those companies want isn't entirely predictable and may not be Stanford, which brings me back to that *Wall Street Journal* survey of employers, the one that ranked ASU fifth as a source for entry-level hires. The schools that ranked first through fourth were Penn State, Texas A&M, the University of Illinois and Purdue. Sixth through tenth were the University of Michigan, Georgia Tech, the University of Maryland, the University of Florida and Carnegie Mellon. The only Ivy in the top 25 was Cornell (No. 14).

SEVEN

AN ELITE EDGE?

"I think there's a conceit, a myth, that you can go and sit in a university and things will come to you. They don't. You have to go to them."

—Condoleezza Rice

The *Wall Street Journal* survey that lifted Penn State, Purdue and the University of Maryland so high isn't a full and accurate portrait. It requires a few qualifications and explanations, which the *Journal* story that accompanied it provided or at least suggested. Recruiters weren't exactly saying that students from the schools that they put at the top of the list were better educated and more intellectually nimble in some overarching sense, or that they had brighter careers ahead of them. The recruiters were saying that when it came to filling entry-level jobs that require discrete skills, state universities had proven more reliable pools of eager workers with specific, relevant training. In an uncertain era of unusually high unemployment for young men and women just out of college, that's worth noting and heeding. But so, in fairness, are a few other realities.

For example, certain firms are more likely to visit and interview students at highly selective schools than at the *Journal* survey's top 5. A few of these firms may go to those highly selective schools alone. They're trying to put a cap on the amount of time, manpower and money that they devote to recruitment, and they're regarding and taking advantage of the rigorous admissions processes at elite colleges as a prescreening that has whittled down an unwieldy universe of potential hires to a manageable group of finalists who can be presumed to possess some baseline of drive, poise and intelligence. To that end some of the richest banks and funds on Wall Street and some of the most highly paid consulting firms have developed close, sturdy relationships with Harvard, with Princeton, with the University of Pennsylvania.

And once a critical mass of people from an elite school set up shop somewhere, they tend to bring aboard yet more people from that school, because it's a place they have pride and faith in, because the compliment they're paying to the school is a form of self-validation and because they and their new hires all share points of reference, speak a common language and are products of the same culture. In rocky marriages, familiarity breeds contempt. In finance, law and other fields, it can breed comfort and job offers.

For those reasons and others, schools like Stanford and Harvard placed high—in the top 25—when the federal government in September 2015 presented information that ranked colleges based on the median annual earnings of alumni ten years after graduation. The information was part of a "College Scorecard" assembled by the Department of Education, which used college financial aid information, federal tax returns and other data to put together as detailed a financial portrait of the fates of college students—how many had completed their degrees, how much debt they'd emerged with, what kinds of salaries they attained—as had ever been assembled. When the report was released, some news coverage focused at least partly on its affirmation of highly selective schools, whose graduates seemed to fare well, at least in terms of money, in the job market. (One important note: Statistics on the minority of graduates who'd received no federal aid at all could not be, and weren't, factored into the numbers.)

But the picture presented by the College Scorecard was in fact more nuanced and complicated than any such validation. Most striking, for example, was how many small, specialized schools devoted to sciences, health care or technology placed in the top 25, ahead of Harvard and Stanford. The SUNY Downstate Medical Center was No. 1, and the top 10 also included the Albany College of Pharmacy and Health Sciences, whose graduates were making \$110,600 annually. It placed just ahead of MIT (\$91,600), and the Cochran School of Nursing (\$87,700) was just ahead of Harvard (\$87,200). Yes, these are utterly different kinds of academic experiences, drawing utterly different kinds of students, but the figures bolster a point that transcends this comparison: Your earnings say more about what you chose to study, and with how much of a practical and salary-minded agenda you chose it, than they do about the luster of a school's name.

And even among schools with robust liberal-arts traditions, graduate earnings, at least as measured by the College Scorecard, didn't precisely reflect the selectiveness and fame of the institution. Graduates of Villanova (\$73,800) outpaced those of Columbia ($72,900). Graduates of Fairfield University ($71,500) reported higher incomes than graduates of a school just a bit farther up the turnpike in Connecticut, Yale ($66,000). This could mean many things, including that the highest-earning graduates of Columbia and Yale never got financial aid and thus weren't captured by the survey. With most sets of numbers, you can never know with precision what the right message and moral are, and anxious parents and students navigating the marketplace of higher education forget that too quickly and easily.

They should bear in mind some of the questions raised and dynamics explored by the renowned business writer James B. Stewart in his weekly "Common Sense" column in the *New York Times* in October 2015. Reflecting on the College Scorecard and various salary-centric rankings of schools, Stewart wrote: "There is no way to know what, if any, impact a particular college has on its graduates' earnings, or life for that matter." That's because it's impossible to separate out the ambition, talent and family connections of the person who entered the college from the college's influence on his or her trajectory. Jerry Z. Muller, a professor of history at Catholic University who specializes in misplaced and misunderstood metrics, stressed to Stewart that graduates of schools like Harvard and MIT have high earnings because Harvard and MIT are "incredibly selective about who they let in.

"And many of them come from privileged backgrounds, which also correlates with high earnings," Muller told Stewart, referring to the students at those schools.

Stewart then spoke with Jonathan Rothwell, a fellow at the Brookings Institution who had been gathering and analyzing information about the earnings of graduates of different colleges. Rothwell crunched those numbers in a very particular way: He looked at what a person might be expected to earn based on his or her characteristics (such as test scores and family background) before entering college. He looked at what they ended up making years after college. And he adjusted for the fact that earnings would invariably be higher for people who'd attended science-focused colleges and gone into science-related fields. The idea was to measure the "value added" by various colleges.

Using this yardstick, Stewart's column presented what he christened the "Brookings–Common Sense" rankings, and the top 10 schools were Colgate University, Carleton College, Washington and Lee University, Westmont College, Kenyon College, Wagner College, Marietta College, Manhattan College, St. Mary's University and Pacific Lutheran University.

"No Ivy League schools made the top 20 on this list, suggesting that many of those students have an edge heading into college," Stewart wrote. "The highest-ranked Ivy was Brown, at No. 45." Elite colleges may well set their graduates up best for continued studies beyond a bachelor's degree. There's a disproportionate presence of alumni of highly selective colleges at revered graduate schools—in business, law, medicine and other disciplines—that can be magnets for recruiters and springboards to some of the best-paying jobs. Wendy Zupac, Devin Mauney, Peter Hart and other interview subjects of mine who went from state universities to Ivy League law or business schools said that they met plenty of people there like them, but they also said that the fraction of their fellow students who'd been to the most selective undergraduate schools seemed to be at least slightly higher than the fraction who'd been to less selective public colleges.

The elite graduate schools don't routinely publicize information analyzing the undergraduate alma maters of their students, but the Yale Law School did precisely that in 2013 and again in 2014, looking at all of the hundreds of young men and women at various stages of study there. Just over 40 percent of them had gone to the eight schools in the Ivy League. Seven of those eight—all but Cornell—were among the ten colleges that had sent the most alumni to Yale Law. In contrast, graduates of state schools represented well under 20 percent of the student body—and that was even when you counted the many graduates of top-ranked public universities like UC Berkeley and UCLA at Yale Law.

My sense from scattered data is that the distribution of students at top business schools and in other graduate programs isn't nearly as flattering to the Ivy League as that snapshot from Yale Law. But whatever the case, there's a crucial caveat about how to interpret the composition of Yale Law and how to think about several studies that have suggested that graduates of elite colleges earn more across their lifetimes than graduates of less elite ones. It's obvious, and it's this: Did the elite college make the Yale lawyer and the robust breadwinner, or do the characteristics and priorities of a Yale lawyer and a robust breadwinner dovetail with the characteristics and priorities of a person who aims for the elite college and studiously and diligently succeeds in putting together the sort of high school resume that wins over the admissions committee there?

Because this question is ultimately unanswerable—how do you design a study that builds in the right controls?—it's too seldom asked whenever big, sweeping assertions about education and earnings are made. It's left on the curb.

Take the recent discussion and documentation of the enormous income gap between college graduates and others. There's no doubt that much if not most of that gap is attributable to skills picked up in college or the greater confidence an employer will have about a college graduate. Many employers won't look at someone without a college diploma, even if it's not specifically necessary for the position being filled. But some of the gap is almost certainly attributable to variables that aren't products of a college education but are merely associated with it. A person's odds of graduating from college rise exponentially if he or she comes from a family of means, and people from such families probably have more connections to draw on, greater confidence about their fitness for lofty jobs, bigger expectations and a host of privileged experiences throughout their youths that point them in a propitious direction. College graduates may have more discipline, or at least discipline of the right kind. College didn't create it, but getting to and through college reflected it, and that same discipline could be essential to hunting down a good job, keeping it and being promoted over time. And similar dynamics could well be at work in any discrepancy between the achievement levels of elite-college alumni and the achievement levels of graduates of less selective schools.

A 2011 study done by Alan Krueger, a Princeton economics professor who served for two years as the chairman of President Obama's Council of Economic Advisers, and Stacy Dale, an analyst with Mathematica Policy Research, tried to adjust for that sort of thing. Krueger and Dale examined sets of students who had started college in 1976 and in 1989; that way, they could get a sense of incomes both earlier and later in careers. And they determined that the graduates of more selective colleges could expect earnings 7 percent greater than graduates of less selective colleges, even if the graduates in that latter group had SAT scores and high school GPAs identical to those of their peers at more exclusive institutions.

But then Krueger and Dale made their adjustment. They looked specifically at graduates of less selective colleges who had applied to more exclusive ones even though they hadn't gone there. And they discovered that the difference in earnings pretty much disappeared. Someone with a given SAT score who had gone to Penn State but had also applied to the University of Pennsylvania, an Ivy League school with a much lower acceptance rate, generally made the same amount of money later on as someone with an equivalent SAT score who was an alumnus of UPenn.

It was a fascinating conclusion, suggesting that at a certain level of intelligence and competence, what drives earnings isn't the luster of the diploma but the type of person in possession of it. If he or she came from a background and a mindset that made an elite institution seem desirable and within reach, then he or she was more likely to have the tools and temperament for a high income down the road, whether an elite institution ultimately came into play or not. This was powerfully reflected in a related determination that Krueger and Dale made in their 2011 study: "The average SAT score of schools that rejected a student is more than twice as strong a predictor of the student's subsequent earnings as the average SAT score of the school the student attended."

When I interviewed Krueger, he explained: "The students are basically self-sorting when they apply to colleges, and the more ambitious students are applying to the most elite schools." The inclination to consider UPenn, not attendance *at* UPenn, is the key to future earnings. Or maybe it's the inclination coupled with assertiveness and confidence, two other attributes suggested by the fact of applying to a college or colleges where admissions are fiercely competitive.

"Another way to read my results is: A good student can get a good education just about anywhere, and a student who's not that serious about learning isn't going to get much benefit," Krueger told me.

There was, though, one wrinkle to the findings. Krueger and Dale found that even after their clever adjustment, minority students and those from disadvantaged backgrounds *still* seemed to make out better, in terms of income, if they'd gone to more selective colleges. The two researchers theorized that for these students, the networking opportunities at selective colleges were more important than for other students, who had access to fruitful networks apart from the one established in college.

I don't believe it's right or especially useful to view and evaluate colleges primarily as bridges to riches, but even a kid who is approaching higher education that way would be wise to look less at the names of institutions and concentrate more on what he or she plans to study. *Majors* make a greater difference. In one recent study, Georgetown University's Center on Education and the Workforce determined that the median annual earnings of college graduates who'd chosen the most lucrative major, petroleum engineering, were more than four times higher than the median of college graduates who'd chosen the least lucrative one, which was counseling/psychology. The likelihood of simply being employed varies just as greatly with major. Graduates who'd studied pharmacology had a

100 percent employment rate. Graduates who'd studied social psychology had a 16 percent one.

"It matters a lot less where you went to college than it used to," the Georgetown center's director, Anthony Carnevale, told me. "What really drives your earnings is your field of study. If you go to Harvard and become a schoolteacher, you're not going to make more than another schoolteacher who didn't go to Harvard."

But even your major recedes in importance once you've been out in the workforce for a while and have an actual performance to be judged by, a track record to be assessed. In early 2014, Gallup released the results of a nationwide poll in which business leaders were asked to characterize the importance of four different factors when making hiring decisions. Those factors were the amount of knowledge a job candidate had in a particular field, a candidate's "applied skills," a candidate's college major and where a candidate had received a college degree. They could characterize each as "very important," "somewhat important," "not very important" or "not at all important." Field-relevant knowledge was by far the employment criterion that business leaders most frequently called "very important." Nearly 85 percent of them described it that way. But where an applicant had gone to college? Only 9 percent of the leaders described *that* as "very important."

Interestingly, the same Gallup survey showed that average Americans' impressions of how business leaders made hiring decisions were different from what those leaders said. Nearly one in three respondents indicated a belief—erroneous, if the leaders' own answers were trustworthy—that where a job candidate had gone to college was very important.

As Rusenko's success and Altman's comments suggest, the

tech world in general and Silicon Valley in particular may be the most vivid arenas in which ideas and know-how muscle educational pedigree out of the picture. This was captured in two 2014 columns in the *Times* by my colleague Tom Friedman that promptly went viral. Titled "How to Get a Job at Google" and "How to Get a Job at Google, Part 2," they contained many insights and pieces of advice from Laszlo Bock, the supervisor of all of Google's hiring. As recounted by Friedman, Bock paid no particular heed to prestigious colleges.

"To sum up Bock's approach to hiring: Talent can come in so many different forms and be built in so many nontraditional ways today, hiring officers have to be alive to every one—besides brand-name colleges," Friedman wrote. "Because 'when you look at people who don't go to school and make their way in the world, those are exceptional human beings. And we should do everything we can to find those people.' Too many colleges, he added, 'don't deliver on what they promise. You generate a ton of debt, you don't learn the most useful things for your life.'

"Google attracts so much talent it can afford to look beyond traditional metrics, like GPA," Friedman continued, later adding: "Beware. Your degree is not a proxy for your ability to do any job. The world only cares about—and pays off on—what you can do with what you know (and it doesn't care how you learned it). And in an age when innovation is increasingly a group endeavor, it also cares about a lot of soft skills—leadership, humility, collaboration, adaptability and loving to learn and re-learn. This will be true no matter where you go to work."

I got that same message from Parisa Tabriz, whom I

reached out to because she'd appeared on that 2013 list of 30 Under 30 in *Forbes*. She'd found her way to Google from the University of Illinois, where she received undergraduate and graduate degrees in computer science. Now thirty-one, she manages Google's Chrome Security Team and is involved in the hiring for it and for other security teams at Google.

"When I look at candidates' resumes, whether they have a degree or not is a data point, but I've never been especially interested in where they got a degree," Tabriz said. "I'm much more interested in what kinds of organizations they're involved in. I work in information security—finding security bugs, making software more secure—and I'm looking for experience doing that, which they wouldn't do in a classroom." They might do it, she said, in their free time, as a hobby. Or maybe while they were at school, they participated in some special, outside-of-class research project along those lines. That's what matters to her. That's what moves her.

"My experience at Google has really made me question how necessary a university degree is in the first place," she said. "If you have access to the Internet, you can teach a lot of this stuff to yourself. I have a Polish engineer—he's brilliant—who taught himself English by reading engineering manuals and participating in community forums and panels on the Internet. A degree in computer science isn't worthless, but getting an A in computer science doesn't mean you're a good programmer."

Well beyond Silicon Valley, many employers talk about trying to size up potential employees in ways that get beyond the window dressing of diplomas. Stuart Ruderfer, who runs a large marketing agency in Manhattan, told me that he's less concerned with the prestige of an applicant's college than with his or her GPA, which is often a barometer of how goal-oriented and hardworking someone is. He's also impressed when he sees or hears about aspects of an applicant's involvement in campus life: Did he or she run an organization? Stage an event or fund-raiser that was wildly successful? Pull off some difficult project? And Ruderfer pays careful attention to how applicants present and comport themselves in an interview. That's a harbinger of what they'll be like to work with, both for colleagues and clients.

"If you're looking only at the elite schools, you're going to miss some very talented people," Ruderfer said. "There are a lot of reasons why people go and don't go to the elite schools. There's money, geography. In some cases, people were perhaps not as focused in high school, so they don't have the grades or such, but then they get to college and they turn it on with a level of intensity that, for whatever reason, they hadn't turned up earlier in their lives. But they've got it now. And that's what you want. That intensity is going to be a much bigger factor in their success."

The longer a person has been out of college, the less relevant a college is to an employer. By the time someone is forty years old, it probably doesn't matter at all, but even by thirty-five or thirty, there's a whole new body of information to judge him or her by, and it's what most employers will choose to judge.

"Demonstrated success and a track record relevant to the need we're trying to fill is far more important to me than where someone went to school eons ago," said Kevin Reddy, the chief executive officer and chairman of Noodles & Company, a Colorado-based chain of restaurants that's one of the biggest success stories of the last few decades in what's called the "fast casual" space. Kevin has the ultimate say in hiring the chain's senior management.

His own rise didn't involve elite schools. It did involve an entrepreneurial spirit and work ethic that predated college and can't be taught. When he was eleven years old, he struck up a conversation one day with the man who delivered milk and eggs to the houses in his suburban Pittsburgh neighborhood. The man complained that the eggs were his fragile enemies, because they could break so easily and thus prevented him from moving too quickly as he made his rounds. Kevin told the man that for a modest fee, he'd take the eggs off his hands and deliver them himself to all of the houses near his family's. He'd just put them in his wagon and be sure to pull gently on it. "I wanted to earn a little money," Kevin said, "so I could buy a baseball glove."

His parents weren't particularly well-off, so Kevin always worked. He took a job at McDonald's when he was fifteen. "It was growing and advertising a lot, and there were several that were reasonably close to my house and I could get there quick enough. I told them, 'Here's my school schedule, here's my sports schedule, other than those times, I'll work whenever you want.' When I was that young, I wasn't allowed to cook on the grill, so I cleaned the dining room, cleaned the bathrooms. I worked the shake machine. Gradually I made it to the point where I could get to the grill." During his last years of high school he spent up to twenty hours a week at McDonald's, and he continued to devote the same amount to McDonald's during college, although by that point he had managerial responsibilities and, in his junior and senior years, worked in the corporate offices. It helped pay his college expenses.

He went to Duquesne University, a Catholic school in Pittsburgh. "I lived at home, because I couldn't afford to live in the dorms," he said. He majored in business and accounting, but when I asked him to recall a class that had held particular meaning for him, he mentioned one outside of those areas. It was called Marriage and Family Relationships and taught by a priest.

"He had this constant theme about not overreacting and not underreacting in times of stress," Kevin recalled. "And he said that you can't really argue with, debate or change somebody's mind if you don't understand their belief system, and so you really need to listen. For all walks of life, that was very sound advice. Let's face it: The business world is about relationships. You've got to have intelligent people. But once you understand the intellectual plan and you've analyzed it, you still have to bring it to life. And you bring it to life through relationships, through being able to work with people." Kevin said that while he honed those skills in college, he didn't need a college of any particular altitude to do that, and he'd honed those skills at McDonald's as well.

"There's so much more than raw intellect if you're going to influence people and accomplish things, and I don't think you can map it all out as some of the Tiger Moms are trying to," he said. "In the short run, college opens doors. But I think real success, enduring success, in life, in any arena, requires substance, and that substance is much more about what people do every day than where they went to school or where they grew up. It's a function of choice and persistence and being a student of *life*. Once you get out of college, so much of life is being able to relate to people, to influence people, to take risks, how well you listen. I don't think people's real character and real skills shine until they've been doing something for a long time, had their asses kicked and had to get up off the ground a few times."

When he's hiring, he's asking not only whether a candidate has precisely what the position needs but also, he said, "What kind of person are they? Are they genuine? Do they respect other people? Are they passionate?" He can sometimes sense that from interviews. He can sometimes glean it from references, or from noting the sequence of jobs that the candidate has held over time, the frequency and manner in which he or she has been promoted. But from the college a person attended? Not really. Not usually.

Shortly after I spoke with Kevin, I had a conversation with Bradley Tusk, someone I first met nearly fifteen years ago, when he was the communications director for U.S. senator Chuck Schumer of New York. Since then he's been a deputy governor for the state of Illinois, a senior vice president with Lehman Brothers, a special assistant to Mike Bloomberg when Bloomberg was mayor of New York City, and the manager of Bloomberg's 2009 reelection campaign. He currently runs Tusk Strategies, a political and strategic consulting firm based in New York City.

"Over the last twenty years," Tusk said, "I've hired hundreds and hundreds of people." And while he himself went to UPenn for college and the University of Chicago for law school, he said that he has not found that elite schools are any guarantor or predictor that someone will turn out to be a great employee and excel. "In most jobs, there's a base level of intelligence that's needed, and after that, success is typically determined by other factors: work ethic, hustle, instincts, communication skills, street smarts, character, creativity, persistence. I haven't seen any evidence that going to an elite school inherently means you have any of these skills (other than work ethic). And I've found that people who've had to struggle a little will often develop more of these skills—especially persistence—and they also don't have the same kind of entitlement and expectations you sometimes see from employees from top schools.

"So at least based on my experience in government, politics and business, I haven't seen any particular reason to focus our hiring on students from elite schools," he summed up. Then he laughed, because it occurred to him that he had recently made three offers for senior jobs to people in their thirties and, he said, "I don't know where any of them went to college. I *think* I know where one of them went, but I'm not sure. The two others? I have no idea."

Toward the end of 2013, in mid-December, Gallup and Purdue University announced a partnership, supported by funding from the Lumina Foundation, to "build and conduct the largest representative study of college graduates in U.S. history." The study was christened the Gallup-Purdue Index, and its goal, according to the initial press release, was to "measure the most important outcomes of higher education—great careers and lives that matter—and provide higher education leaders with productive insights." The index is a telling indication of just how consumed Americans have become with the question of college: why it costs so much; whether its returns warrant the investment; how it can best be used to students', and the country's, advantage.

"As it finally did in K–12, an accountability era has begun for higher education," said Mitch Daniels, the president of

Purdue and the former two-term governor of Indiana, upon the unveiling of the project, which would quiz college graduates about what was described as "five key dimensions of well-being: purpose, social, physical, financial and community."

In May 2014, the first annual report, based on a survey of more than thirty thousand graduates, came out. The headline on the summary distributed to the news media: "It's Not 'Where' You Go to College, But 'How' You Go to College."

"There is no difference in workplace engagement or a college graduate's well-being if they attended a public or private not-for-profit institution, a highly selective institution, or a top 100–ranked school in *U.S. News & World Report*," the first paragraph of that summary proclaimed. Right out of the gate, Gallup and Purdue confronted the obsession with elite colleges, and right out of the gate, they confronted the unwarranted obeisance to *U.S. News*. They understood the era, and it was as if they were taking aim at a mass psychosis.

The report didn't measure graduates' salaries: a poor stand-in for achievement and a flawed, irrelevant predictor of happiness. Instead it measured their own professed satisfaction with their jobs (the "workplace engagement" referred to in the summary). Its separate (though related) verdict on their well-being was cobbled together from those key dimensions, meaning how much the respondents said that they liked what they were doing (purpose); how supportive they found the relationships in their lives (social); whether they felt healthy and energetic (physical); whether they felt that they were managing their economic lives in a way that made them less stressed and more secure (financial); and whether they felt connected to, and proud of, the places where they lived and spent most of their time (community). Depending on their own assessments of these criteria, they were characterized as thriving, struggling or suffering.

According to the report, which will be revisited annually over a five-year period, student debt had a significant impact on well-being and workplace engagement. Graduates with between $20,000 and $40,000 in loans, which the report defined as the average student loan debt, were much less likely to be thriving than graduates without any loans to repay.

People's lives were improved if, in college, they'd found some sort of academic mentor. "For example," the report said, "if graduates had a professor who cared about them as a person, made them excited about learning, and encouraged them to pursue their dreams, their odds of being engaged at work more than doubled, as did their odds of thriving in their well-being.

"And if graduates had an internship or job where they were able to apply what they were learning in the classroom, were actively involved in extracurricular activities and organizations, and worked on projects that took a semester or more to complete, their odds of being engaged at work doubled also," the report said.

In other words, the nature and quality of the time spent in college—including, as it turned out, the major someone chose and the efficiency with which he or she zipped toward a diploma—were paramount. Employed graduates who'd majored in the arts and humanities or the social sciences were slightly more engaged at work than those who'd majored in science or business. And graduates who'd finished school in four years or less were much more likely to be engaged at work than those who'd taken longer.

These conclusions of the initial report were validated in a second report, issued in late September 2015, by which point the index's canvass of college graduates had grown to sixty thousand people, of all ages. A few weeks before the report was released, during a visit to Purdue's campus in West Lafayette, Indiana, I sat down with some of the Purdue and Gallup researchers and analysts who are responsible for the project.

Brandon Busteed, who leads Gallup's education work, stressed to me that the more people surveyed, the more clear it was becoming that specific college behaviors correlated with greater contentment down the road. And he said that analysts were factoring in and adjusting for the personalities of respondents, to be sure that the results weren't merely showing that certain *kinds* of people approached college in a fruitful way. What was obvious, he said, was that actual behaviors, independent of character type, had enduring benefits.

Speaking of those behaviors, he singled out deep, sustained participation in a campus group or pastime—note the phrase "*actively involved*" in the summary of the initial report—and emphasized that this is distinct from minimal attachment to an indiscriminate range of things. And he said the importance of such commitment suggests that the transcript-gilding, resume-padding practice of dabbling in a profusion of extracurricular pursuits is just a showy waste of time. "There's an area where we're literally guiding kids wrong in terms of the values we're teaching them," he told me.

For this second report, the Gallup-Purdue Index added a question that examined whether exposure to diversity in college had a measurable impact. It did, within limits. While graduates who strongly agreed that they'd interacted regularly with people from different backgrounds were no more or less likely to be thriving in all five dimensions of life, they were more than twice as likely as other college graduates to say without reservation that their education was worth the cost.

And if they'd finished college in the last five years, they were almost one and a half times as likely to be committed to and enthusiastic about their jobs. Exposure to diversity had discernible upsides but no obvious downsides.

I asked Busteed if the Gallup team could run the numbers to compare outcomes not just for public-university graduates versus private-college graduates but also to compare graduates of the top 50 national universities in the *U.S. News* rankings, graduates of the top 50 liberal arts colleges and the overall sample of college graduates. I was looking for a more granular breakdown than the first report had provided. He indeed produced one for me.

It showed that 10 percent of all graduates described themselves as thriving in all five dimensions of life. The figure inched upward only to 11 percent for graduates of schools ranked among the top 50 national universities and to 13 percent for graduates of schools ranked among the top 50 liberal arts colleges.

As for graduates' engagement in their employment, 39 percent of all respondents professed serious commitment to, and enthusiasm about, their jobs. The breakdown of this again suggested little advantage to a private school or an especially selective one. While 39 percent of public-school graduates were engaged in their work, 40 percent of graduates of private nonprofit schools were. For graduates of national universities in the top 50, the figure was 41 percent. It did increase—but merely to 47 percent—for graduates of top 50 liberal arts colleges.

Other yardsticks in the index revealed greater differences but never profound ones. While only 24 percent of all graduates strongly agreed with the statement that they could not imagine a world without the school they attended, 35 percent of graduates of top 50 liberal arts colleges and 34 percent of graduates of top 50 national universities said as much.

And while only 29 percent of all graduates and 33 percent of graduates of top 50 national universities strongly agreed that their schools prepared them well for life, 40 percent of graduates of top 50 liberal arts colleges did. Highly ranked colleges outperformed highly ranked universities by a bit in several categories. But if you looked to the Gallup-Purdue Index for glaring signs that the alumni of the most widely venerated and exclusive schools felt enormously better about their experience in higher education, and felt significantly more fulfilled in their subsequent lives, you couldn't, and didn't, find them.

How you use college. What you demand of it. These dynamics get lost in the admissions mania, which overshadows them, to a point where it makes them seem close to irrelevant. But their importance is vividly underscored by the histories of just about every successful person interviewed for this book. I think back to Peter Hart and his involvement at Indiana University in both its business fraternity and a modest real estate enterprise of his own; to Jenna Leahy and her short trips to Mexico and long ones across the Atlantic to study abroad; to Condoleezza Rice and her lust for extracurricular involvements, along with her habit of arriving to office hours early, with flattering comments at the ready; to Bobbi Brown and her creation of a nonexistent major that she could get truly excited about; to David Rusenko and his strategy for plucking precisely what he needed from Penn State.

I also think of Jillian Vogel, twenty-five, who did a thorough job of maximizing her four years in college precisely because she didn't end up where she'd hoped to and was determined to turn the consolation prize into something more, into the trophy itself.

Brown University had been her dream, and it hadn't seemed to her like such an impossible one, given that she was in the top 5 of roughly 100 seniors at a selective, well-regarded public school in New York City. She applied to Brown for early admission, was deferred and had a good guess why, because her guidance counselor and others around her had warned her about the problem. She'd scored only 24 out of 36 on the ACT.

After Brown deferred her, she resolved to charm the gatekeepers there into accepting her during the general-admission period in the spring. She drew and sent them a comic strip of all the stuff she'd been up to since she'd first applied. She wrote and mailed them a letter, which she addressed to that cursed 24 on the ACT.

"Dear Composite Score," it read. "It has come to my attention that you are unimpressive. While you represent the hours in a day, the title of a television drama and the product of 3 times 8, you are not an ideal ACT score. I have only a hazy memory of the Saturday morning of your conception, as it was so long ago." It said that back then, "I could not foresee what you would represent and the amount of power you would come to hold over me," and it took issue with that power, arguing that her mind and her potential couldn't be distilled into two measly digits. At the bottom of the letter, Jillian had a dozen of her teachers sign their names in support. "That's 12 signatures," she wrote, "to compensate for the 12 points" between her 24 and a perfect 36.

Brown did not admit her. Nor did Middlebury, Tufts or Emory. "I felt so rejected," she told me. "I've never felt that kind of rejection before." She ended up with a choice between the University of Vermont and UNC. She headed to the South, feeling lucky to have Chapel Hill but still feeling the sting of not being wanted by all of those other places.

She turned that sting into resolve. She sprang into action. She sought the most interesting classes that she could find, some of them intensive, some of them offbeat, and she wheedled or stormed her way into them. One of the most beloved seminars in the English department, with just twelve to fifteen students per session, was a fanciful exploration of style and usage called Gram-o-Rama. Students in it composed songs, dances, skits and pieces of performance art that were devoted to, or showcases for, the fine points of grammar and wordplay. It was reserved, supposedly, for kids on a creative-writing track; Jillian was a communications major. But she'd met the professor. She pleaded with her. And it worked.

With a ruminative essay about growing up kosher, she also managed to get into a word-of-mouth class about food science and food culture for students in the honors program, which she wasn't even a part of. Limited to fifteen kids, it had an extraordinarily ambitious, encyclopedic syllabus of books and magazine and newspaper articles about everything from overfishing to obesity. It welcomed a who's who of guest speakers. It included a long weekly dinner at the professor's house off-campus, and it culminated in a five-day trip to the Bay Area replete with visits to several of San Francisco's most famous restaurants and to a vineyard in the Napa Valley.

Jillian said that if she wanted an exhilarating experience or an academic challenge at UNC, "I could find it. It just took a little more effort. I was extremely satisfied there, but it took everything I had to make it happen. I couldn't be passive. I had to be proactive." And she carried that gumption back to New York with her, pressing it into the service of a job hunt that led, ultimately, to a position recruiting and developing talent for CollegeHumor Media, an online entertainment company that produces and curates comedic skits, pictures and articles aimed at a young audience.

Then again, she had that gumption all along. It was abundant in her entreaties to Brown, and while it didn't get her an invitation there, I suspect that it will have more to do with what happens to her through the years than will anything else, including which college she went to. The best that college, any college, could do was to draw on it and to draw it out—to give it even more muscle. UNC accomplished that, and UNC taught her, or reaffirmed for her, that you have more options than you initially think you do, if you hunt for and insist on them.

In fact at UNC she discovered and took advantage of something most students there are oblivious to: If there's a course at nearby Duke University that fits into what you're studying and isn't replicated at UNC, you can make arrangements, space permitting, to take it. She did that for a lecture class on contemporary documentary filmmaking. It was terrific, she said, largely because renowned documentarians would drop in to address the roughly 150 students.

But many of those students wouldn't even pay much attention, she said. "Everybody in the classroom had their computers on and Facebook up," she recalled. "And it was like: What are you guys doing? This person is talking to you!" She got the feeling that Duke students had become accustomed, even numb, to the kinds of special opportunities that UNC students appreciated more.

"Maybe I'm just seeing what I wanted to see," she told me. "But I'd sit there and I'd think: Don't take this for granted, guys."

EIGHT

STRANGLED WITH IVY

"Presidents, deans and professors rarely tell students simple truths, for example that the strategizing and diligence that got them into the college of their choice may not, if followed thoughtlessly, lead to an adult life they will find worth living."

—Harry Lewis, a former dean of Harvard College, the undergraduate wing of Harvard University, in his 2006 book, Excellence Without a Soul

While the advantages of going to an elite college aren't questioned as often as they should be, the disadvantages are even less frequently broached, perhaps because a great many people can't imagine that there'd be any. William Deresiewicz can. He's devoted no small part of the last decade to grappling with and articulating them. He does this provocatively, but with some standing and credibility: From 1998 to 2008, he taught English at Yale, and for six years before that, he was a graduate instructor at Columbia University, which is where he got his undergraduate degree, his master's and his

PhD (in English). In other words he's frolicked in the Ivies. Only he doesn't make it sound so frolicsome.

In 2008, as he left Yale, he published an essay in the *American Scholar* titled "The Disadvantages of an Elite Education." "Our best universities," said an introductory summary of the essay, "have forgotten that the reason they exist is to make minds, not careers." This was the seed of a book, *Excellent Sheep*, which was in turn previewed, just before its publication in August 2014, in the *New Republic*. The magazine found even sexier language for Deresiewicz's perspective, because that's what magazines do. "Don't Send Your Kid to the Ivy League," read the headline that it slapped on the preview. No equivocation. No qualifications. And the subhead cannily appropriated a booming pop culture trend, warning: "The nation's top colleges are turning our kids into zombies." Bolt your doors and say your prayers. They're on the loose—the flesh-eating hordes from Haverford, the walking dead from Williams.

What Deresiewicz dwells on, and what's so important to keep in mind, are some themes I mentioned earlier in this book, for instance when exploring Rebecca Fabbro's dissatisfactions with Yale, Howard Schultz's satisfactions with Northern Michigan University and the philosophy behind *Washington Monthly*'s evaluation of schools: There's ideally a whole lot more to higher education than a springboard to high-paying careers, and an elite school composed almost entirely of young men and women who have aced the SATs or ACTs isn't likely to be the most exciting, eclectic stew of people and perspectives. It doesn't promise to challenge extant prejudices and topple old expectations. And that's largely because there's a surfeit of students who traveled to their elite destinations on an on-ramp of familiar perks and prods.

"When I speak of elite education, I mean prestigious institutions like Harvard or Stanford or Williams as well as the larger universe of second-tier selective schools, but I also mean everything that leads up to and away from them—the private and affluent public high schools; the ever-growing industry of tutors and consultants and test-prep courses; the admissions process itself, squatting like a dragon at the entrance to adulthood; the brand-name graduate schools and employment opportunities that come after the BA; and the parents and communities, largely upper-middle class, who push their children into the maw of this machine," Deresiewicz wrote in the *New Republic.*

And in the *American Scholar*, this: "Elite schools pride themselves on their diversity, but that diversity is almost entirely a matter of ethnicity and race. With respect to class, these schools are largely—indeed increasingly—homogeneous." He added that because the schools also "cultivate liberal attitudes, they leave their students in the paradoxical position of wanting to advocate on behalf of the working class while being unable to hold a simple conversation with anyone in it." He cited Al Gore and John Kerry, the Democratic presidential nominees in 2000 and 2004 respectively, "one each from Harvard and Yale, both earnest, decent, intelligent men, both utterly incapable of communicating with the larger electorate." Their successor, Barack Obama, was capable, sort of, but even his route to the Ivy League wasn't consistently hardscrabble, and it didn't give him an automatic rapport with working-class Americans. He attended a private secondary school in Honolulu, called Punahou. It's arguably the best known and most exalted in Hawaii.

Deresiewicz observed that the students at an elite school

are prone to vanity, because they are constantly told that they are the chosen, their presence there a testament to how special they are. "There is something wrong with the smugness and self-congratulation that elite schools connive at from the moment the fat envelopes come in the mail," he wrote. "From orientation to graduation, the message is implicit in every tone of voice and tilt of the head, every old-school tradition, every article in the student paper, every speech from the dean. The message is: You have arrived. Welcome to the club. And the corollary is equally clear: You deserve everything your presence here is going to enable you to get. When people say that students at elite schools have a strong sense of entitlement, they mean that those students think they deserve more than other people because their SAT scores are higher."

If you think that sounds like an exaggeration, I'd point you to an acceptance letter from Lawrenceville, a New Jersey prep school that feeds the Ivy League and presages the affirmations that flow so freely there. It came to my attention after its recipient posted it on Facebook. Dated March 10, 2014, it read: "This is the moment a door opened to reveal an educational journey that can shape the rest of your life. Welcome to Lawrenceville. Welcome to the next chapter in your life as a Lawrentian." It proceeded to praise "the remarkable sense of balance our students possess" and to ask its recipient, "Are you ready? We think so, and so do your future classmates." The heart flutters. Goose bumps rise.

Deresiewicz expressed additional concerns. He said that at elite schools you find "the self-protectiveness of the old-boy network, even if it now includes girls," which means that no one is ever challenged all that mightily or held to stern account, and many students settle into a complacent mediocrity.

This, he said, is embodied in the man who kept both Gore and Kerry from the presidency, George W. Bush, who attended both Yale (undergrad) *and* Harvard (business school).

And Deresiewicz's plaint didn't end there. He fretted about a lack of imagination and a dreary careerism in the students at elite schools, which don't challenge those leanings but, rather, instill or amplify them. And he contended that the homogeneous group of overachievers who make it to Princeton or Yale have, to that point, known only one triumph after another, largely because they've been given extensive preparation to master precisely those tasks that the elite educational track values. They can be strangely weak, not strong, as a result.

It's one hell of a laundry list, and I heard some of the same worries expressed by other educators who'd worked at highly selective schools. I saw bits and pieces of his lament all over the place.

"I think we're really screwing them up badly in the long run," said Bruce Poch, the former admissions dean at Pomona, referring to the way in which kids who wind up at elite schools are pointed in that direction from an early age, monitored ceaselessly by their jittery parents and made to believe that a great job and a contented life are a matter of faithful adherence to a program. "These kids are not equipped to get knocked on their tail. At Pomona, one of the things I got really nervous about was looking at these kids who'd had nothing but success. There was a stunning fragility to some of them. The parental bubble wrap and the boot camps got them to their one and only goal in lives," a top-ranked school. Once there, they're sort of frozen, adrift.

And they respond by taking cues from the herd and following what they believe to be the script, because script-following is precisely what they learned to do, and script-following is what got them this far. Act I was admission. Act II is heading in a professional direction deemed worthy of the elite school whose name will be stamped on their diplomas. This means a direction that's reliably lucrative. They avoid risk, because they can't brook the possibility of failure. They conform.

In *Excellent Sheep* Deresiewicz charts the grim ascendance of economics as a major—and finance or management consulting as careers—for a shocking percentage of young people who attend the most highly selective colleges. He writes that while economics was the most popular major at only three of the top 10 national universities in *U.S. News* and three of the top 10 colleges in the mid-1990s, it has tended to reign supreme at 26 of the top 40 schools—the top 20 universities combined with the top 20 colleges—over recent years. There have also been recent years, he writes, when nearly half of the students graduating from Harvard and more than half of the students graduating from the University of Pennsylvania have gone into consulting or finance, while more than a third of students graduating from Cornell, Stanford and MIT did so. In 2011, more than a third of Princeton's graduates went into finance alone, he reports. And the focus on just a few professions means the neglect of so many others. "Whole fields have disappeared from view: the clergy, the military, electoral politics, even academia itself, for the most part, including basic science," he writes in *Excellent Sheep*. A lack of imagination and a fear of experimentation constrict, rather than expand, their opportunities.

That same viewpoint is expressed in a small study published in May 2014 by three researchers with an initiative called the Good Project, which is housed within the graduate school of education at Harvard. The authors conducted interviews with forty members of Harvard's undergraduate class of 2013 during their final, senior year. And they concluded that a Harvard education had "a funnel effect."

"Though students enter college with a diverse set of interests, by senior year, most of them seem to focus on a narrow set of jobs," the authors wrote. "The culture at Harvard seems to be dominated by the pursuit of high earning, prestigious jobs, especially in the consulting industries." In students' minds, only some jobs "live up to the degree."

The authors noted that one of the seniors had done some teaching and had loved it, but she eschewed the classroom for "a job at an education-consulting firm," because it felt "more aligned with the kind of work that many of her peers choose to do." Another senior was a fanatic for rare books and rare objects and wrote a thesis on World War II treasures. She then went to work for a medical software company.

This isn't a pattern peculiar to Harvard. Anushka Shenoy, who graduated from Columbia in 2008, told me: "It didn't occur to me to study anything other than economics and go into a banking or consulting career." That's what the people around her at Columbia aspired to and worked toward. That was the vogue. "I didn't know anything about management consulting except that it was really hard to get into," she said. "And I thought, 'Okay! I'll try that!' "

She landed an enviable job at Bain & Company, and moved to San Francisco to work for that management consulting firm there. But after a few years, she realized that she had no passion for what she was doing and that, in retrospect, she'd never really paused at Columbia to take adequate survey of what her heartfelt interests were. Everything there moved too fast for that to happen. It was as if there was no space to wander, no license for it. Once she took a breath and thought more deeply about it all, she changed tacks—and how. Now twenty-nine, she's in medical school in Portland at Oregon Health & Science University. And she's much happier.

What Shenoy felt at Columbia and what the authors of the funnel-effect paper noticed at Harvard are part of what the writer Junot Díaz refers to as "the commodification of the university as a trade guild, a very expensive trade guild." I contacted Díaz, who won the Pulitzer Prize in 2008 for his novel, *The Brief Wondrous Life of Oscar Wao*, and received a MacArthur Foundation "genius grant" four years later, primarily because he'd gone to a state school, Rutgers, and has spoken of how well it served him and how much he loved it. But he has an additional vantage point on higher education and on today's admissions mania, because he's on the faculty of one of the most selective institutions in the country, MIT. He's been teaching creative writing there for twelve years.

"The idea that a university directly feeds into a job: This is sacred law now," said Díaz, forty-seven. "When I went to school, yeah, the university was going to help get you a job, but there was an entire experience around the university that was about your life and being educated in ways that weren't about markets. Nowadays, most of my students have a very, very painful or excruciating or overbearing market prerogative on them. The idea that you would go to a university for an education at the level of your soul is considered absurd, and to me that's heartbreaking."

He was speaking of higher education in general—he has taught at Syracuse University and New York University, too—and his observations dovetailed precisely with the results of an annual survey of incoming freshmen at hundreds of colleges nationwide. Administered by the Higher Education Research Institute at UCLA, it shows a striking change in the stated priorities of students over the last half century. For example, in the mid-1960s, only 42 percent of freshmen said that being able to "make more money" was a "very important" goal in their decision to go to college. That number rose to just over 73 percent in the survey results published in March 2014. Between the mid-1970s and 2014, the percentage who said that getting a better job was a "very important" motivation to attend college rose from 67.8 percent to 86.3 percent. Over that same stretch of time, the percentage of students who attached considerable importance to developing a meaningful life philosophy fell sharply.

But the particular culture that Díaz can best vouch for, the one in his mind when he mentions "most of my students," is MIT's. "I've literally had a front-row seat on this crap," he said. "It's just crazy."

An immigrant from the Dominican Republic, Díaz grew up among poor and working-class people who struggled and generally didn't have college educations. "I was a kid stranded in a neighborhood next to the largest active landfill in New Jersey," he said. "Rutgers gave me a passport to the world." It introduced itself to him as the name and logo on a sweatshirt worn by a friend's sister, who went there, and it became a symbol of hope for Díaz, a promise of something larger and better, a focus of his aspirations. "For us working-class kids, it seemed a gold mine," he said.

And it rejected him, at least the first time he applied. In high school he hadn't gotten the grades he'd needed to, and so he spent a year at Kean College (now Kean University) in Union, New Jersey, proving to himself and to Rutgers that he could do better. He transferred to Rutgers for his sophomore year, majored in English and lived in a residence hall favored by students interested in writing. He also worked: pumping gas, washing dishes. And, more than any of that, he opened his eyes to a newly kaleidoscopic community. Communities, really.

"I had never met feminists," he said. "I had never met activists. I'd never met anyone who was openly gay and would organize around that identity. All of this stuff, I'd never had access to. My pre-Rutgers life was like black-and-white television. It was like the first few minutes of *The Wizard of Oz* before the color kicks in."

Is MIT that kind of rainbow? Are any of the elite schools?

Not in Díaz's experience.

"If you look at the family backgrounds of my kids, you're not getting a very diverse student body," he said. "They can claim it's diverse. But you're not getting the kind of diversity that I had at Rutgers, where you had kids who were Ivy League–qualified but their parents didn't want to spend that money, and kids like me, immigrants busting their humps. We have in so many ways narrowed it down."

Echoing Poch, he said that what he sees when he looks at many of the students at MIT and at the other revered university in Cambridge, Massachusetts, are what he called "fragile thoroughbreds." They've been trained to peak performance on tests and in term papers, but not to the unpredictability and tumult of adulthood. Many of them come to MIT for specific preparation for a career they've already decided on. They're after a credential they've been told they need. They're executing a plan they brought with them. And the university helps them with that, indulging who they are rather than challenging it, because elite colleges—maybe all colleges—are businesses in the end.

"Customers come in and they want their pickles on their burger," Díaz said. "They don't come in for you to upend everything."

Maybe I got lucky, because my Princeton students didn't seem as intellectually incurious as Deresiewicz found most of the kids at Yale. One was learning Farsi and plotting an ambitious, months-long summer backpacking trip along what used to be the Silk Road, and she wasn't doing this with a big pile of money from her parents, who didn't have it, or to impress the admissions committee, which she'd already done, or with a career in mind, because she hadn't yet decided on one. She was just doing it.

Another, though bound for the world of management consulting and scarily fluent in the ways of Princeton's status-ratifying eating clubs, had read an array of fiction and nonfiction that only someone who's following his heart and brain rather than any syllabus reads: cult mysteries, bestselling thrillers, books about food, Jonathan Franzen, David Foster Wallace. And another wrote a final paper of such detail, depth and polish that I almost got choked up as I graded it, or rather showered it with compliments. She'd already sewn up an A in the class and was pretty much on track for employment following her imminent graduation, but she had grown fascinated by the topic, was determined to become an expert on it, and seemed interested in doing excellent work for excellent work's sake.

The sixteen kids in my class didn't seem all that fragile, either, though they were less accustomed to criticism than I expected students to be. Isn't digesting negative feedback and turning it into positive fuel the very metabolism of education? Isn't school supposed to humble you?

That's not how it played out at Princeton, which seemed more expressly designed to pump up and prop up its students. I hadn't yet interviewed Díaz, and didn't do so until the semester was long over, but the word *customer* frequently entered my own thoughts while I was teaching there. From the moment I arrived on campus to the moment I left, I got the message that the students were my clients, and I was told more often about what I owed them, in terms of unambiguous explanations, in terms of support, than about what they owed me, their professor.

While I was instructed not to be lavish with A's, I was also informed that virtually nobody got C's. If a student seemed to be descending to a C-plus or even a B-minus, I should check in. I should intervene. Something might be wrong, and it was incumbent on me to look into what that was, whether it could be fixed, and if there was an aspect of the course or of my instruction that wasn't quite working. I caught one student cheating, and when I raised the matter with other faculty, looking for advice, I was asked whether I'd spelled out the rules of the class and the specifics of the assignment with sufficient clarity. And I was encouraged to give the student a do-over.

I liked most of the kids in my class immensely. They were warm and polite. Several had charm to burn. But more than a few of them operated with a literalism that I found dispiriting. They wanted to know *exactly* the minimum number of interviews necessary for a given assignment. They wanted to know *exactly*, point by point and step by step, what they could do to lift the B-plus they'd just received for one paper to an A-minus for the next. They seemed to be calibrating their efforts and meting out their exertions with pinpoint precision, focused on discrete markers instead of anything larger. I kept wishing for less cunning and more heart.

In many ways I was in awe of Princeton. It's a magnificent haven, gorgeous to look at, brimming with talent, rich with world-renowned faculty. But I was sometimes unsettled by many students' tone deafness to the good fortune embedded in all of that, to the stereotype of Ivy League kids as the cosseted denizens of an aloof caste.

I learned that one of the eating clubs hosted an especially raucous, beer-soaked party known as "State Night," the idea being that on this sloppy occasion, everyone would party as if at a state school. They were encouraged to wear T-shirts or sweatshirts with the names of such institutions—I'm sure that Díaz's alma mater, Rutgers, made the occasional cameo—though some kids would come in garb from other, supposedly lesser rivals in the Ivy League, which, they would reportedly joke, might as well be public universities. Another eating club had "Titanic Night," when partygoers were assigned to different classes of the ship—steerage, et cetera—and told to dress as they imagined those status-sorted seafarers would.

But I was most struck by something I noticed in my own seminar, which was devoted to food writing. Before it began, more than forty-five students signed up for the sixteen slots. In situations like that, the university has them write letters of application to introduce themselves and describe their interest in the course; the professor then makes the cut. I read the letters, with a smile and with welling excitement. These kids were so mature, articulate, enthusiastic.

Then, deep into the semester, I realized that more than half of my sixteen students hadn't written anything *for* the class that showed the verve and care of their letters. I mentioned this to several full-time professors at Princeton. All nodded, unsurprised. They explained that what many Princeton students excelled at, as demonstrated by the fact that they were there, at a school with an acceptance rate that's now about 7 percent, was *getting into* things, and that the message these kids had received from the college admissions mania was that gaining access, besting the competition, was the principal goal and primary accomplishment. You rallied your best self, or struck your comeliest pose, for that. You didn't worry as much about what came after.

Those same full-time professors theorized that Wall Street was such a common destination for Princeton's graduating seniors precisely because the process of getting the most desirable jobs there was a competition among peers that was familiar from the college admissions sweepstakes. It gave their college years a rhythm, shape and purpose that they recognized, pointing them toward another culling, and promising, if all went well, the satisfaction of having acquired something that many classmates didn't.

One Princeton student, not in my seminar, and not willing to be identified, told me that his lack of interest in any future as a financier left him feeling lost, because he'd never stopped, on his path to Princeton, to figure out what he expected to get out of the university. He just knew that he was supposed to fight for admission to it. After he arrived on campus, he said, he experienced a palpable letdown, a loss of velocity. "A lot of my friends have experienced similar things," he said. "In high school, getting to college was what everyone's doing. That's what everyone is focused on. And then once you get to college, it becomes ambiguous. I kind of felt like I put so much energy into getting in in the first place that once I got in, I didn't know what to do."

"What's that last line in *The Candidate*?" asked Bruce Poch, referring to the political classic, starring Robert Redford, about the triumph of process over substance, image over truth. At the very end of the movie, Redford's character wins his election but seems lost, and asks his equally victory-focused team what happens next. "The whole thing was getting it, getting it, whoring himself in ways that are just stunning, and then they find that they don't know what to do," Poch remembered. He said that there's an element of that in the kids who wind up at elite colleges.

I put this observation to Anthony Marx, the former Amherst president, who fell silent for about fifteen seconds. I couldn't tell if he was mulling whether he agreed with it or just trying to choose his words with diplomatic care. Finally he spoke: "It's interesting to think about how this is shaping America. If our elite is to some extent being formed by this powerful experience of frenzied admissions, does it suggest that we're creating a culture in which the sale is more important than the product?"

That's just one of the frenzy's many troubling implications. The kids who strap themselves into it get the signal, or convince themselves, that they must assemble their high school records in a particular way—this many AP courses, that many extracurricular activities, a memorable summer job, an area of study to which they show profound attachment—whether it tracks with their real interests or not, whether it's who they are or some contrived mannequin. A contrived mannequin is okay.

"We've spent so much time talking about packaging that it suggests that the real trick of the collegiate endeavor *is* to be packaged," said Andre Phillips, the senior associate director of recruitment and outreach at the main campus of the University of Wisconsin. There's too little emphasis on authenticity, which has too unreliable a reward.

And there's so much talk of the trickery that applicants employ, of the connections they exploit and of favoritism and gullibility in admissions offices that too many kids feel licensed, even compelled, to do whatever it takes: hired guns, massaged credentials, outright lies. "The message a kid hears is: I can't do it on my own, I'm not worth enough," said Lloyd Thacker, the executive director of the Education Conservancy, a nonprofit devoted to changing and restoring calm to the admissions process.

"There's real evidence of the deleterious effect—the cumulative impact—of this process," he said, alluding to scattered cheating scandals around the country, both among kids taking the SATs to get into college and kids already there. He recalled that a few years ago, "I'm giving a talk at a school in Bellevue, Washington: Bill Gates territory. I talk about bad behavior in gaming the system, and the audience is really quiet. Then the counselor tells me that two weeks earlier, kids were caught breaking into the principal's office to change their AP scores. And a mother then asked a counselor at the school,

'You're not going to change the recommendation you wrote for Johnny because of this, are you?' "

From him and others I kept hearing the same apprehension: If you hold up certain metrics as the very determinants of children's futures, if you invest those metrics with too much importance and allow too blinding a focus on them, don't you essentially instruct kids to define and see themselves in terms of those very measurements? Isn't it unconstructively clinical, and doesn't it turn them inward on themselves rather than outward toward the world?

"The kids in my grade—the 'smart' ones—grade their success purely on a points system," Jess Silverman, who was then a seventeen-year-old senior at a New Jersey high school, marveled to me in late 2014. "They measure everything down to the decimal, charting their happiness based on a test curve. It's given me an ideal to strive against. It scares me to become so dependent on a number, because that's not what I am." But, she added, it's what the culture around her seems to want her to be.

I worry just as much about the pecking order that the admissions process creates, or at least affirms. That order is so entrenched and pervasive that even Deresiewicz, who is clearly and rightly disapproving of it, falls prey to its vocabulary in a passage that I quoted above, referring to "prestigious institutions like Harvard or Stanford or Williams as well as the larger universe of *second-tier* selective schools." The italics are mine, used to point out that even within the stratum of selectivity, there are yet more tiers, yet finer gradations. From these microcategories kids develop lists of "reach schools" and "safety schools," of fantasies and fallbacks. They stretch hopefully for some. They settle dejectedly for others.

And they are acutely aware of where they end up. This

came through in a letter published in response to a column in the *Times* in 2012 by Andrew Delbanco, a professor of American studies at Columbia University and the author of the book *College: What It Was, Is, and Should Be*. Delbanco had written that there was "a germ of truth" to the charge that elite colleges bred self-satisfaction, and he expressed the wish that they "encouraged more humility and less hubris."

"A germ?" asked the author of the letter. "Has he ever been to a sports event where one team is an Ivy League school and its entire student section engages in the chant 'Safety school! Saaaaa-fety school!' at the opponents?"

Caste consciousness also popped up in a conversation I had with Harry Segal, a senior lecturer in psychology at Cornell. Segal was reflecting on the way that people in general and today's kids in particular can lose sight of how fortunate they really are, always glancing around them and spotting someone with a seemingly better lot. He was also remarking on the unnecessary distinctions made in contemporary America. And he told me that because he's fascinated by those habits and curious about them, he routinely puts a particular question to the two-hundred-odd students in his largest lecture class. He asks how many of them feel bad that they didn't get into Harvard or Yale.

"Lots of hands go up," he told me. "Probably sixty percent of the class. And the ones that don't? I'm not convinced that they don't want to go up."

This is a lecture with seniors, juniors, sophomores. They're years past the college admissions process. They're *in* the Ivy League. And they're still thinking of what might have been, and still mulling their exact place in the nonsensical college hierarchy that our society has constructed.

NINE

HUMBLED, HUNGRY AND FLOURISHING

"Whenever I do graduation speeches, I always tell students: Yes, yes, often the name of your university can open doors for you. But in the end, it is so up to you. I know that's a cliché. But I think that sometimes the very, very fortunate people who've gone to the Ivy League or Cambridge or Oxford are a little entitled, and I don't think entitlement is good for a career."

—*Christiane Amanpour, CNN anchor and a 1983 graduate of the University of Rhode Island*

Justin de Benedictis-Kessner won't lie. He did not arrive at the College of William and Mary in the fall of 2007 thinking, "This is really for the best." He did not arrive with the belief that everything happens for a reason or with any other, similarly sunny platitude in mind.

He arrived skeptically, even bitterly, still aware, he said, that "this is my safety school," and still smarting over his inability to go elsewhere. Although William and Mary is routinely ranked among the top 50 national universities by *U.S.*

News, it wasn't what prep school graduates like him aspired to; only two students from his class at Exeter would be joining him there, many fewer than were heading to any given Ivy League school. "I arrived on campus a naive and preemptively arrogant freshman, ready to excel in classes and to get the whole college thing done with," he said. And he feels embarrassed about that now.

Raised in Berkeley, California, he went to Exeter because his father had gone there many years before and because he was given a scholarship that covered all of his expenses, which his parents weren't in a position to afford. When junior year dawned, the talk about college spiked.

"They've got the process down to a science there," he said, explaining that there were perhaps eight full-time college counselors and that each student was assigned to a specific one, who would provide advice about "how to structure your classes, what classes you might want to take, whether you should focus on grades or leadership activities." And as he and his classmates began to obsess about admissions, people outside the school assured him that he'd fare brilliantly. "They'd say, 'Oh, you go to Exeter? You'll get into Harvard, Yale or Princeton, because it's a feeder school,'" Justin recalled. "And my dad echoed that."

He didn't apply to those three schools, but he did apply to Dartmouth, Middlebury, Tufts, Swarthmore. "I was really, really into Swarthmore," he said. "And then, as a backup, I applied to Kenyon, William and Mary and some California state schools." After he got his acceptances and rejections, he was left to choose among UCLA, UCSD, UC Davis, Tufts, George Washington University, Kenyon and William and Mary. Of those schools Tufts excited him the most by far. It was in the

Northeast, where the lion's share of his friends would be attending college, and it was somewhere Exeter kids routinely went. But neither it nor GWU nor Kenyon was offering him as much financial aid as William and Mary was, and, he said, "My parents were adamant that I not take on a lot of debt for college.

"I took the train down to Tufts, because I was dead set on it," he recalled. "I thought I wanted to study developmental psychology and do this particular program there. I visited the financial aid office. They laid out the books: Here's your family's situation, here's why we can't give you more money. I'm pretty sure I was in a chair crying. I was as close to begging as you can get without being on the floor."

So William and Mary it was. And while regret trailed him there, he was smart and practical enough to try to convert it into a kind of gameness. "That sense of disappointment motivated me," he said, and he set about making William and Mary its own adventure—not the one he'd wanted, not the one he'd planned, but a worthwhile side trip, a diversion that surely had virtues all its own.

Because William and Mary was a relatively small school and he didn't feel intimidated by it, he signed up for stuff. He joined groups—the rowing team, for example. He'd been, in his own estimation, "a mediocre rower" at Exeter, so he hadn't resolved to continue the sport in college. But William and Mary's team was modest and approachable.

"I had the chance to be in some of the varsity boats as a freshman and to excel in a sport that I loved," he said. "That was awesome, and it couldn't have happened at some of those other schools. I ended up being the president of the rowing team by the time I left. I even raised a bunch of money for the school, helped to build the boathouse."

On William and Mary's stage, he became a star, a leader. "I ran for the student honor council," he said, and he was elected, so he spent several years adjudicating ethics violations like plagiarism cases. It fascinated him. "I learned a lot about how people's minds work," he said.

And in his government and psychology classes—he was a double major—he found that he stood out and that professors noticed and appreciated him, extending opportunities his way. During his freshman year, a psychology professor invited him to help with a research project over the summer, and he eagerly agreed to. Another professor later put him on another research project, actually hired him for it, paid him and then wrote him a glowing recommendation for grad school.

"He's the reason I'm here," Justin said, referring to MIT, where he's pursuing a doctorate in political science and working as a research coordinator in the political experiments lab. His dissertation examines how public services and government accountability at the local level influence and interact with people's political opinions, and he said that it could logically lead to a job in academia or in the private sector, doing data analysis. He hasn't decided which he wants.

But he's sure that he's on the right page. And he's grateful for his years at William and Mary, where he had not only a great time but also a meaningful one that pointed him as sharply as he could be pointed in an academic and professional direction that feels exactly right. Justin doesn't wonder what Swarthmore might have meant to him or what Tufts might have done for him. He doesn't feel so much as a twinge of regret.

"There was a lot more that I could do in a new environment than I could have done if I'd gone to a college with a huge bunch of people I'd been to high school with," he explained. William and Mary, he said, was nothing less than "a chance to reinvent myself."

It's impossible, and therefore foolish, to say definitively that some students are better served by going to colleges that aren't their first or third or fifth choices; that aren't quite as prestigious as the ones that they had hoped for or actually decided to pass up; or that aren't on anyone's list of elite standouts. And the students themselves are perhaps the worst judges of the situation. After all, it's a human tendency, and a merciful one at that, to develop and hold tight to a conviction that the assigned or chosen course turned out to be the optimal one, especially if the alternatives are no longer in play. Regret is corrosive; many people surrender it as quickly as possible. And if they can't be with the one they thought they would love, well, they love the one they're with.

But some of these students, like Justin, really do develop an assurance that might have been suffocated on a campus of kids with a more uniform academic fluency and more obvious self-possession. They sidestep the peril, explored by Malcolm Gladwell in a passage of his book *David and Goliath*, that threw one Brown University student he profiled off her longtime desire to be a scientist. "She was a Little Fish in one of the deepest and most competitive ponds in the country," Gladwell wrote, "and the experience of comparing herself to all the other brilliant fish shattered her confidence. It made her feel stupid, even though she isn't stupid at all." In a less daunting body of water, she might have escaped the currents of self-doubt.

And some students at smaller, more obscure colleges discover that what these schools lack in a bounty of resources they often make up for in the availability of the resources that do exist. This was the experience that Todd Martinez had at Calvin College, in Grand Rapids, Michigan.

I briefly mentioned Martinez, forty-eight, a Stanford chemistry professor and (like Díaz) a MacArthur Foundation "genius grant" winner, earlier in the book, in connection with his belief that there's not likely to be all that much difference between the prowess of students at a school with a 5 percent acceptance rate, like Stanford's, and students at a school with a 20 percent acceptance rate. He went to Calvin College largely because it's run by the Christian Reformed Church, for which his father was a missionary. It has about four thousand students and an acceptance rate now of just under 70 percent. He then did his graduate work at UCLA and taught at the University of Illinois as well as at Stanford, so he has seen the world of higher education through disparate lenses.

And he told me that at many small schools like Calvin, "you have much more access much earlier to both equipment and to professors." He gave the example of a nuclear magnetic resonance, or NMR, machine. "Most schools that have a chemistry program will have an NMR machine. But at UCLA, where I was a grad student, the undergraduates are not going to touch it, whereas we at Calvin were able to take apart the NMR machine if we wanted." It wasn't the fastest, most powerful, most sophisticated kind of NMR machine, he said. But it was theirs. They could have at it. Similarly, he said, professors were approachable in a way that they sometimes aren't at larger schools.

The novelist John Green, who wrote the bestselling phenomenon *The Fault in Our Stars*, certainly found that to be true when he was a student in the late 1990s at Kenyon, in Gambier, Ohio. It has about 1,700 students, and Green told me that he got to know many professors there extremely well. An exchange with one of them stays with him always. It had no small bearing on his ability to forge a career as a writer after he graduated, he said.

At Kenyon, Green took an introductory fiction-writing class, after which he applied to take another, more advanced one. It was open to only twelve students. A total of sixteen, including him, wanted in, and he was one of the four turned away. "I was decimated," he said. "I thought, 'If you can't be one of the best twelve writers in your class at your tiny Midwestern college, how are you ever going to have a career?' "

Fred Kluge, the professor who taught the class that Green had completed but not the follow-up, took note of his reaction. "Without me even saying anything to him, he invited me to his house," Green recalled. "He sat me down. He poured himself a glass of Scotch. He poured me a glass of seltzer water. And he told me I was a good writer, 'a solid B-plus writer,' as he put it, and then he told me that the stories I told before class and on breaks were really, really good, and if I could figure out a way to write the way I told those stories, I could have a life in writing." Green's problem, Kluge suggested, was that he was trying too hard to be lofty and literary; he wasn't writing from emotion, in a true voice.

The advice was precise, and it was pivotal.

"I needed someone to tell me that I had potential, but I also needed someone to tell me why I didn't get into that class," Green said, adding that Kluge's intervention "was *way* above and beyond the call of duty." Green holds on to, and sometimes revisits, a particular photograph from his graduation ceremony at Kenyon, and the reason isn't the way he looks in it but the fact that Kluge can be seen in the background, watching over him and smiling.

Green, who is now thirty-eight, said that before Kenyon, he wasn't an especially good student, and had perhaps a 2.9 GPA at the prestigious boarding school he attended in Birmingham, Alabama. His SAT scores were "reasonable," he said; he did better, oddly, in the math than in the verbal component. Many of his classmates applied to Ivy League schools. He didn't dare. As he remembers it, his applications went to Emory University, Grinnell College, Kenyon, Macalester College and Guilford College, in Greensboro, North Carolina. He was put on the wait list at Emory, rejected at Macalester and got into the rest. Back then, he said, Kenyon took more than 50 percent of its applicants. These days it takes between 35 and 40 percent.

"It isn't any better or worse a college," he laughed. "It's mostly the same teachers as when I went."

And he thought it was terrific. He loved it. He did a double major in English and religion, and he said that most of his classes had between eight and thirty students. One had four. It was called "Reading *Ulysses*," he said, and it was devoted entirely to James Joyce's masterpiece. One of the other three students was Ransom Riggs, who went on to write the bestseller *Miss Peregrine's Home for Peculiar Children*.

"Looking back on it, I got such tremendous value out of the classes," Green said, and he recalled many of them with a detail that made clear just how much they'd meant to him. He talked about a class on Islamic history. He also talked about a class on Jesus in which he learned that "the idea that there were sons of gods wasn't in any way uncommon in the first century," he said. "That wasn't the radical idea. The radical idea was that Jesus of Nazareth was *the* son of God. And that just blew my mind."

He relished his excursions into nineteenth-century British romantic literature. "There's just so much stuff in those classes that I use in my books," he said. "I'm always cheating and stealing from them. I wish that I could go to college again, so that I could have four more years to steal and cheat from.

"There's something magical about that time," he continued, and it's not primarily that you're living among all your friends or going to so many parties. It's not the beauty of a campus or the first taste of something verging on adult independence. It's the permission to sit still, to *think*. It's the lull, the space and the freedom for that. "Spending six hours on a Sunday reading *Jane Eyre* and *Jane Eyre* criticism is by far the best use of your time," he said. He wishes he'd done more of that.

And while he could have done it at any number of schools, he said that he's not sure that many of them would have served him nearly as well as Kenyon did. And that's not because Kenyon is famous as a cradle for writers, the school that gave birth to the *Kenyon Review*, which is still published in Gambier. It's because of Kenyon's personal touch, its intimacy. One of his religion professors, Don Rogan, would invite him over for evenings when various professors recited poetry. And he became a coach and an audience for Green when Green found his way back to fiction writing.

Green said that after the rejection from the advanced class, "I stopped for about a year and felt totally useless, but started up again my senior year and wrote a story that—while still very bad—was a huge leap forward for me. It was about a recently ordained Lutheran minister traveling home to perform a wedding who ends up also overseeing a funeral, and it was longer than anything I'd ever written and I remember it as *brilliant*, but then of course I dredged up a copy and it turns out to be pretty awful. These things should live in memory, where they can glister.

"Anyway," Green continued, "Don treated the story with total respect and encouraged me to finish it, and I still remember his comments about it after I gave it to him upon my graduation. He said, 'This is a very promising story. The funeral went on too long, but then, funerals generally do.'"

Reflecting on Rogan, reflecting on Kluge, Green said, "I do think that those relationships were more available to me than if I'd gone to Harvard.

"My closest friend in high school went to Princeton," he said. "A couple of months after he started, he sent me an email: 'There are a lot of stupid people here.' He got 1600 on the SATs and was searingly brilliant. He was really offended that all of these people didn't live up to his expectations." Green wasn't making a dig at Princeton. He was making the point that the experience a person has at any school depends on hopes, prejudices, unforeseeable interactions, attitude. It's subjective.

"I believe that you can get a good education at most American universities," Green said. "You can also get a not-good education anywhere. You can scrape by." That's what he sees when he looks at the people and the world around him.

"I might be wrong about this," he said, "but I don't think it matters that much where you go."

I'm inclined to agree, but then I recognize just how right Kenyon was for him and William and Mary for Justin. I consider how many kids seem to find, at schools well outside the Ivy League, a reassurance, an impetus or a spark that they might not have found at schools inside of it. Those schools do seem to matter. They do seem to make a difference. Just as Harvard is the crucial launch for one person, the University of Maryland or the University of Rochester can be essential for another.

I cite Maryland for a reason. I interviewed one young lawyer who went there, but only after rejections from Columbia and UPenn that were such a "personal blow to my identity," he said, that he posted them on the wall above his bed in his boarding school dormitory room, "to remind myself to do better." At Maryland he was a standout in the criminal justice department, because he resolved to be and because he could be. As a result, he got into the highly regarded law school at New York University. Upon his graduation from it last year, he nabbed a coveted associate's position with a major Manhattan firm.

And I cite Rochester because that's Joseph Ross's alma mater.

Ross, now forty-one, attended high school in the suburbs of Buffalo, and he said that his best friends in his graduating class headed alternately to Harvard, Yale, Amherst, UPenn and Smith. "I was the dumb one among them," he said. "I applied to UPenn and Cornell. Didn't get into either."

So he went to Rochester, where he didn't feel at all like the dumb one. "My high school had been very competitive," he said, "and I did much better in college." He developed an assertiveness, academically speaking, that he hadn't possessed before, and he stretched further than he might otherwise have, attempting and completing not only two majors, in psychology and neuroscience, but also a minor in creative writing.

When he turned his gaze toward becoming a physician, he didn't bother with the top-ranked medical schools. After all, Rochester had wholly satisfied him, and it didn't sit at the summit of rankings. As best he can recall, he applied to just two places, SUNY Buffalo and SUNY Syracuse, both of which made sense in terms of cost. He ended up at SUNY Buffalo, and eventually made his way to where he is now: on the faculty of the Yale University School of Medicine.

He teaches internal medicine there and also writes frequently and extensively for various blogs and publications, a passion that has been helped enormously by classes he took at Rochester. At an unusually young age, he's an associate editor for *JAMA Internal Medicine*. "I can't imagine a better job," he told me. As for the way he got there, he said, "I think that what served me well, and this is part of what I look for when I'm selecting research fellows, was focusing on what I was passionate about rather than focusing on getting into School X." Perhaps partly because of Rochester, Ross concentrated on deeds, not labels.

And perhaps partly because of Northwestern Oklahoma State University, Travis F. Jackson, who is also forty-one, concentrated on working harder than many of the people around him.

Jackson is a Los Angeles–based lawyer with a nationwide firm that's a major player in the health-care industry. His career has gone about as well as he could have imagined, and it has taken him far from the Oklahoma farmland where he grew up. "My town had a population of about one thousand," he told me, "though I think there may have been some cattle in that count."

He went to college at Northwestern Oklahoma State because it was nearby and affordable. He graduated summa cum laude. He went to law school at the University of Notre Dame because he got a scholarship that paid for enough of his expenses to keep his student loan debt manageable. He graduated summa cum laude there, too.

At Notre Dame he was around many alumni of elite colleges, and he's been around many more of them since. And he said that because his own undergraduate alma mater doesn't have any particular glimmer, "I was intimidated to compete with these people. But that made me not take things for granted.

"With all due respect to some of my friends who have gone to Ivy League schools," he said, "I think they have a tendency to do that." They're not as intent on proving themselves, because in their own minds, their diploma has already made their case for them. And consciously or unconsciously, they count on it to be a safety net. "If I didn't put the effort in," Jackson said, "I didn't have anything to fall back on."

Indeed, students at less lavishly celebrated colleges are sometimes motivated by their institutions' lack of luster. They don't assume that the names of their schools will propel them into the job market and through life, so they take greater care to acquit themselves in a way that might. Nor do they assume that the college atmosphere they inhabit is so rich with positive influences that they'll simply prosper by osmosis. They're prodded to be scrappier, and that can turn into its own advantage.

"You're going to be forced to be more entrepreneurial at a small school," said Martinez, reflecting on his experience at Calvin. He developed an interest in theoretical chemistry early on there, and the college couldn't offer him every last bit of instruction he craved. But it had a library and affiliations and concerned, generous faculty. He discovered that he could improvise and patch together what he needed. Looking back, he sees enormous merit in having been compelled to take that kind of initiative.

"It's not necessary to get into a highly selective school in order to be successful," he said. "What's necessary is to understand what you want to do and how to do it well, and to be a self-starter."

As I listened to Jackson, Ross and others whom I interviewed, I searched for any and all commonalities, themes, ways of thinking and strategies for behaving that departed from a lockstep striving for the school with the "best" name. And I spotted, in the stories of many of the people happiest with the way things had turned out for them, an openness to serendipity that sometimes gets edited out of the equation when you're blindly accepting the marks that your parents and your peers have all agreed on and you're dutifully hitting them, one after the other. I noticed a nimbleness in adapting to change, a willingness to shoot off in a new direction and an attention to the particular virtues of the landscape right around them rather than an obsession with the promised glories of the imagined terrain around the bend.

I saw qualities that two longtime educators told me were in insufficient supply among students these days. One of these educators was Barry Schwartz, a renowned psychologist who has been teaching at Swarthmore for about four decades—and who, interestingly, has come to believe that some sort of lottery system should replace the way that college admissions is now done. I asked him if the students who'd survived the current admissions frenzy and managed to get into Swarthmore were noticeably different from the ones he taught in the past, and he said yes: "I think that these kids want to be given a clear and unambiguous path to success. They want a recipe. And that's the wrong thing to be wanting. The cutting edge of intellectual life isn't about recipes. Progress isn't made by recipe. Recipes create cooks. They don't produce *chefs*. And if we don't manage to produce chefs at Swarthmore, where are we going to produce chefs?"

Hiram Chodosh, the Claremont McKenna president, made a strikingly similar observation with different, though equally vivid, language. He remarked on, and rued, a "propensity to be very linear" in too many of today's overachievers. He conceded that this wasn't a wholly new phenomenon, remembering his time at Yale Law School and the way many of his peers there drew up and executed their plans to become law professors down the line. Their thinking, he said, went like this: "I need to get a great federal court clerkship, ideally with the Supreme Court. To get that, I need to have a recommendation from a prominent Yale law professor. To get *that*, I need to TA for him my third year. To do *that*, I need to work for the law review under their supervision my second year."

As Chodosh flashed back on that, he shook his head. "You don't become a great academic because you're trying to become a great academic," he said. "You become a great academic when you look out the window and you have something to say about what's wrong with this picture that's unique."

Not enough of the students arriving at elite schools are looking out the window. Instead, he said, "There's this job they want, and they've benchmarked someone's career, and they've created a straight-line path. Frankly, I don't know people who've been successful who've worked in a straight line. Maybe they exist, but I don't know them."

I know some, but their straight lines usually didn't begin all the way back in kindergarten or for that matter middle or high school, and their mile markers weren't SAT scores and enrollment at a college with an acceptance rate below 15 percent. Their focus was the actual work they intended to do: preparing themselves for it, picking up the skills they needed, snatching small chances to show what they were capable of and then using those to grab hold of even bigger chances. That's how success generally happens.

It's how it happened for Christiane Amanpour, the CNN correspondent who occupies an altitude in the news business so lofty that when the writer Sheila Weller chose three TV journalists to profile in her 2014 book, *The News Sorority*, she grouped Amanpour with Katie Couric and Diane Sawyer. I'd met Amanpour a few times and knew her a bit before I thought to inquire about where she'd gone to school. I can be as pitiful a slave to stereotypes as anyone else, and the erudition that she exhibits on air, coupled with her plummy English accent, led me to expect Oxford or Cambridge. The University of Rhode Island surprised me.

Amanpour grew up in privileged circumstances in Iran and indeed attended boarding school in England. "My original desire to be a doctor didn't pan out," she told me. "I didn't get the right grades. I was a bit lost and roaming in the academic wilderness. And I didn't go to school again after high school for a number of years."

The revolution in Iran sharpened her interest in international affairs and gave her the idea of becoming a journalist, but it also wiped out her parents' funds and put many colleges out of financial reach. She knew she wanted to study in America—it was where so many friends had fled—and was steered to the University of Rhode Island because it didn't cost as much as many private colleges and because a family friend knew the school's president. The reasons were that mundane and the process that quick and blunt. Like Dick Parsons, Condoleezza Rice, Howard Schultz and so many others, she pivoted to college in a manner that bore positively no relation to what so many kids and parents today put themselves through.

Partly because Amanpour didn't start college until she was twenty-one and partly because money was a concern, she did a swift sprint toward her diploma, beginning school in January 1980 and finishing, after six semesters, in December 1982. She worked during that time, at a local television station in Providence, about a forty-minute drive from the school's location in Kingston, Rhode Island. And, she said, "I did not live on campus. I lived with friends in Providence, who, actually, hilariously, were at Brown, so I got the best of both worlds." (For one period, one of those housemates was a Brown student by the name of John F. Kennedy Jr.)

She said that the education she got in her journalism classes was helpful, but her time off-campus was at least as important, and what mattered most of all was that she had figured out what she wanted—a journalism career—and she summoned a drive to match that direction. Perhaps it had to do with the upset of the Iranian Revolution and with being so far from home. "My life experience made me much more worldly than most of the freshmen, sophomores and juniors I encountered," she said, adding that her subsequent success "was a combination of the education I got and a deep, deep commitment and understanding that I had to work hard in the world. It was my own personal motivation. I climbed the ladder very systematically and dogmatically—internships, ground level at CNN, up the ladder. At no point did the name of my college make any difference in my career."

My friend Scott Pask could—and would—say the same about the name of his college, and with him, as with Amanpour, I didn't know for the longest time which college that was. I was aware that he'd received a master's in fine art at Yale University and that he'd done so when he was around thirty, and not right after his undergraduate education. But where that undergraduate education happened didn't come up in our conversations until several years into our friendship, which goes back about a decade now. Pask went to the University of Arizona.

He's a prodigiously respected Broadway set designer, with three Tony Awards to his credit, along with a slew of additional nominations. And he's exactly the kind of person Hiram Chodosh envisions when he sings the virtues of not working in a straight line.

Scott grew up in Yuma, Arizona, without much money, so cost was a major consideration when he decided on college. He chose the University of Arizona. He wanted to study architecture—"I loved drawing houses," he said, "and I loved looking at houses"—and according to his research, Arizona was a fine place to do that. He enrolled in its College of Architecture, which he said was "a very small and rigorous institution within the greater structure of the university." And he quickly came to know the other students and the professors in the college well. The conversation among them was constant, enlightened, intense.

He reveled in that. Even so, he didn't tamp down interests other than architecture when they flared. Didn't tame or limit his curiosity. Occasionally, Broadway musicals would come to town, and he found himself drawn to them. Watching the spectacle of *Cats*, he wondered who conceived and built the sets and how the whole process worked. "I thought it was some elaborate hobby that people had," he said. "I couldn't imagine that these were jobs: the design and the costumes and lighting. I thought, 'Wow, how do they have the time to do that?' " They were surely doing something else, something real, to pay the bills.

Although the theater program at Arizona was mostly limited to students who had chosen it as a major, Pask was determined to sign up for a set design class that he'd learned about. "It had all these prerequisites, none of which I had," he said. "But I took over some models I'd been building, and they let me in." After that he persuaded someone to let him help with a campus production. "It was like a light going on," he said.

He went ahead and got his architecture degree, but there were new thoughts bubbling in his head, new schemes being entertained. He set out for New York City without any detailed agenda. His first steady job was in a Paul Smith clothing store on Fifth Avenue. He usually manned the counter, though sometimes he folded shirts. "I was an ace folder," he said. "I was also really good at accessories." One year, he was even allowed to decorate the Christmas windows.

He assiduously cultivated friendships with the artists and performers he met, and he seized opportunities for obscure, offbeat collaborations with them. He volunteered to create huge murals for regular parties at a New York nightclub. He contributed the scenery for the modest shows of aspiring dancers. And when he started to get paying jobs in set design, he threw himself into them, not principally out of ambition but because he loved what he was doing. It wasn't until he was nearing thirty that he realized he had the makings of a lifelong career and enrolled at Yale, eager to expand his knowledge and raise his game.

He now runs his business—and it's a serious, successful business—out of a studio in Manhattan, and college students and recent graduates routinely ask to stop by. He says yes as often as he can. And he's frustrated by how many of them are looking not for general advice or inspiration but for step-by-step marching orders. They want it all laid out for them.

"There is no map!" he told me, his voice rising, his words emphatic. And if someone insisted on drawing one, with a destination of his brilliant career, they probably wouldn't put Arizona and a Paul Smith store on it.

TEN

FIRE OVER FORMULA

> *"If you are extremely smart but you're only partially engaged, you will be outperformed, and you should be, by people who are sufficiently smart but fully engaged."*
>
> *—Britt Harris, the former chief executive of the Bridgewater Associates hedge fund and a 1980 graduate of Texas A&M*

College has long been seen as a pivotal gateway—even *the* pivotal gateway—to professional success and overall fulfillment. Parents have long had strong feelings about where their kids should go. Kids have long felt enormous pride about where they were welcomed. And a hierarchy of colleges, with some eliciting more admiration than others, isn't anything new. So what explains the particular fever of the college admissions process over the last decade? Why has the temperature risen so high?

When I sat down with Anthony Marx, the former Amherst president, and asked him what he thought was driving the admissions mania, he first brought up something that was also very much on my mind: the heightened preoccupation in America with status and labels and the thoroughness with which higher education has been absorbed into that. "People don't advertise their names, their hometowns or their high schools," he said. "What do people put on the back windshields of their cars? Colleges. Surely that says something about the branding aspect of higher education. Yes, we hope for our kids to get great educations and meet friends who will change their lives. And they do. But there is also the halo effect."

That can't be all or even most of it, though: The stickers have been around for decades. A factor that hasn't is the cult of the expert. Twenty years ago, you never heard about personal trainers; people believed in the possibility of squatting, sweating and slimming on their own. But trainers are now ubiquitous in the upper-middle-class neighborhoods of major metropolitan areas, whose most pampered, indulgent denizens may also have nutritionists and therapists and personal shoppers, in a few cases for their children as well as themselves. Many people of means seem to believe that there's no problem, from a belly's sprawl to a child's sloth, that isn't best fixed by throwing money and a specialist at it. Anything can be delegated. Everything can be outsourced. This mindset is the fertile climate for all of those independent college consultants, whose proliferation has invariably turned up the heat of the admissions process, both for the families who use them and the families who are then forced to worry about a possible penalty for not doing so.

The cost of college aggravates the situation. Parents poised to spend as much as sixty thousand dollars a year on tuition, room and board want whatever's deemed to be the luxury model and push their kids to attain it, while the children of the much greater number of parents who can't swing a bill that enormous vie for scholarships whose acquisition and generosity hinge on board scores and GPAs higher than those of their peers.

Several college placement counselors told me that the oft-rued narcissism of the so-called selfie generation may sometimes come into play, with kids intent on going to a revered institution that validates their self-regard. It's where they belong. It's what they deserve. On top of that, social media has given kids ways to keep track of one another and to issue widely seen bulletins about their lives that didn't exist before, and what kids often want and choose to do with those bulletins, whether the news is related to college or something else, is impress. Check out the Facebook pages of high school seniors around the days that early-admission or general-admission notices are released, and you'll see a blizzard of updates communicating who got in where. The process, like so much of modern life, is public as never before.

But counselors said that mothers and fathers are the principal agents of the frenzy, which is the apotheosis of their efforts to micromanage every last moment of their children's lives and protect them from all injury, especially to their self-esteem. If they've been run-of-the-mill helicopter parents up until they start plotting college, they become Black Hawks at that point.

"Parents have put so much into kids, kids have put so much work in," said Tim Levin, the head of the tutoring service Bespoke Education. "You get to this process that you don't have a lot of control over—maybe for the first time in your life—and it's so quirky that even if you do everything right, you may not get what you want. And that drives parents crazy. They've chosen the right schools, the right tutors, the right museums. They've controlled *all* the variables. And suddenly they get to something that they can't control so well, and they can flip out a bit."

Especially because many of them sense that this passage in American life isn't like others. That's a key part of all of this, maybe *the* key part of all of this. The world is a more competitive place, in which the hegemony and influence of the United States are no longer the givens that they were in the past. The gap between the haves and the have-nots has widened, raising the stakes of which side of the divide you wind up on. "The difference between being in the top one or five or ten percent and not is bigger than ever before, so if people think going to a highly selective school will get you there, they're going to care more," said Alan Krueger, the Princeton economics professor.

Like Krueger, Catharine Bond Hill, the Vassar president, is an economist, and like him she sees "increasing income inequality" behind the college admissions mania. "The reward for getting into the top X percent of the income distribution now is a multiple of what it was thirty or forty years ago, and people perceive the access to that as coming through these elite schools."

There are fewer and fewer well-paying jobs for people without college degrees and, over recent years, there hasn't been any surfeit of great options for people *with* college degrees. The fear and awareness of this among young people were captured in a short graphic and story that ran in the summer of 2014 on Mic.com, a news and commentary website aimed at an audience of those under thirty years old. It showed that from 2000 to 2010, the number of people between eighteen and twenty-four who were enrolled in college climbed by 29 percent; during the same period, the number of college-educated janitors rose by 69 percent. The post framed this, melodramatically, as possibly "the saddest economic statistic ever."

For most of the last decade, the gross domestic product has grown at a snail's pace, and the optimism that once seemed inextricable from the American spirit has flatlined. In this century, there have been only three fleeting points when most Americans signaled satisfaction with the direction in which the country was headed, and all came at tense, fraught junctures when Americans had reasons to will themselves into a sort of defensive confidence: the month when George W. Bush took office, which followed the furious legal contest over vote counting in Florida and the intervention of the Supreme Court; the days following the 9/11 terrorist attacks; and the month when the United States invaded Iraq. All of those came in the first four years of the century.

Over the next ten years, which the Democratic political strategist Doug Sosnik has referred to as "a decade of anger and dissatisfaction," polling by the *Wall Street Journal* and NBC News continuously showed that the number of Americans who believed the country was on the wrong track exceeded those who thought that it was on the right track. "For the first time in our country's history," Sosnik wrote in a political memo that he shared with the newspaper and website *Politico* in late 2013, "there is more social mobility in Europe than in the United States."

Americans had been so humbled, and become so pessimistic, that when a Gallup poll asked them in mid-2014 which country was the world's "leading economic power," 52 percent said China, while only 31 percent gave the correct response: the United States. It was the sixth consecutive year in which more Americans had mistakenly answered China instead of our own country. And that downbeat, doubting frame of mind came through in a *Wall Street Journal*/NBC News poll in August 2014, when 76 percent of Americans ages eighteen and older said they weren't confident that their children's generation would fare better than their own. That same survey showed that the percentage of Americans who felt that the United States was on the wrong track had shot up to 71.

"It's been a long time since Americans felt that way or at least had that aggregate fear," said Anthony Marx. "So, understandably, you look for every angle that you can that will give your kid an advantage." And a selective college that commands pronounced respect is perceived as one of those angles. In the eyes of apprehensive parents, it's a possible guarantor, or at least an extra arrow in the quiver.

So they meddle and wheedle and marshal whatever resources they have toward the goal of a college that gleams in the public eye, convinced that this is the responsible, caring thing to do. Or at least too many of them do this, setting their children up for what is very likely to be disappointment, infusing the effort with an emotionalism that can turn that disappointment into heartbreak and planting the notion that there's a clear winner's circle and, outside of it, a tundra of uncertainty.

"It's ironic because what, in the end, do parents really want?" said Andrew Delbanco, the American studies professor at Columbia. "They want their children to be happy. And

I don't see how buying into the college admissions process is accomplishing that."

I don't, either. And I have two particular complaints about the mania that I'd perhaps put above others, two primary reasons that I wish kids and their parents wouldn't be drawn into it. The first is this, and it's an echo of the laments and concerns raised by Scott Pask, William Deresiewicz, Barry Schwartz and Hiram Chodosh: The mania's focus on such a limited number of acceptable outcomes, coupled with its attention to minutely detailed instructions for achieving them, suggests that life yields to meticulous mapping and plotting. That's a comforting thought but a fraudulent one. The second reason is that the admissions mania perverts the true meaning and value of hard work, in a manner that I'll return to shortly.

As for plotting, Steve Schmidt, the McCain campaign strategist, told me that his interactions with students at elite colleges over recent years had given him a set of impressions about them much like Chodosh's. "I'll talk to a group at Stanford and I've spoken at the Kennedy School at Harvard on any number of occasions," he said. "You have a bunch of hyperambitious kids, and they're nice kids, they're earnest, they're engaged. But they have their notepads out. 'How did you get where you are?' They're almost looking for you to give them a formula: 'On Day 246 of your career, you should do this.' I said to one kid, 'I'm going to give you a piece of advice. You should go and get a job working on a sailboat in the Caribbean for six months. Or maybe work behind a bar.' He was shocked. And I said, 'I'm serious as a heart attack. Life isn't reduced to a formula. Luck enters into it. It's a chance event.' "

How true. And this happens to be perfectly illustrated by the career, or rather careers, of another high-powered campaign strategist, one who can be added to the long list, at the book's beginning, of political operatives who aren't alumni of elite schools. I'm referring to Joel Benenson, who was the chief pollster for Barack Obama's 2008 and 2012 presidential campaigns and was subsequently chosen to be one of the principal architects of Hillary Clinton's 2016 presidential campaign. I got to know him well in 2015, and the jagged arc of his life speaks volumes about higher education, the liberal arts, indulging your passions, allowing for digressions and not sweating the immediate relevance and payoff of each and every step you take. His biography has similarities to those of Dick Parsons, Condoleezza Rice and so many other accomplished, contented people, in that it's not so much formulaic as accidental, and it suggests the importance of coloring outside the lines and surprising yourself.

Benenson, sixty-three, grew up in Queens, the youngest of three kids. His father died when he was eighteen months old and his mother, who worked as a bookkeeper and office manager, never remarried. For higher education, he chose a public school, Queens College, which is part of the City University of New York (CUNY), because it was free and he could live at home. He majored in theater, thinking he'd become an actor. He studied, and even performed in, Shakespeare's plays.

But after college, for most of his twenties, he co-owned a beer distributorship in the Crown Heights section of Brooklyn. Then, through a fluke, he segued into journalism at a New York tabloid and ended up covering politics. But it wasn't until his early forties that he fully awoke to his enthusiasm for the kind of work that he does now and pivoted to it.

The lesson for young people, he told me, is not to think too much "about what you want to do for the rest of your life. Think about what you want to do next." Maybe, he said, you "have a big goal out there and pursue it, but along the way, that line from A to B is not a continuum. The key will be identifying what you are passionate about in each of those steps along the way." And you shouldn't make hasty assumptions about what course of study will or won't be relevant down the line, he added.

"I can personally attest to the value of Shakespeare in my current profession," he said, explaining that parsing *Hamlet* and *Macbeth* gave him an "understanding of the rhythm and nuance of language" that's as useful to his political work as any fluency in statistics or any political science seminar could be. "College is about learning how to think critically, learning how to write and communicate your ideas," he said, and that can be accomplished at any number of institutions in any number of ways. If you're set on just one path and you resist or freak out about any deviation from it, he stressed, "I think you don't discover yourself."

I complained earlier that the admissions mania also perverts the integrity of hard work. I could add that it perverts the integrity of learning. And when I say those things, I think of a conversation I had in the fall of 2015 with Rachel Petrella, a college counselor at the Pacific Ridge School in the San Diego area. I asked her what she dreads most about every admissions season. She said that she shudders at a statement that she hears time and again, from one disappointed student after another. A student will get notices from all of the schools to which he or she applied. The ones that he or she coveted most will not offer admission. And the student will invariably respond: "I did all of this for nothing."

"How can that be the message in your house?" Petrella said. "They didn't get that one acceptance letter: 'I did all of this for nothing.' For nothing? What about training and preparation for a purposeful life? That's what you do it for." Her point, a crucial one, was that education isn't just a means to an end; it's a journey all its own, a process of growth, an act of betterment. And hard work shouldn't be framed, or thought of, only in terms of a specifically defined goal and merely as a humdrum bridge to some imagined promised land. Hard work bears the ripest, sweetest fruit when it's approached as an act of passion, a lifetime habit, a renewable resource.

And hard work is what nearly all of the most accomplished people I've interviewed attribute their achievements to. They sometimes call it different things, dress it up in different semantic finery. But it's always there in the gist of what they're saying, the cream of their advice. And the work they're talking about isn't the narrowly targeted kind that goes into anything as prosaic as an SAT score, a science project or an essay. They're talking about something that overarches all of these and is sustained well beyond them.

It's what Sam Altman of Y Combinator identified when I asked him what distinguished the entrepreneurs behind the startups that took off from the ones behind the startups that went nowhere. He said that what mattered most in the end was a true, deep attachment to whatever you're making, whatever you're selling, whatever you're doing. He praised intensity and stamina. "Sheer determination" was how he put it. It sounded to me like a synonym for hard work, which is at the very least a component or by-product of it.

It was about a week after my phone conversation with him that I happened to meet and have drinks with Britt Harris, the rich financier who teaches the Titans of Investing course at Texas A&M, his alma mater. He told me that largely because of the Titans class, he had given extensive thought to the real secret of the most successful people. Ambition? Sure, they all had that, but many unsuccessful people did as well, and sometimes in greater measure. Competence? Yes, but that doesn't take a person all the way to the top. Mentors? Those helped, and anyone who finds a shrewd and generous one should by all means make the most of him or her. But mentors weren't the decisive edge.

Harris shared his conclusion with me by recounting a guest lecture that he'd given to a hundred or so students at Princeton about five years ago. He told the students that he was humbled to be appearing before them and conceded as much, saying to them: "Your level of intelligence is literally off the charts. I want to admit to you—and this is not false humility—there was never a day in my life when I could reasonably be considered to be accepted into Princeton. I would have rejected myself!

"I'm in my fifties," he recalls telling them. "I've run seven relatively important organizations, and I've been fortunate enough to have people from Princeton work for me. But I've never worked for somebody from Princeton. How do you explain that?"

He then gave them *his* explanation for it: "I'm fully engaged. If I decide to get involved, I'm all in. Every day is one hundred percent." That's his greatest asset, he told them and, later, me, explaining that a robust and lasting energy for hard work is always going to be more consequential than any college.

Few of the parents I know would dispute that. Most feel it in their bones. It's common sense. And that's exactly what the college admissions mania squeezes out of us. It makes us forget what we inherently know.

We know, for instance, that many people hit their strides late in life—later than college, sometimes by decades—and that who they are when an admissions office evaluates them and even who they are when they finish their higher education isn't who they'll be years later. We know that extrapolating too far from the present into the future is a fool's game: At different times, we're different versions of ourselves. One version exists on the cusp of college. There will be other versions down the road. And they'll be dealing with circumstances, professionally and personally, that we can't begin to imagine.

We know that many of the attributes that best position someone for professional success—and for contentment, which isn't the same thing—aren't fully reflected in a high school transcript or easily distilled in a college admissions application. Many people flourish in their careers and their relationships because of the buoyancy of their spirits, their talents for establishing a positive rapport with everyone around them and the emotional wisdom with which they separate what's vitally important from what's not. Their gift isn't their measurable intellect but their personality, and while it may come through in better grades and flattering references from teachers who take a shine to them, or in leadership positions attained by dint of their popularity, it's probably not going to show up as readily in the material that an admissions officer evaluates as other, more quantifiable gifts do.

We know that people are often defined as sharply by setbacks, and by their responses to them, as by getting what they want when they want it, including a "yes" from Yale or a welcome from the University of Chicago. One of the most potentially meaningful aspects of the college admissions process is, in fact, rejection. And that's partly because college is, or should be, disruptive. It's about becoming a new person, not letting the ink dry on who, at seventeen or eighteen, you already are. In that sense defeat can be a springboard. And figuring out how to rebound from disappointment is infinitely more beneficial than any diploma.

We also know, or should know, that by infusing the choice of a college with so much anxiety, we're taking an exhilarating crossroads and turning it into something sour and sinister and gratuitously injurious. *Going to college*: That phrase—that adventure—has lost some of the thrill it once had, and not just because so many Americans now pursue higher education, making it a more routine occurrence. No, we've sucked some of the magic from college by letting college get sucked into our tedious, soulless preoccupation with status.

But not entirely, at least not yet. And that's what keeps Tara Dowling, who has worked as a college counselor at Choate and other schools, moving forward, despite all of the parents who ask her why their kids didn't get into an Ivy, despite the cynical games that some students play, despite their insistence on looking past and down on so many terrific but underexposed schools, despite every other facet of the frenzy.

"Every year I ask myself: 'Do I want to do this again?'" Dowling said. "'Do I want to do this one more year?' But in the end, as a first-generation college student who got no help from a counselor and whose life was changed by college one hundred percent, I believe in the transformational power of higher education and the self-awareness and self-actualization that comes from the process of applying to college."

If students are steered through it correctly, if at least some measure of calm can be made to prevail, "kids become aware of who they are," she said. "Kids become aware of what they want. I love being part of that process: watching the light bulb go on, watching them work their buns off. And in the end they all go to college, and their lives *are* changed."

There's something else we know, and it's the forgetting of this that's perhaps most curious, and saddest. We know that where we go to college will have infinitely less bearing on our fulfillment in life than so much else: the wisdom with which we choose our romantic partners; our interactions with the communities that we inhabit; our generosity toward the families that we inherit and the families that we make. We know that no college can compete with getting any one of those things right, let alone getting several or all of them right. Then the admissions process comes along, and it shoves all that knowledge to the side.

That's what baffled and horrified Susan Bodnar.

ELEVEN

BEYOND THE B-PLUS

"We just don't stack up. We're just not going to stack up."

—Susan Bodnar, stressed-out parent

You met Bodnar in an earlier chapter. She was the one whose son, Ronen, was rejected from an elite preschool. It was his frog that was only hopping. When I corresponded with her in the spring and summer of 2014, as Ronen finished his junior year and began his summer break before senior year, she told me, "It feels a bit like that right now. His frog is only hopping."

We were on the phone, and it was one of Ronen's last days of school, and he was awaiting word on a final paper in an English class for which he desperately wanted an A-minus. He feared that he'd get only a B or B-plus. Because English was supposed to be one of his strengths, a B or B-plus wouldn't look good to an Ivy League school.

"My son is texting me his final grades right now," Bodnar said at the start of our conversation. Her voice was tense. She knew that. She apologized for it. She hated herself for being so wound up but she wasn't sure how not to be. She vowed to stop mentioning the imminent English grade. She repeatedly broke that vow. "He's going to get a B in English," she predicted. "His first B. End of his college dreams."

Ronen goes to Manhattan's Trinity School, which I mentioned earlier in terms of its low kindergarten acceptance rate. His sister, who is younger than he is, goes to Horace Mann, another private school in New York City's "Ivy Preparatory School League." But Bodnar, a psychologist, and her husband, a technology researcher, don't have the kind of money that Trinity and Horace Mann cost; both kids are on half scholarships. And up until Ronen's junior year, she took pride in not leading a life as posh and pampered as so many of the other families with children at those schools, at not participating in all of their expensive rituals, at having to find ways at home to economize, like most Americans do.

For their vacations, the family doesn't go to fancy resorts. They hike and camp. Dinners out in restaurants are rare. "I cook all of our meals," Bodnar said. And while other families turned to caterers and decorators for their kids' birthday parties, Bodnar felt that she could do as well with her own efforts and ingenuity. "There was a way that we felt we were on some sort of equal footing, and everything was hunky-dory," she said.

Then, she said, "It was like someone skied into me and I was knocked on my face."

What happened was all the junior-year talk at Trinity about college admissions. Belatedly, she realized that the families and kids around her and Ronen had been doing all of this concerted prepping, all of this vigorous strategizing. She also had her eyes opened to just how unforgiving the odds for getting into the most selective schools had become. Ronen was an exemplary student; she'd always assumed he'd go to the school of his choice. But exemplary wasn't good enough anymore.

She said that as summer approached, "one friend said to me very casually, 'My son is going to Yale for pre-law for a week and then studying [acting] with Stella Adler for four weeks and then going to Harvard for a pre-med program.' He's between his *sophomore* and junior years. You hear that and you shrink. You just shrink. My son's going to music camp, again, for the fourth year, because he really loves music."

Trinity provides dedicated SAT tutoring for small groups of its students, and Ronen had of course participated in that. But he didn't do an additional private tutor: That was outside the family's budget and their sense of how much privilege and entitlement anyone should exploit. Ronen was already going to what was considered one of the finest secondary schools in New York City. All these add-ons seemed sort of obscene. Still, Bodnar wondered: Had it been a mistake not to sign her son up for them, to figure out a way?

For instance, she said, "It never occurred to us to put him in a Saturday pre-college program. It turns out that's a big deal. And there are people in the summertime who aren't hiking or camping but going on world community-service trips that cost a lot of money." But not Ronen.

She'd never fretted about that stuff before, she said. She'd never measured herself and her family so carefully against others. She didn't want to do so now. But she also wanted her son to have every option in life and, yes, every advantage, including a school with a name that snapped people to attention, at least if that was the school he preferred. And she didn't want him doubting himself or feeling hurt. But they were hurtling toward a junction that seemed designed to diminish him.

"Suddenly we have been transported to an alternate universe known as the potential applicant," she wrote to me in an email. "We speak a new language with words like *legacy* and *diversity* and *institutional priorities* and *Ivy League*. Suddenly our son is being looked at through rubrics, assessments and cutoffs." She didn't want Ronen to buy into all of that but wasn't sure how to pull out of it responsibly. "We don't know how to get off this train," she continued. "I haven't slept since we went on our college tours during spring break. I wake up crying and hurting. I'm considering medication. Yes, me. Ms. Natural, who never even takes cold medicine."

What Bodnar found especially odd about her susceptibility to all of this was that she saw, in her very own psychotherapy practice, how damaging it could be when a kid was allowed or encouraged to become too invested in the admissions game and its results. She treated young people in their teens and twenties who'd been pulled into "the vortex," as she called it. "It's like we are mass-producing perfect robots posing as kids," she wrote to me in one email.

And on the phone she said, "They have no space to be kids. They're not feeling that the work they're doing is their own. They're succeeding, but it's not coming from within. And they're having a lot of psychological problems because of it: obsessive-compulsive disorder; freaking out because they're not perfect." She wondered aloud about some of the blackout drug-taking and binge drinking that's happening on college campuses. Were the roots of it in the high-pressure, overprogrammed secondary school experience that a kid doggedly pursuing the most elite colleges has?

The possibility spooked her, so she was working on some kind of balance. She was trying to celebrate Ronen for who he was, whether it turned out to be admissions bait or not. She was reminding herself that a place like Harvard or Princeton or Yale probably wasn't even right for him. "He's not an alpha male," she said. "He loves the woods. He loves poetry. That kind of school could be a disaster, not a boost. So who knows? Where's he going to feel happy? Where are they going to like him? We're telling him: Be honest. Be yourself. His Common Application essay is going to be about his joy of being in the wilderness. Is that going to be a winning essay? Probably not. But it's who he is."

The verdict on his English paper did arrive before the end of the phone call during which she'd been waiting for it. He got a B-plus, which would also, then, be his grade for the course. The next day, Bodnar emailed me and told me that Ronen had come home "angry with himself for failing" to do better. "He believed he failed his passion," she wrote. "He is 16!

"This is what we told our son," she continued, and in her message I heard echoes of the reassurance that Diana Levin had given her son, Matt, the boy who'd fantasized about Yale, Princeton and Brown but was heading off to Lehigh instead. Bodnar said to Ronen: "This is not the end of your journey. This is a learning experience. You will be better at whatever college you attend because you have had this experience. You still have time to develop the competence to match your passion. It will happen. Trust your inner voice and one day it will match up with what you can demonstrate on the outside. Do not give up."

Here is what I would like to say to her: Those very words prove that your son has something so much more essential and nourishing and lasting than whatever he's going to get on whichever campus becomes his home, because that's only his temporary home. You've given him his real home, the one he had before college and the one he'll have after, and just look at all that it brims with, and consider all that it will bequeath him.

You once told me that when he and his sister and you and your husband go camping, you not only "talk a lot" but "sing together." Ronen will always have that music. You once told me that for you and your husband, your family "has been the center of our existence, and our love for our children our heartbeat." That rhythm will forever be his. So will the wilderness and so will poetry, so long as he isn't permitted to lose sight of them.

You told me that "enthusiasm inhabits his every gesture." If that stays true through this crazy college crossroads and remains the case beyond it, he'll be a graced man. Probably a happy one, too.

AFTERWORD

A few weeks following the publication of the first edition of this book in March 2015, I received an email from a friend who is roughly my age. He was writing to me about someone else in our generation, a woman who'd gone to a prestigious private high school and was expected by her parents to go to an equally prestigious college, and he was reflecting on how much less frenzied and ridiculous the college admissions process had been back then. The email said:

> *My friend Deb recalled taking the SATs back in the Spring of 1981, when we were high school juniors. She lived in Manhattan, and was taking the test early on a Saturday morning up in the Bronx... Because of the early start-time, the infrequent weekend subway service, and her desire to be at the test well-rested and on-time, she asked her father if he could drive her up to Riverdale on the morning of the test. He declined, stating that he had an excellent parking spot, and did not wish to relinquish it for fear that his carefully orchestrated alternate-side-system would be upset. Another friend's father was planning on driving and there was space in the car for her, but this*

arrangement fell through as well because that father's Saturday tennis game was starting earlier than usual and prevented him from driving the kids. So they got up early, took the subway, and took the test. No ride—because a parking spot and a tennis game were more important to the parents. This was definitely not 2015.

No, it wasn't. And I present this recollection not just because it captures the change so well and so humorously. I present it because it focuses on parents and because I've increasingly come to believe that they're the answer to this madness, the best hope we have of finding a way out of it, the contributors to it who can perhaps get the many other contributors to reform their ways as well.

The colleges that fetishize low acceptance rates and move heaven and earth to achieve them are responding to a marketplace that wrongly equates exclusiveness with quality, and the prime movers in that marketplace are parents. The admissions consultants who ratchet up the anxiety wouldn't exist in such plenitude and possess such power if parents didn't write big checks for their services. The high school counselors who guide students through the application process would put less emphasis on colleges ranked high on the *U.S. News* list if they didn't have to answer to administrators who keep track of how many of the school's kids get into the Ivies, and those administrators wouldn't keep track if parents weren't constantly asking, worrying, needling. As for the kids who think they'll be affirmed only by acceptance to a school that takes one in five or one in 10 or—best of all!—one in twenty applicants? They're influenced by their peers, yes. But they're influenced more by their parents, who are the chief agents of the climate in which they and their peers dwell (and too often flounder).

I don't mean to vilify parents. I have enormous sympathy and respect for them, because while some are indeed motivated by vanity, and want their children to be flattering and validating mirrors of themselves, many more are simply trying to ensure happy and successful lives for their offspring, to create the most opportunity for them, to safeguard their welfare in uncertain times. And as I've mentioned before, they see the right college as a way to do all of that, and they respond to the countless cues out there that the right college is the one that's the hardest to get into, the object of facile (and often misinformed) envy.

It's because parents care for their children and endeavor to do best by their children that I have hope. Parents just need to be reminded and educated about all of the damage the admissions mania does, and this can't be a subtle or a fleeting campaign. They need to understand that if they pump kids too full of the belief that a highly selective school is the be-all and end-all, and if they point kids too obsessively in that direction, they're tempting and courting a great deal of potential harm.

Some of that harm, which I've flagged before, is a matter of warped values. If you're among the affluent Americans who can afford to layer tens of thousands of dollars of fees to independent consultants on top of the private-school tuition you're already paying, and you indeed choose to do this, are you telling your children that an advantage is something that's purchased and that success is rightly bought? If you spend hour upon hour talking with your children about how to get into an exclusive college and only a fraction of that time discussing what they should do—and learn!—once they get there, are you saying that acquisition and not experience is the utmost concern, the real key? Are you perpetuating the idea that all of life is a pecking order? I often feel that among the most fortunate Americans, higher education has been turned into a mall with tiered department stores: Neiman Marcus over there, Nordstrom right here, J.C. Penney down the way. Oh, and across the highway, on the other side of all that messy traffic, lies a Wal-Mart. With any luck, the shoppers stuck there will find what they need.

But some of the harm is less theoretical, less abstract: It's evident and measured in physical and psychiatric terms. At Alice Kleeman's high school in Silicon Valley, teachers and administrators actually decided a few years ago that they had to take bold steps to address the sleep problem among their students. And when I say "sleep problem," I don't mean that kids were sleeping too much, failing to wake up on time, getting to class late. I mean that so many kids were so stressed out about taking the right number of Advanced Placement classes, getting perfect grades, acing standardized tests and establishing perfect transcripts that they weren't allowing themselves enough rest or able to *fall* asleep.

The school brought in outside sleep experts. It created a sleep curriculum. It trained students as "sleep ambassadors." It even held a contest among students for the best sleep slogan.

The winner? "Life is lousy when you're drowsy."

This high school serves students from Atherton and from Menlo Park, which is right next door to Palo Alto, home to Stanford and its precedent-setting acceptance rates. In Palo Alto there are train tracks, and when I was there in the spring of 2015, I noticed, at several of the spots where roads cross those tracks, orange-vested safety workers. Sentries.

They were on a suicide watch.

Between May 2009 and January 2010, five Palo Alto teenagers ended their lives by stepping in front of trains. And between October 2014 and April 2015, another three Palo Alto teenagers killed themselves that way. The *Palo Alto Weekly* refers to the deaths as a "suicide contagion."

While mental health professionals in the area were being rightly careful not to oversimplify or trivialize the emotional anguish behind the suicides by focusing on any one possible factor, the contagion had prompted a heartfelt examination of the kinds of pressures felt by high school students in epicenters of overachievement. The local media was rife with commentary, from many perspectives, on this situation.

One junior at Palo Alto High School wrote: "As I sit in my room staring at the list of colleges I've resolved to try to get into, trying to determine my odds of getting into each, I can't help but feel desolate." She confessed to panic attacks in class, to menstrual periods missed as a result of exhaustion. "We are not teenagers," she added. "We are lifeless bodies in a system that breeds competition and hatred and discourages teamwork and genuine learning."

Such suicides aren't just a secondary-school phenomenon. Over recent years there have been rashes of suicides at Tulane, MIT and Cornell. There were six suicides at the University of Pennsylvania during one recent thirteen-month period.

They're extreme cases, and not indicative of some staggering rise in the suicide rate. But apart from suicide, there's much evidence of psychic trouble among achievement-oriented students from relatively affluent backgrounds. They're leaning harder on the mental health services on college campuses than their counterparts did in the past. They're reporting unusual levels of anxiety and depression. As Susan Bodnar noted, they're engaging in substance abuse and binge drinking.

Suniya Luthar, a renowned developmental psychologist now teaching at ASU, has done extensive research that shows higher incidences of certain self-destructive behaviors and of feelings of distress and despair among children from wealthy suburbs than among those from inner cities. "The evidence all points to one cause underlying the different disturbances documented: pressure for high-octane achievement," she wrote in a summary of her research for *Psychology Today*.

I reached out to her and asked how big a component of "high-octane achievement" admission to the "right" college was. Very big, she told me. And she said that the "kids who say that their parents overwhelmingly value *achievement* are the most depressed. They do the most drinking. And they don't have the better grades." In contrast, she said, kids who say that their parents value decency and integrity are better adjusted and in many cases perform better, too.

I don't think that parents have to, or should, stop exhorting their children toward excellence. Fulfilling your potential is part of being fully alive. But why not frame it that way? Why not talk about acing a course as a measure of having ingested all of its valuable information and insights? Why not talk about running a fast race and even breaking a record because it can feel electric, joyous, to discover the length and strength of your stride? Don't discuss these accomplishments in terms of how they might facilitate acceptance by an elite college. Eliminate references to the strangers on admissions committees in Palo Alto or Cambridge or Amherst, Massachusetts. Stop oohing and aahing when the kid next door heads off to Brown. Stop introducing an accomplished adult by mentioning what his or her alma mater is. Stop beginning every conversation with a high school student by asking where he or she hopes to go to college, with an emphasis on the *where*. There's plenty else to talk about.

"You can listen to what your kids' needs are in a loving way, and let them do it *their* way, and they can still get into a good college," Bodnar said to me when I caught up with her in late 2015, many months after Ronen's college admissions odyssey was done. In the end, she said, Ronen applied to about twelve schools, including several Ivies: Yale, Dartmouth, Cornell. He wasn't accepted by those three. Parents of other students at his private secondary school told me that this threw Bodnar for more of a loop than she admitted to when she and I had our catch-up conversation, by which time she sounded relieved about, and grateful for, the options Ronen did have. They included McGill, Tufts and the University of Chicago, which offered him not just admission but also a sizable merit scholarship. He chose Chicago.

He also chose to defer enrollment for a year while he used the money he'd made from a summer job as a busboy to travel to Western Europe, where he was going to work on, and learn about, farms in France, Italy and Germany. Then he would return to the United States and realize his ambition to hike the Appalachian Trail. This news thrilled me, as it did Bodnar, because it showed that Ronen wasn't just racing toward a diploma and a predetermined career. He was taking the time to get to know himself and the world a whole lot better, and he was flexing, and developing, the muscle of independence.

Bodnar told me that with her daughter, Binah, who was

three years away from college, there'd be less consciousness of, and attention to, elite schools. "Ronen's sister is saying, 'I'm just going to step aside from all these crazy people,'" Bodnar told me.

Her words put me in mind of another bit of commentary I'd read on a Palo Alto news site. It was from Adam Strassberg, a psychiatrist and the father of two Palo Alto teenagers. Sifting through all the damage to the community's children, he recommended lightening their schedules, limiting the number of times that they take the SAT and—the part that especially caught my eye—lessening the message that it's Stanford or bust.

"I will never be neutral on this issue," he wrote. "The 'Koala Dad' is the far better parent than the 'Tiger Mom.'"

There's one more email I'd like to share, this one not from a friend of mine but from a friend of my father's. It, too, came to me shortly after this book first appeared. It, too, was a response to the book's message. Its author is someone who grew up with my father in the Italian section of White Plains, New York, among kids who, like Dad, would be the first in their families to attend college.

I need to fill you in about Dad: His parents were Italian immigrants who still struggled with English when he was in middle and high school. He attended Dartmouth, thanks to an enormous scholarship, and did not only his undergraduate work there but also got his MBA from its business school, Amos Tuck, after which he went to work for a big accounting firm, eventually becoming one of its senior partners. For him Dartmouth was a special point of pride, because it was so far from his gritty childhood neighborhood and because it represented the kind of trajectory he associated with kids who had more comfortable lives and more educated parents. In fact his parents balked at the idea that he'd be in a place they'd never laid eyes on.

His childhood friend wrote to me:

> *For what it's worth, I certainly agree with your premise that the student is more important than the school in determining the ultimate outcome. Lots of children—especially those of immigrants—did, and do, very well being educated at non-top-tier institutions.*
>
> *Your father once told me your grandfather really wanted him to go to Fordham, not Dartmouth. Your father's choice of Dartmouth obviously worked out very well. But another kid about your dad's age, and in similar circumstances, Mario Gabelli, chose Fordham. Since he is one of the highest paid executives in the country, I guess his choice worked out fine too.*
>
> *At the end of the day, I've always believed smart, highly motivated kids will succeed wherever they get their education.*

I read that email quickly and pretty much forgot about it, possibly because Gabelli's name didn't ring any bells. One of the highest-paid executives in the country? I suspected some exaggeration in that description.

Then, a few days later, I was riding in a taxi from my apartment on Manhattan's Upper West Side toward Penn Station to catch a train. As Columbus Avenue turned into Ninth Avenue, I looked to my right, in the direction of Fordham's Manhattan campus, adjacent to Lincoln Center. And I noticed something that I'd never registered before. Emblazoned on one of the buildings were these words: Gabelli School of Business.

Gabelli?

I went back to the email, then did some rapid research, and learned that my father's childhood friend hadn't exaggerated at all about the worth and might of Gabelli, an investment wizard whose biography in some ways mirrored Dad's. Like Dad, Gabelli was born to Italian immigrants. He grew up in the Bronx, not White Plains, but also like Dad, he'd relied on a scholarship to pay for college. And like Dad, he'd risen far above the economic station of his youth—in his case, so far that he'd been able to make a $25 million gift to Fordham. (If Dad has a sum like that, he's hiding it from me.) That's why that building bore the Gabelli name.

For one striver, Dartmouth. For another, Fordham. In both cases, a bright future and a meaningful life, because in *all* cases, it's as much the person as it is the path.

Suggested Reading and Resources

There are many fine alternatives to the *U.S. News & World Report* rankings: books and guides that focus not on the panicked effort to get into a highly selective school but on making an informed college match and staying sane along the way. There's also a subgenre of nonfiction that exposes some of the prejudices and shortcomings of the admissions process, and there's a rapidly, mercifully growing body of literature that questions the excessive competition at many secondary schools, giving parents and kids much-needed encouragement to adopt a healthier attitude and more constructive approach.

These are just some of the titles I'd recommend. They are in no particular order. Not all are readily available at bookstores, but in the age of the Internet, new or used copies of each should be findable online.

College Unranked: Ending the College Admissions Frenzy edited by Lloyd Thacker. In this useful and wise volume, Thacker compiles essays from people with inside knowledge of the admissions process, but their goal—and his—isn't to help applicants game that process. It isn't to produce some ridiculous short list of schools to which all secondary school students should aspire. No, it's to demystify admissions and explain why too much importance is placed on a school's exclusivity. That this was originally published in 2005 shows how long we've been locked in the frenzy, which has only worsened since then.

Fiske Guide to Colleges by Edward B. Fiske. Most of the college counselors I trust most consider this the gold standard of reference books with raw information on hundreds of colleges, and they applaud it for steering clear of some of the status consciousness that's detectable in other guides. It's updated regularly.

The College Finder and ***College Match*** by Steven R. Antonoff. Antonoff's books emphasize which types of colleges might be especially good *fits* for which types of applicants, and they promote an investigation of college options that goes beyond—that ignores, really—a school's questionable rank on subjective lists. One counselor praised *The College Finder* as "broad-reaching," "incredibly inclusive" and "my go-to book for list-making with kids." That's not just high praise but the right kind of praise.

Colleges That Change Lives by Loren Pope, updated by Hilary Masell Oswald. The whole idea behind this book, which has become something of a classic, is that there are special schools less concerned with their rankings and less interested in being coveted than in creating and maintaining unique, nurturing learning environments that work spectacularly well for the right students. I love its attention to untraditional, quirky schools and its very clear message that college is an experience, not an acquisition.

A Review of Fifty Public University Honors Programs by John Willingham. As I explained at length earlier in *Where You Go Is Not Who You'll Be*, honors programs and honors colleges at state universities have much to recommend them and warrant serious consideration. This straightforward analysis of the best ones gives them the spotlight they deserve.

College Admission: From Application to Acceptance, Step by Step by Robin Mamlet and Christine VanDeVelde. While a big part of my message is *not* to turn the application process into a full-time occupation by studying up on every move, it's helpful, even necessary, to have at least one intelligent how-to manual, one revelatory map. Mamlet and VanDeVelde provide that, in a book that covers, for example, the fundamentals of early admission and the fine points of financial aid. Their approach is calming and level-headed enough that it drew compliments from the National Association for College Admission Counseling, which called it "beneficial to students of *any* background at *any* stage of their college search."

Debt-Free U: How I Paid for an Outstanding College Education Without Loans, Scholarships, or Mooching Off My Parents by Zac Bissonnette. Here's what I like about this book, and why it's important: Bissonnette wrote it while *still* a student in college, at the University of Massachusetts, so it's a perspective from the inside, not the outside. It explains the advantages of a state university. It discusses the circumstances under which community college makes sense. It urges students to be independent and seize responsibility. Above all, it addresses a problem much bigger and more important than admissions anxiety—namely, the cost of college today.

I'm Going to College—Not You! edited by Jennifer Delahunty. Delahunty, who is quoted several times in *Where You Go Is Not Who You'll Be*, was the longtime dean of admissions at Kenyon College and has a knack for understanding how the college admissions process drives people crazy and what sorts of words and salves might help. *I'm Going to College—Not You!* is very smartly conceived, combining essays by obsessed, distressed parents and essays by admissions officials. And as its title suggests, it gets at something fundamental and important: the degree to which some parents approach their kids' college application process as a referendum on child-rearing and a final opportunity to exert control before the nest empties.

Crazy U: One Dad's Crash Course in Getting His Kid into College by Andrew Ferguson. The proper response to the ridiculously competitive, overly emotional odyssey that many parents and kids embark on is wonder, laughter and a significant measure of mockery, all present in Ferguson's book. His description of what others go through and the road he himself was drawn down will force parents and students to question their own approach and ask some of the right questions about what they want and don't want to do in the service of acceptance.

The Chosen: The Hidden History of Admission and Exclusion at Harvard, Yale, and Princeton by Jerome Karabel. This is an ambitious, thoroughly researched, *epic* book recommended only for readers with time, patience and a deep interest in the subject. I include it, though, because it goes back decades in time to illuminate something much larger than the subtitle suggests: the ways in which student bodies at elite institutions are molded by more than merit.

The Price of Admission by Daniel Golden. Golden won a Pulitzer Prize for his reporting in the *Wall Street Journal* on the favoritism that Ivy League admissions offices show to certain applicants, principally wealthy ones and legacy cases. This book expands on those *Journal* stories and provides, in a briskly written manner, what *The Chosen* does as well: a reminder that the admissions process is far from a meritocracy and that those applicants who don't get what they want shouldn't see that as any indictment of their abilities. In Golden's eye-opening, forcefully argued view, elite schools are instruments with which the "ruling class" perpetuates itself.

The Gatekeepers by Jacques Steinberg. Like *The Chosen* and *The Price of Admission,* Steinberg takes readers deep inside the decisions made by admissions offices and illuminates dynamics that applicants are blind to and have no control over. For one whole admissions cycle, he was granted extraordinary access to the process at Wesleyan University, and he describes the thinking of both the decision makers and the applicants yearning to win their favor.

Lost in the Meritocracy by Walter Kirn. Kirn is a spectacularly lively and gifted writer, and this memoir traces his ascent from an undistinguished Minnesota high school to Princeton, which it skillfully demystifies. It's useful because it traces some of the unsavory aspects of the Ivy

League summit and because it asks some of the right questions about how people get there. "I've topped the hill," Kirn writes, "thanks to an education and a test that measured and rewarded...what, exactly? Nothing important, I've discovered. Nothing sustaining. Just 'aptitude.' That's why we're all here: we all showed aptitude. Aptitude for showing aptitude, mainly."

The Price of Privilege by Madeline Levine. Years before the tiger mother sang her battle hymn, Levine identified the type, if not by feline sobriquet, and sounded an alarm about what can happen to kids subjected to excessive parental pressure. Mothers and fathers who are starting to fill their children with worry about getting into an exclusive college might want to pause and read Levine.

The Blessing of a Skinned Knee by Wendy Mogel. In a vein similar to Levine's, Mogel takes issue with, and aim at, certain kinds of overzealous parenting. This book and other writings of hers exalt self-reliance, resilience and ethical behavior—all of which can be overlooked and undervalued when parents become intricately involved in, and obsessed with, a specific sequence of accomplishments that will supposedly ensure their kids admission to a "top college" and a future of material success.

The Gift of Failure by Jessica Lahey, and ***How to Raise an Adult*** by Julie Lythcott-Haims. Two of the heirs to Levine's and Mogel's work, these books, both published in 2015, provide an updated perspective, and Lythcott-Haims writes from the vantage point of someone who was a dean at Stanford and is raising her own children in the pressure cooker of Palo Alto.

Acknowledgments

If I named all of the people who helped me in some way—with interviews, with suggestions, with encouragement, with friendship—I'd need pages and pages. I hope that all of you know who you are and that you have my gratitude. I'll confine this very short list to those people without whom this book simply wouldn't exist. Thank you, thank you, thank you to Tom Nickolas, Elinor Burkett, Jennifer Steinhauer, Alessandra Stanley, Gail Collins, Trish Hall, Andy Rosenthal, Barbara Laing, Anne Kornblut, Ben Greenberg, Maddie Caldwell, Jamie Raab, Lisa Bankoff, Robert Niles, Alex Halpern Levy, Susan Bodnar, Diana Levin and my uncle James Bruni, the educator in the Bruni clan.

About the Author

Frank Bruni is an op-ed columnist for the *New York Times* and writes frequently about higher education. During his two decades at the newspaper, he has been its Rome bureau chief, a staff writer for its Sunday magazine, one of its White House correspondents and its chief restaurant critic. *Where You Go Is Not Who You'll Be* is his third bestseller, following the memoir *Born Round* and a chronicle of George W. Bush's 2000 campaign for the presidency, *Ambling into History*.

Index

-in-Chief: Barrie Pitt
: David Mason
rector: Sarah Kingham
e Editor: Robert Hunt
tant Art Editor: Denis Piper
er: David A Evans
ation: Michael Flanagan
graphic Research: Carina Dvorak

hs for this book were especially selected from the following archives: from left to right pages 2-8
chtliches Bildarchiv, Munich; 10 US Library of Congress; 11-12 Ullstein GmbH, Berlin; 13 US
rchives, Washington; 14 Archiv Gerstenberg; 15 Süddeutscher Verlag, Munich; 16 Library of
18 Ullstein; 18 Bundesarchiv, Koblenz; 19 Ullstein; 19 Gerstenberg; 20 Ullstein; 20 Bundesarchiv;
tscher; 22-23 Gerstenberg; 23 Library of Congress; 25 Radio-Times Hulton Picture Library, London;
ein; 30 National Archives; 31 Zeitgeschichliches; 32-33 Ullstein; 34 Bundesarchiv; 36 Süddeutscher;
hichliches; 40 Staatsbibliothek, Berlin; 41 National Archives; 42 Süddeutscher; 43 National Archives;
berg; 45 National Archives; 46 Gerstenberg; 46 Bundesarchiv; 47 Ullstein; 48 Bundesarchiv;
chichliches; 50-51 National Archives; 53 Staats; 56 Süddeutscher; 56 Ullstein; 57 Süddeutscher;
tenberg; 61 Ullstein; 62 Süddeutscher; 63-65 Ullstein; 66-67 National Archives; 68 Süddeutscher;
of Congress; 70 Süddeutscher; 72 Bundesarchiv; 73 Ullstein; 74 Süddeutscher; 75 Keystone Press
7 Gerstenberg; 77 Bundesarchiv; 78-79 Gerstenberg; 79 National Archives; 80-81 Süddeutscher;
; 83 Library of Congress; 84 Staats; 86 National Archives; 86 Ullstein; 87 Süddeutscher;
hichliches; 89 Ullstein; 89-93 National Archives; 94 Zeitgeschichliches; 95-96 Süddeutscher;
berg; 97 Süddeutscher; 98-99 Ullstein; 99 National Archives; 100 Süddeutscher; 101 Zeitgeschichhliches;
al Archives; 103-105; 106 Bundesarchiv; 107 Ullstein; 108-109 Süddeutscher; 110-111 National Archives;
archiv; 114 Suddeutscher; 115 Staats; 115 Bundesarchiv; 116 Ullstein; 117 Süddeutscher;
n; 119 Zeitgeschichliches; 120-121 Ullstein; 122 Bundesarchiv; 124-125 National Archives;
stenberg; 128 National Archives; 129 Staats; 130-131 National Archives; 132 Zeitgeschichliches;
l Archives; 134-135 Bundesarchiv; 136-137 National Archives; 138-139 Süddeutscher; 139 National
41-142 Ullstein: 144-145 Süddeutscher; 146 Bundesarchiv; 148-149 Süddeutscher; 150-151 National
52 Süddeutscher; 153 Bundesarchiv; 154-155 Süddeutscher; 156 Popperfotos, London; 157 Staats;
deutscher; Front and back covers Zeitgeschichliches Bildarchiv

inting: August 1972
in United States of America

ne Books Inc.
Avenue New York NY 10003

t Publisher

Night of t
Long Kni

Nik

Edito
Edito
Art D
Pictu
Cons
Desig
Illust
Photo

Photogr
Zeitgesc
Nationa
Congres
20 Südde
26-29 Ulls
37 Zeitge
44 Gerste
51 Zeitge
58-60 Gers
69 Library
Agency;
82 Ullste
88 Zeitges
96 Gerste
102 Natio
112 Bunde
118 Ullste
126-127 Ge
132 Natio
Archives
Archives
158-159 Sü

First P
Printed

Ballant
101 Fift

An Inte

Contents

Throughout the years of his dictatorship Hitler was at pains to emphasise the 'constitutionality' of his seizure of power and of all his subsequent acts as Chancellor and head of state. Not for him, ran his implicit and often explicit claim, the cruel and criminal path of revolution along which the Communists would have led their German followers; not for him the destruction of the nation's institutions that they might be replaced by alien models; not for him rule by decree of tribunal and commissar. Whatever his contempt for the Weimar Republic and the democratic system which it falteringly practised, he had not stooped to illegality in his defeat of it but had beaten it fair and square on its own terms: direct appeal to the electorate. And however unparliamentary his personal style of government, it was a system for which the last German parliament had voted a lawful basis by a clear majority.

In a country without a free press, these were difficult claims to counter. Even today it will take a competent historian some time to expose their hollowness: the 'minority' chancellorship, the gerrymandering of the Enabling Law and the *Gleichschaltung* in which Nazi supplanted non-Nazi in every significant organ of German state and society. Hardest of all to refute is Hitler's claim to have achieved power by non-violent means for the good reason that if we are talking of January 1933, when he became chancellor, or of March, when he achieved a coalition majority in the Reichstag, it is in the simplest sense a true one. On neither of those occasions did Hitler, his opponents or the army, the guarantor of the state, resort to arms.

But Hitler, of course, had no personal objection to the use of violence to secure his ends. Indeed, he rather approved than disapproved of violence, on philosophical as well as practical grounds, had often employed it or sanctioned it in the past and

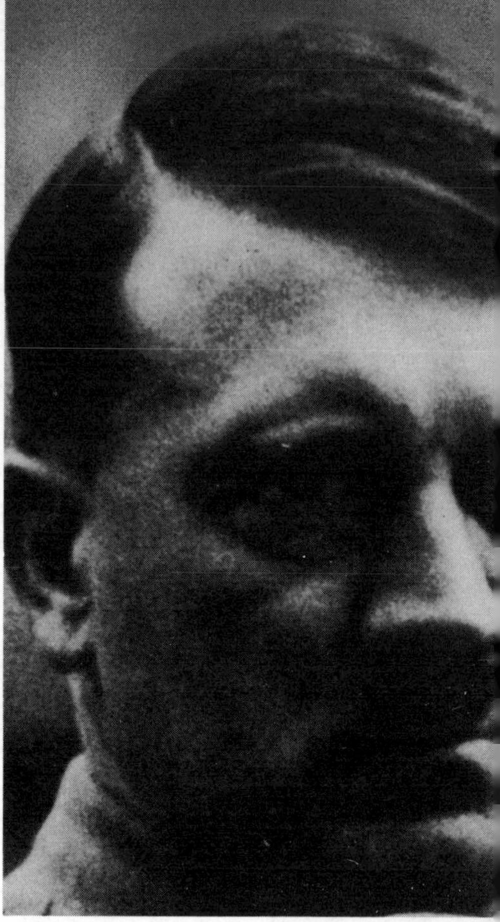

would do so in the future. If he eschewed its use in 1932 and 1933, it was for good cause. He had tried once before to sieze power by force, in November 1923, had failed humiliatingly, had suffered imprisonment and had emerged to find his movement in ruins. Worst of all in a state dominated by generals, he had earned the disregard of the army. Almost amid the echoes of the shooting on the Odeonplatz, he vowed that he would not take on the army again. Next time he would win with votes.

And so he did. But he had preached and condoned violence too often to escape the consequences altogether. The irony of his victory was to be that it forced him to kill when killing was apparently no longer useful and, in

Hitler's blood purge

Introduction by John Keegan

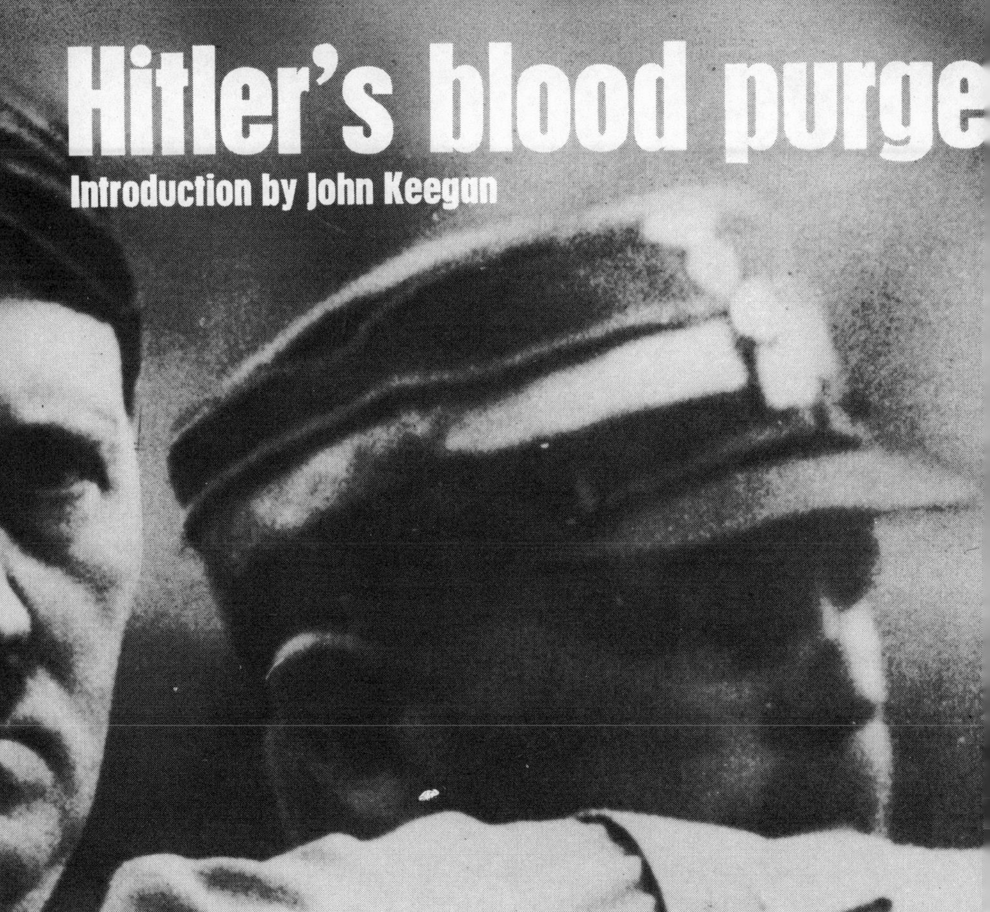

killing, to choose his victims from among his friends. As in 1923 it was the attitude of the army which determined that his policy should lead to bloodshed. Then the army – which in truth did no more than deny its support to him – had very properly been safeguarding the existence of the state. In 1934, the army was chiefly concerned to safeguard its own military primacy, which it saw threatened by the SA *(Sturmabteilungen)*, the brownshirted Nazi militia whose marching masses had swayed votes in half a dozen elections and whose fighting squads had battled with the communist Red Guards for the streets of working-class Berlin. The seizure of power had encouraged the Brownshirts, but particularly their leader, Röhm, to expect tangible rewards. A professional soldier from outside the traditional officer class, he looked to see the amalgamation of the regular army with the SA, preferably under his command. He also desired a genuine social revolution, and of that the army disapproved almost as strongly as it did of his military ambitions. However – to be fair to the army's record of apoliticality – it was the military side of Röhm's programme which prompted the generals to urge Hitler to have done with him. Whether it was the will of the generals alone which moved Hitler to unsheathe the Long Knives in June 1934 is a question which Count Nikolai Tolstoy explores compellingly in the account which follows.

Hitler and Röhm

On 8th November, 1923, the thirty-four year old demagogue and revolutionary Adolf Hitler made his first and only open attempt to seize power in Germany by unconstitutional and violent means. His home state of Bavaria was then under the control of three men: Gustav von Kahr, the State Commissioner; General Otto von Lossow, state commander of the *Reichswehr* (national army); and Colonel Hans von Seisser, head of the Bavarian police. All three on that evening were to be present at a widely-advertised meeting to be held in the Bürgerbräukeller, a large beer hall on the outskirts of Munich, the Bavarian capital.

The opportunity was not to be missed: here was the entire Bavarian leadership vulnerably assembled in a single hall – the pear was ripe for the plucking. Moreover, Hitler had reason to fear that Kahr might be using the opportunity to proclaim a measure near to his heart: the restoration of the Bavarian monarchy. Ancient ties of loyalty and affection linked the staunchly Catholic Bavarians to the illustrious dynasty of the Wittelsbachs, and with the popular Crown Prince Rupprecht on the throne, Hitler's chances of gaining power would be small. His opportunity lay in the chaos and corruption of the Republic, and until his iron grasp was finally confirmed over Germany and Austria, he continued to fear the restoration of the Hohenzollerns, Wittelsbachs or Habsburgs.

Hitler acted swiftly and ruthlessly, as he always did once his mind was made up. Confident in the prestige lent to his cause by the support of the great General Ludendorff, and in the martial spirit of his own Stormtroopers, he surrounded the beer hall with armed supporters and compelled Kahr, Lossow and Seisser at revolver-point to agree to support the Revolution. Meanwhile, Stormtroopers of another allied revolutionary group, the *Reichskriegsflagge*, had seized the War Ministry. The Bavarian government officials had no immediate alternative but to submit, and the jubilant Hitler sent them off to organize the new régime. Never doubting that they had seen the light, Hitler set out for the War Ministry.

The building in the Schönfeldstrasse was in the hands of armed stormtroopers, past whom strode the shabby, nervous figure of the future Führer. He went straight up to the commander of the new garrison and embraced him excitedly. 'This is the happiest and most wonderful day of my life!' he cried out joyfully; 'now we shall see better times – we will all work, day and night, towards our great goal – to rescue Germany from her misery and disgrace!' The brown-uniformed officer, more practical, began to ask what measures were being taken to seize the telegraph office, counter the moves of Crown Prince Rupprecht, or guard against action by the Berlin *Reichswehr*. But these difficulties were waved aside by the overjoyed agitator, confident as he was that von Lossow and von Seisser must even now be busy rallying the army and police to the cause.

The officer to whom Hitler had entrusted so vital an operation as the seizure of the War Ministry was a certain Captain Ernst Röhm. In appearance he was a formidable figure; powerfully-built with a large round head whose grim, solid features were disfigured by numberless scars from old wounds; part of the upper section of his nose had been shot away. His manner was the manner of a soldier, frank and straightforward, if somewhat brutal at times. He possessed a brilliant organisational brain, and had the front-line soldier's contempt for red-tape, 'influence', and all other obstacles placed in the way of efficiency and good management. Be-

Hitler and Röhm at Nuremberg in 1933. Within a year the doomed SA chief would suffer the inevitable penalty for overweening ambition in the Führer's Germany

The first swastika flag, displayed at Tegernsee in 1920

General von Lossow (left), von Kahr (above) and Hans von Seisser (below), the men holding the real power in Bavaria at the time of the Munich putsch

Crown Prince Rupprecht von Bayern

hind this martial exterior, however, lurked a side of his character that was hardly to be expected in the tough soldier of fortune: Röhm was a homosexual. The two men who stood in the Munich Feldherrnhalle discussing measures necessary to confirm their initial successes in the *putsch* were, as can be seen, strangely contrasted. Hitler was a visionary fanatic with an unassailable faith in his own abilities and destiny. Prone to put off decisions and then act with impulsive haste, he knew that it was he alone who could lead Germany to greatness again. His megalomania and egocentricity had already been denounced at an early meeting of his own tiny National Socialist German Workers' Party (NSDAP). He possessed a mysterious, magnetic charm which held the masses spellbound, and which could, on occasion, win over the most improbable people. There was a genuinely romantic streak in his character, and there is no doubt he would have liked to have been a successful artist. Perhaps if he had been, his unquestioning belief in his own rightness and ability might have proved a virtue, or at any rate have been regarded as an amusing eccentricity, tolerable in a man of genius.

Röhm, the tough hard soldier of fortune, undoubtedly fell under Hitler's charm. He also saw in the incipient Führer the man for Germany, but was far from being as blind a devotee of the demagogue as many other Party leaders were. On several occasions he expressed extreme dissatisfaction with Hitler's ideas and measures, but always ended with a resigned: 'Oh, but what's the use of talking! There's nobody to replace Hitler . . . we can't do without him.' Röhm believed, as too many did, that

Ernst Röhm. Hitler entrusted Captain Röhm with the seizure of the Munich War Ministry in the debacle of November 1923

pressure and persuasion could in time bring Hitler round to their way of thinking.

His own political ideas were simple and uncompromising. Born in 1887, the key moment of his life came, as he told in his memoirs *Die Geschichte eines Hochverräters* ('The Story of a Rebel'), on 23rd July 1906, when he enlisted in the German Imperial Army. From that moment he never looked back; he was a soldier before everything else. He himself stated firmly: 'I consider the world, consciously from a one-sided viewpoint, that of a soldier.' With the collapse of the German Empire in 1918, and the restriction by the terms of the Treaty of Versailles in the following year of the once invincible German army to a mere 100,000 men, Röhm saw his task before him.

The German people must be reawakened to military virtues, and their army once again assume its old primacy in the national life. But it

Hitler at the time of his trial in 1924, Röhm on his left, Ludendorff on his right

was not the restoration of the former Imperial Army he desired. The son of a Bavarian railway official, he had nothing but contempt for what he saw of the titled and monocled officers of the old order, and wanted instead a huge, highly-disciplined people's army, where ability, efficiency and merit would be fairly rewarded. So much was he wedded to his work for a resurgent German army, that his political ideas scarcely extended beyond this conception. He hated capitalists and certainly believed in the Socialist side of National Socialism, but had only vague notions of what this would involve. Later, when the brown-shirted SA had grown to a body of nearly 3,000,000 men, he was to talk of 'unit socialism' – the concept of the efficiently-organised, comradely group of the SA *trupp* or *gruppe*, all working for a common purpose, and united under an intelligently applied discipline. What that common purpose implied, however, was a question as cloudy as it was to most other National Socialists.

The Versailles settlement delivers Germany into bondage – and inadvertently promotes the growth of Nazism

It will be seen that, given the very exceptional times in which they lived and their own peculiar abilities, Hitler and Röhm made a formidable combination. Hitler had an exceptional gift of oratory, a faculty for inspiring blind devotion in his followers, and a fund of visionary social panaceas suitable for the terrible times through which the nation was passing. Röhm, on the other hand, was a ruthlessly practical man of action, who could organise a tough and highly-efficient private army, ready at once to obey any order, despite the fact that the 'army' had none of the legal sanctions of reward and punishment possessed by a regular state army. Hitler provided the will, the direction, and the 'ideas', whilst Röhm provided the men, the raw material that would take up Hitler's will and see it enforced.

The Munich putsch 1923

When, on 11th November 1918, the victorious Allies signed the armistice with Germany, millions of former officers and men of the Emperor Wilhelm II's once mighty army came marching back to a Germany thrown into chaos by military defeat and the collapse of the old government. With no clear duties to fulfil and nowhere to go, the hordes of disbanded soldiers were easy victims of frustration and ambition. For not only were there the veterans of France, who still believed they could have had 'another go', but also those divisions who had profited by the triumphant Treaty of Brest-Litovsk to march into and occupy fully a third of European Russia. The German soldier of 1918, unlike his counterpart of 1945, did not feel himself or his army to have been fairly beaten; and it was not difficult for interested parties to gain wide acceptance of the theory of 'the stab in the back', that is, of the heroic German army having been betrayed by corrupt politicians, Socialists and Jews. 'Hang the November criminals!' became the street orator's familiar cry – he was referring of course to Friedrich Ebert and the Social Democrat government which signed the 'unforgivable' Armistice. And when the Treaty of Versailles reduced the German army to frontier-guard and internal security forces, a pathetic *Reichswehr* of 100,000 men, then hundreds of thousands of jobless ex-soldiers swore that one day their time would come again.

Many of them found congenial work in the bands of *Freikorps*, private armies that sprang up to defend the Fatherland against external and internal foes. Ill-equipped, shabbily uniformed and usually unpaid, the *Freikorps* units performed prodigies of valour in the East, defending Silesia against the Poles or fighting with von der Goltz in Estonia against the Red Army. Later they helped to crush the Communist terror in Bavaria, and attempted to overthrow the Berlin government at the time of the Kapp *putsch* of 1920. The gradual stabilising of the eastern frontiers released many *Freikorps* men, but where were they to go? Unemployment was rife, and few would wish to exchange the prestige of the uniform, the comradeship and the comparative security enjoyed in a detachment of freebooters, for the misery and lack of dignity inherent on the life of an unemployed working man. The officers of course would find the fall even greater.

What was the attitude of the new *Reichswehr* to these soldiers of fortune? It must at once be stressed that the new army, emasculated as it was by the terms of the Treaty, was far from being a negligible factor, militarily and politically, in the new Republic. Under its brilliant commander, General Hans von Seeckt, standards of discipline, morale and efficiency were superlative. One effect of its drastic reduction in size was that the *Reichswehr* had the pick of the old German army from which to select its officers and men. An indication of how far the new body benefited from this is indicated by the fact that, at the height of the Imperial Army's prestige and influence, in 1912-13, twenty-four per cent of officer candidates came from families with a strong tradition of military service. Under the Republic, in 1926-27, the proportion was no less than forty-eight per cent. Even when Hitler's private Brownshirt army reached the staggering complement of 3,000,000 men, with machine gun squads and motorised corps; no one, whether regular officer or Brownshirt *Gruppenführer*, doubted for a moment that the *Reichswehr* would be more than a match for any armed force within the country. Even when Röhm contemplated armed revolution, it was on the assumption that the *Reichswehr* would not intervene. As a *Reichswehr* general put it disdainfully: 'It would take five SA to match one *Reichswehr* infantryman.'

Cavalry clear the Munich streets

Above: **1918; welcoming schoolchildren march before Germany's returning troops.**
Below: Freikorps **recruits at weapons practce before the putsch**

Above: **Armoured cars are used during the Kapp putsch of 1920.** *Below:* **SA members man a machine-gun in Munich**

Above left: General von Epp, under whom Röhm served during the overthrow of Johannes Hoffmann's Social Democratic government. *Above right:* Manfred Freiherr von Killinger. In front of him stands Captain Ehrhardt. *Below:* Heines (fourth from left, second row) in a *Freikorps* group photograph

However, the army was naturally by no means content to remain the tiny force allowed by the Versailles Treaty. Under the watchful eye of the Allied Control Commission, it had to keep outwardly to the terms of that treaty. But the threat from the resurgent Poles had to be met, and the army recognised the valuable work being accomplished by their *confrères* of the *Freikorps*. In many cases *Freikorps* members were taken surreptitiously under the *Reichswehr* wing, given secret training, financed and armed from funds granted with the connivance of Ministers of the Republic. This 'secret army' became knows as the 'Black *Reichswehr*', and acted both as a hidden wing of the regular army and a valuable pool of human material for recruiting.

It was to this Black *Reichswehr* that Captain Röhm, lately a Company Commander in the 10th Bavarian Infantry Regiment, naturally graduated. In 1919 he was a sincere supporter of the Bavarian monarchy, and served under General von Epp when the latter with a detachment of the Bavarian *Reichswehr* overthrew the Social Democrat government of Johannes Hoffmann, and set up a right-wing régime under von Kahr; it was Kahr's government, as we saw earlier, that Hitler attempted to coerce into accepting his leadership in the abortive 'beer hall *putsch*.'

Already in the previous autumn, Röhm had made Hitler's acquaintance and the (as yet) tiny German Workers' Party (DAP). Impressed by Hitler's personality and oratorical powers, and also with his possible use as an instrument to bring the workers over from Marxism, Röhm and some of his friends from the *Freikorps* (Heydebreck, Pfeffer von Salomon, Heines, von Killinger) joined the DAP. They gave the struggling movement new strength, as well as directing it towards more military and nationalistic goals. Not only this, but Röhm was able, in his capacity as a regular officer to allocate secret *Reichswehr* funds – and later, arms – to the penniless party.

Röhm remained on the staff of General von Epp, commander of the 7th Division, stationed in Munich. The General was more than sympathetic to right-wing movements of this kind, and supplies were freely available in such cases. What this might entail will be apparent when it is realised that Röhm was entrusted at this time with the formation of a local section of the 'Black *Reichswehr*', the 'Bavarian Home Guard'. As secret 'Quartermaster' to the 'Black *Reichswehr*', he was supplied from the 7th Division's arsenals with 169 light and eleven heavy guns, 760 machine guns, 21,351 rifles, carbines and revolvers, 300,000 grenades, and 8,000,000 rounds of ammunition.

In the summer of 1921, however, the Berlin government abolished the so-called Bavarian Home Guard, and Röhm now began to concentrate all his energies on an expansion of the increasingly vocal Nazi party. Though they were soon to disagree on the role such a body should play in the Party, both Hitler and Röhm were agreed that a 'strongarm' force was necessary to protect meetings from being broken up by Communist and other rowdy opposition elements. Though there was at all times a genuine need for such protection, it was not long before the Nazi 'guards' began to act in as truculent and brutal a manner as their opponents.

Röhm began at once to organise these thugs on a more regular basis. From the men of 19th Trench Mortar Company, he detailed a group of burly veterans under a Captain Streck to deal with over-vociferous or violent opponents of the Party at meetings. This group was thinly disguised under the title of the Party's 'Gymnastics and Sport' section, and formed the germ of the largest private army perhaps the world has ever seen. Their efficiency was soon to be tested in the first of innumerable ferocious brawls that became a fairly regular feature

The SA prepares

of Nazi meetings.

On 4th November 1921 several hundred Communists tried to break up a meeting addressed by Hitler. After a violent struggle, the Communist invaders were ejected. Two men particularly distinguished themselves in this Homeric conflict: his friend Hess and ex-convict bodyguard Emil Maurice.

So it was that at this time a properly-organised strong-arm detachment was set up. The 'Gymnastic and Sports' section became officially known as the *Sturmabteilung* – the 'Storm Detachment' – known generally under the initials SA. It was Röhm, with the backing of the *Reichswehr*, who organized this body into a para-military detachment. He himself of course was still a serving officer, and so could not take direct command. Nevertheless, he transferred into the SA officers from the No 2 Naval Brigade, a unit that had served under a *Freikorps* officer, Captain Ehrhardt, in the abortive Kapp *putsch* of 1920. The first commander of the SA was a young officer, Lieutenant Johann Ulrich Klintsch.

Money and arms were freely available to this new force, but all was not as satisfactory from Hitler's point of view as it might have been. For a condition of this injection of army men and material was clearly that the SA came very much more under the aegis of the *Reichswehr*. This was precisely the aim of Ernst Röhm, who wished to create a secret Reich militia, that could one day (when the iniquitous provisions of the Versailles Treaty had been overthrown) take its place openly alongside the regular army. Hitler, on the other hand, hated the idea of any section of the Party not being wholly under his command. But, owing so much as he

Hermann Göring as fighter ace. Hitler appointed him to the SA command as part of his scheme to take the SA out of the control of its army paymasters

did to *Reichswehr* support, he was obliged for the present to submit to the existing situation.

The SA soon began to develop an *esprit de corps* of its own, with squads rivalling each other for smartness of turnout and efficiency at drill. In his memoirs, the naïve and irrepressible Nazi Kurt Lüdecke describes how he set about forming such a troop. Being fortunate enough in those hard times to have a reasonable private income, he was able to offer free meals (a great inducement) and equipment to volunteers. By the end of 1922 he had 100 men under him, mostly students and unemployed. Arms were stored in Lüdecke's flat. 'Not much was new, but all was in fine condition. Germany was filled with the debris of the war – uniforms, implements, even arms which had been sold by the soldiers or stolen after the armistice from the immense army depots. It was easy to get military goods, but not to get them undamaged. I solved the problem by keeping two Jewish dealers constantly on the lookout for what we needed.' Through appropriate connexions, he was able to use a *Reichswehr* drill-hall for exercise.

Throughout this time, Röhm, from his position of influence on the staff, kept a protective eye on the infant SA. Indeed, the twenty-five-year old Klintsch was little more than a puppet. Thus, in December 1922 Röhm used army funds to purchase the newspaper *Voelkischer Beobachter* for the Party; it appeared twice weekly until 1923, when it became a daily. Again, when Hitler's men caused a violent disruption of a Communist May Day assembly in Munich in 1923, it was Röhm's efforts and influence in high places that saved Hitler from arrest and the Party from dissolution.

Nevertheless, Hitler's overriding concern was to detach the SA from its army paymasters and bring it completely under the Party authority. With a view to accomplishing this, and also to replace Lieutenant Klintsch with a more able commander, Hitler appointed to the SA command a prized new recruit to his cause. This was the former air ace, the brutal, jovial, drug-addict Hermann Göring. An added advantage was that Göring possessed private means, and so Hitler did not have to worry about his salary. Despite Göring's appointment, however, the SA continued very much under army patronage and control. Its separation from the Party was stressed by the fact that it was linked with non-Party *Freikorps* units *(Freikorps Oberland, Freikorps Rossbach*, and *Reichsflagge)* under the blanket title of the *Kampfbund*, run by a Colonel Kriebel. Hitler was discontented, but could do nothing. He could not pay the SA himself, nor could the Party do without its protective force.

To compensate for the near-independence of the SA, Hitler formed a personal bodyguard of his own in March 1923; firstly under the superseded Klintsch, and then two months later under a rough named Berchthold. This select force anticipated to some extent the formation of the SS as an élite body, loyal only to Hitler himself.

Now came Hitler's attempt to gain power by force in the Bürgerbräukeller *putsch*, already described. As we saw, the faithful Röhm, when it came to conflict, appeared in the open and played his part in seizing and holding with his Stormtroopers the War Ministry. But when the *Reichswehr* moved several battalions of troops into the city, and a rather grotesque march headed by Hitler and Ludendorff to relieve Röhm had been thwarted by the police, Röhm realised he had no option and surrendered.

The end of the *putsch* must have seemed to many to be the end of the National Socialist movement. Hitler himself was tried and sentenced to five years' imprisonment – commuted later to less than nine months, however. Most of 1924 he spent in the old fortress, now a prison, of Landsberg, writing the turgid 'Scripture' of the Nazi faithful, *Mein Kampf* ('My Struggle'). Hitler's original proposed title was: *Four and a Half Years of Struggle against Lies, Stupidity and Cowardice* – the title in itself a rather pathetic revelation of early fears and grievances. Like many revolutionaries, Hitler was obsessed with the idea that 'they' were against him, that 'they' could not recognise genius when they saw it, and that a silent conspiracy existed within 'The Establishment' to hold back brilliant young men with dazzlingly original ideas that threatened their stuffy security.

During the war he had never risen beyond the rank of corporal, and he had not shone at school. In 1931 he wrote: 'I was not the child of well-to-do parents, did not enjoy a university education, but was brought up in the hardest school of life, in want and

The revolutionary during his imprisonment. The Landsberg Fortress interlude gave him time to write his testament, *Mein Kampf*

misery. The superficial world never enquires what a man has learned, and even less what he really knows, but, as a rule, unfortunately only what he can show certificates for. The fact that I had learned more than many of our intellectuals was never heeded, but only the fact that I had no certificates.' As the historian Konrad Heiden commented: 'The lack of certificates [was] the ever-open intellectual wound. One is tempted to wonder how often Hitler looked suspiciously over his shoulder to see whether all the Doctors and Lieutenants were not whispering behind his back.'

Again, as is often the case with political revolutionaries, he affected to despise those the social order of the time placed above him. 'These *gentlemen* – these counts and generals – they won't do anything. *I* shall. I *alone*.' So he declared in 1922, after the failure of a right-wing coup.

It is not inconsistent with such a character – common enough in times of social upheaval and unrest – that when Hitler later gained power and prestige, he found he really rather liked to be surrounded by distinguished general officers and smart young noblemen in spruce uniforms. Then he could unbend and relax a little, for after all, these fine gentry were dancing attendance on *him*. He even began to contrast their polished manners and elegant appearance with the rough, uncultured ways of his old companions of the SA. Captain Röhm always spoke harshly to the point, not troubling to disguise the fact that at times he was making threats in order to have his way. His coarse, direct nature disdained the social graces, and his interests were confined to matters of war alone. How very different from the urbane, cultured Minister of Defence, Werner von Blomberg – who was, moreover a real General, commander of a sparklingly

The 'Counts and Generals' of the old school, whom Hitler affected to despise

Werner von Blomberg. Hitler's covert regard for the titled and educated led him to draw comparisons unfavourable to Röhm – particularly with the Minister of Defence, Blomberg

efficient modern army, not of a rabble of brown-shirted street fighters! Röhm sensed the comparison, and resented it.

For Ernst Röhm too had a fierce hatred of titled officers and of the old order in general. Unlike Hitler, he never modified this attitude. Where Hitler found security in identifying himself as the spirit incarnate of the invincible Germanic *Volk*, Röhm perhaps found his in the creation of a ruthlessly efficient and established military force, where attention to duty and hard work were the only requisites for high rank. Whence came Röhm's jealousy and dislike of the governing order? He was after all an officer himself, and one entrusted with important tasks by his superiors.

There was, however, another facet of Röhm's character that we have already touched on which made him a pariah to most of the officer class: his homosexuality. His 'depravity' was all too notorious, and barred him effectively from mingling on social terms with his fellow-officers. He held in contempt the bigoted attitudes of the times: 'Those hypocrites! . . . Homosexuality isn't a sufficient reason for removing an able and honest leader from any position, so long as he is discreet, such a more or less 'natural' abnormality is nobody's business. I do as I please within my own four walls, like anyone else . . . But to hell with pederasty.' And again: 'Nothing is more false than this so-called social ethic. I declare straight away that I am not one of the morally upright and entertain no ambition to become one. I will on no account be reckoned among the "moral men", since I learned by experience that the "morals" of these "moral men" do not as a rule go very far . . .'

Thus two men, both with deep-felt grievances against the world in which they lived, performed mighty works together, and then, with success, grew apart. For Hitler's brilliant achievements, culminating in his attaining the Chancellery of the Reich in 1933, placed him in his own and everybody else's eyes above those lofty generals and princes whose position had before seemed so remote and unattainable. Röhm, on the other hand, found that despite his position as Chief of Staff of the 3,000,000 strong *Sturmabteilungen*, he was no nearer proving his position in the real army than before. For the majority of *Reichswehr* officers, from Field-Marshal Hindenburg down, looked on him with undisguised contempt and disgust. Hitler could compensate for his own weakness and insecurity; Röhm could not. So the seeds of division between the two old revolutionary comrades existed from early days; one day they were to sow a terrible crop.

But to return to the failure and aftermath of the 1923 *putsch*. Hitler,

Hindenburg disliked Röhm intensely. Most of the armed forces chiefs did likewise

The racial theorist Alfred Rosenberg, appointed party leader during Hitler's stay in prison – mainly because his inefficiency would prevent his becoming a serious rival to Hitler

as we have seen, was sent to prison. Göring, the head of the SA (for Röhm of course helped to direct it only from his position as a regular officer on the Munich *Reichswehr* staff), escaped to Austria and later went into exile in Sweden. There he underwent a cure for drug addiction, and stayed until a political amnesty in Germany allowed him to return there in 1927.

Röhm was at last obliged to leave the regular army, having been convicted of open rebellion, and was imprisoned for a short time in the Stadelheim Prison in Munich. He was soon after released on parole, but emerged to find the Party seemingly destroyed beyond redemption. The *Kampfbund* (the front organisation for the SA and its Freikorps fellow units) was dissolved and proscribed by law, the Party newspaper, the *Voelkischer Beobachter*, was banned, and a jail sentence of up to fifteen years hung over the head of anyone attempting to revive the Nazi Party.

Nonetheless, the Party was not regarded with complete disfavour by all in authority, and a thinly disguised remnant continued its activities under the leadership of a misguided racial theorist, Alfred Rosenberg. Hitler had deliberately chosen him to hold the vacant post on the grounds of his incompetence: he feared that he might emerge from Landsberg to find a rival in his place.

On his release from prison, Röhm at once contacted Hitler and obtained permission to try and revive the *Kampfbund*, banned as we have seen by the Bavarian government. Hitler agreed, perhaps feeling he had little choice, and Röhm at once set to work. Now for the first time able to concentrate all his energies on the organization, he very soon began to obtain startling results. Drawing on the one hand on his very considerable organizational powers, and on the other on his contacts with the *Reichswehr* and former *Freikorps* leaders, it was not long before the resuscitated *Kampfbund* (disguised under the name of

Frontbann) claimed some 30,000 followers. Arms and uniforms were supplied from various clandestine sources and it was at this time that the notorious Brownshirts appeared. They originally formed part of a consignment intended for troops serving in German East Africa. They then came into the hands of a *Freikorps* leader, Lieutenant Rossbach (a homosexual and friend of Röhm), who in turn supplied them to the *Frontbann*.

The political structure of the Nazi Party was in a state of disorganization, largely as a result of Hitler's absence, and Röhm began to demand that the *Frontbann* should, as the military arm, be autonomous and so free to concentrate on the task of building up a national military movement. To accomplish this, he suggested a division of responsibilities, with Hitler heading the political side and Ludendorff (the nominal head of the *Frontbann*) the military. But Hitler was as adamant as ever that all sections of the Party, including the *Frontbann*, should be entirely under his sole leadership. And as Ludendorff despised Hitler after what he considered his cowardly and incompetent handling of the Beer hall *putsch*, he in turn refused to co-operate with him.

It was at this point that the Bavarian government decided to step in, and arrested some of Röhm's chief lieutenants for their illegal activities. On the grounds that Hitler was implicated, his commutation of sentence was deferred until December of 1924. Realising he was in no position to assert his views on the relation of the *Frontbann* to the Party so long as he was in confinement, Hitler delayed making a final decision until his release.

At a Party conference on 27th February 1925, Hitler insisted that the *Frontbann* come entirely within the Party. Röhm refused, pointing out how successful the military wing had become, and that this success might well be jeopardised if the existing organisation and discipline were inter-

Rossbach, homosexual and friend of Röhm, who channelled the Brownshirts to the *Frontbann*

fered with. The argument raged for two months, with Hitler adamant and Röhm vainly trying to reason with him. On 16th April Röhm presented Hitler with a reasoned memorandum of his case, and appealed to him to concede so vital a point for the sake of the *Frontbann's* successful future. Hitler rejected this demand out of hand, and the following day Röhm wrote offering to resign from the organisation. Not receiving the courtesy of a reply, he sent in his resignation on 30th April. Hitler still made no overt reaction, but Röhm's letter of resignation was published in the *Voelkischer Beobachter*. Hitler had in fact accomplished his aim; he would rather have no 'military' wing to the Party than one that was not wholly under his command.

It must seem strange that Röhm should have submitted so meekly, when apparently arguing from a position of strength. The *Frontbann* itself, after all, was prepared to back him in the struggle. The answer lies in part in Röhm's curious relationship with Hitler, and in part in the increas-

The French evacuation of the Ruhr helped to reduce discontent, making matters more difficult for the Nazi movement

ing weakness of the *Frontbann* itself. Whilst he was outspoken in condemning Hitler's vacillation (what he termed *Osterreichische Schlamperei* – 'Austian sloppiness') – arbitrary rule, and flagrant unacknowledged borrowing of other people's ideas, he nevertheless confessed himself in part dominated by Hitler's magnetic personality. 'But nobody is perfect', he remarked, 'and he has his great qualities. Apparently there's nobody else who would do better than he.' Alongside this very real admiration lay an occasionally-expressed fear of the 'sword of Damocles' that hung suspended over him all his days; the tacit threat that Hitler could always destroy him because of his weakness. Of course, this in turn worked the other way too; Röhm felt a pathetic appreciation of the fact that Hitler was one person who appeared to accept him for what he was and *not* allow Röhm's morals to affect his (Hitler's) respect for his abilities. Hitler, until it suited him otherwise, always referred to Röhm's homosexual tastes as an 'entirely private matter'.

According to Röhm himself, his abnormality had only started in 1924. However this may be, by 1925 the matter became public through an unpleasant scandal widely reported in the newspapers. He (rather foolishly, it would seem) took to court for alleged theft a Berlin gigolo, Hermann Siegesmund. The question of the crime itself was unimportant; what stirred public interest was that it turned out that Röhm had picked up this young man at the Berlin Marienkasino, taken him up to his room, and proposed an obscene act to him.

Aside from all this, however, the *Frontbann* was going through a difficult period. The economic situation which, when bad caused an immediate influx of recruits to the *Frontbann*, now took a temporary course for the better. The French evacuation of the Ruhr, too, gave the Republic a boost in Nationalist eyes; and divisions and the partial suppression of the Party detracted from the 'military' sector's raison d'être. In addition, General von Seeckt and the *Reichswehr* refused to accept the *Frontbann's* proposed link with the army. Hitler's forcing of Röhm's resignation was in reality the straw that broke the camel's back, and Röhm had little alternative but to leave.

For a while the disillusioned ex-Captain worked as an engineer; then he took advantage of an offer from Bolivia and set off for La Paz, where he became military adviser to the government.

Röhm, Brownshirt chief

Röhm had transferred command of the *Frontbann* by an order of 1st May, 1925 to Count von Helldorf. However, this gesture had little practical meaning, as Hitler was resolved to break altogether with the *Frontbann*. In fact it was a year and a half before a new para-military body came officially into being again. Clearly it would be necessary to revive the SA or a comparable body before long, but the Leader was in no hurry. Firstly, he wanted to make certain that he had re-established his control over the Party before recreating so potentially divisive a body. Secondly, an SA revived immediately after the break with the *Frontbann* might give people within and without the Party cause to think it was merely the *Frontbann* under a different name (the *Frontbann* was, after all, a disguised continuation of the *Kampfbund*). A continued *Frontbann* under whatever name would have meant a standing threat to Hitler's absolute authority, engaged as he was in establishing control over the Party.

Nonetheless, some sort of protection was necessary for the Party's work, and Hitler encouraged local Party units to organise their own SA, provided they were recruited from local Party members and did not bear arms. This meant of course that these so-called SA detachments were not organised on a uniform basis, and that such as they were they came under the entire control of local Party leaders. As the whole was intended from the beginning as a temporary measure, however, the leadership was not unduly worried.

At last the time came when Hitler felt he could safely revive the SA on a permanent basis. Nevertheless, it was to be severely modified to obviate against any possibility of a revival of its claim to independence. On 1st October 1926 Captain Franz Pfeffer von Salomon was appointed the first chief of the new SA, *Oberste SA Führer*. Von Salomon appeared to agree with Hitler's idea that the SA should come entirely under the Party wing, and at first all went well. The new body was deliberately isolated from the army and other military organisations, and was in addition forbidden to carry arms. The men were trained in boxing, wrestling, ju-jitsu and other sports with a view to fulfilling their prime purpose, that of acting as the 'fist' while the Party proper acted as the 'brain'.

This situation did not last long. With its own hierarchy, organisation, training programme and revived *esprit de corps*, the SA soon began to think of itself as a corporate entity again. The process was speeded up by the effect of Pfeffer von Salomon's personality. While agreeing in principle with the idea of the SA's subordination to the Party, the instincts of the old officer soon revealed themselves. A stickler for order and discipline (he had the military man's love of interminable abbreviations in his directives), he introduced a number of ex-*Freikorps* officers who also imported army notions of corporate loyalty and obedience.

Certainly all seemed well at first. The SA order of 1926 declared obediently that the 'SA is a means to an end', and in June of the following year it was decreed that only Party members were eligible to join the SA. But gradually Pfeffer's military instincts began to assert themselves and, like Röhm, he began to demand a measure of independence for his organisation, while always recognising Hitler's supremacy in the leadership. Hitler announced that no order signed by the *Oberste SA Führer* was valid unless also countersigned by himself. Von Salomon ignored this move; and indeed he displayed in general a reprehensible lack of deference to the illustrious leader, both he and his officers not having a very high opinion of the civilian sector of the Party.

When the beginnings of the effect of

SA *Gruppenführer* Ernst marches before Röhm

Count von Helldorf, to whom Röhm transferred command on his resignation

the 1929 Wall Street crash were felt in Germany, unemployed men (mainly young ones) began to flock into the movement, eager for SA free meals. By 1930 the SA numbered perhaps 75,000 men, and Captain von Salomon may well have felt that the commander of such a body was entitled to a measure of independence in deciding policy. He also began to announce in public that the SA was the vehicle for the full scale German army of the future – the notion that had cost Röhm his position.

Among the greatly swollen bands of Brownshirts under von Salomon's command, there was however one section whose devotion to Hitler was unshakable. Though small in numbers, its tight discipline and smart black uniforms attracted favourable attention out of all proportion to its size. Sworn to undying loyalty to the Führer, the members of the *Schutzstaffeln* nurtured an exclusive pride in the special rôle allotted them. And, just as the title *Sturmabteilungen* was universally shortened to SA, so *Schutzstaffeln* became SS.

The history of this body dates back to March 1923, when a special *Stabswache* (Headquarters Guard) was formed to protect Hitler. Three of its original members were Emil Maurice, Hitler's chauffeur, Ulrich Graf, a butcher and wrestler, and Christian Weber, a beer hall 'bouncer'. It had been led by *Freikorps* officers from the Ehrhardt Brigade (involved in the 1920 Kapp *putsch*), but these Captain Ehrhardt later withdrew. A new bodyguard was accordingly formed, this time it was termed the *Stosstrupp* ('Assault Squad') *Adolf Hitler*. Nearly all its members were working- or lower middle-class, and bound together by a blind devotion to the godlike Adolf Hitler. However, the *Stosstrupp*, in common with all other Nazi bodies, was banned after the beer hall *putsch* and obliged to come to life under a new name.

In April 1925 the *Schutzstaffeln* came into being. Its member No 168, who

Hitler put the revived SA under the direction of Pfeffer von Salomon who was at pains to instil the military virtues of order and discipline

The Sturmabteilung, originally disguised as a sports club of the infant Nazi Party, achieved notoriety among the Freikorps of the early 1920s. Similar paramilitary groups fought as the private armies of the different political parties in the earliest days of the Weimar Republic; each chose a distinctive military uniform. The colour adopted by the SA was brown. Its head gear was modelled on the ski cap of the elite mountain riflemen of the Kaiser's army. The high laced boots were legacies of the trenches, while the Sam Brown belt was a borrowing from the British army

The Leibstandarte (Body Guard Regiment) came into being in 1927 as Hitler's Stabswache (Staff Guard) and was given its new title in 1934 in recognition of the loyalty shown to the Führer by the SS during the 'blood purge'. The Leibstandarte was originally the only permanent unit of the SS, and eventually it became the famous 1st SS Panzer Division. This SS-Mann (Private) is wearing the all-black SS uniform and the piped collar patch and shoulder straps appropriate to his rank. The cuff band was worn by all ranks

Behind Hitler are Graf and Weber, both moustached. They were original members of Hitler's bodyguard, instituted in 1923. *Below:* Emil Maurice, organizer of the bodyguard officers

joined shortly after, was an insignificant looking bespectacled schoolmaster's son named Heinrich Himmler. Within a year he had been appointed deputy Führer of the SS, and in January 1929 he was made *Reichsführer* SS. Blindly loyal to his Führer, Himmler was the ideal tool to keep a check on the unwieldy SA. In November 1930 Hitler announced: 'The task of the SS is primarily to carry out police duties within the party.' SS methods of acting on these instructions were not over-scrupulous. As early as 1925 they had started keeping dossiers on party members as a check on their loyalty; but it was not until 1931 that this began to be done on any very large or efficient scale. For it was in that year that Himmler's most brilliant and evil lieutenant joined him: Reinhard Heydrich.

But in the twenties the SS was still a barely considered factor in the Party, though their increasingly self-conscious assertion of their position as the élite of the movement attracted

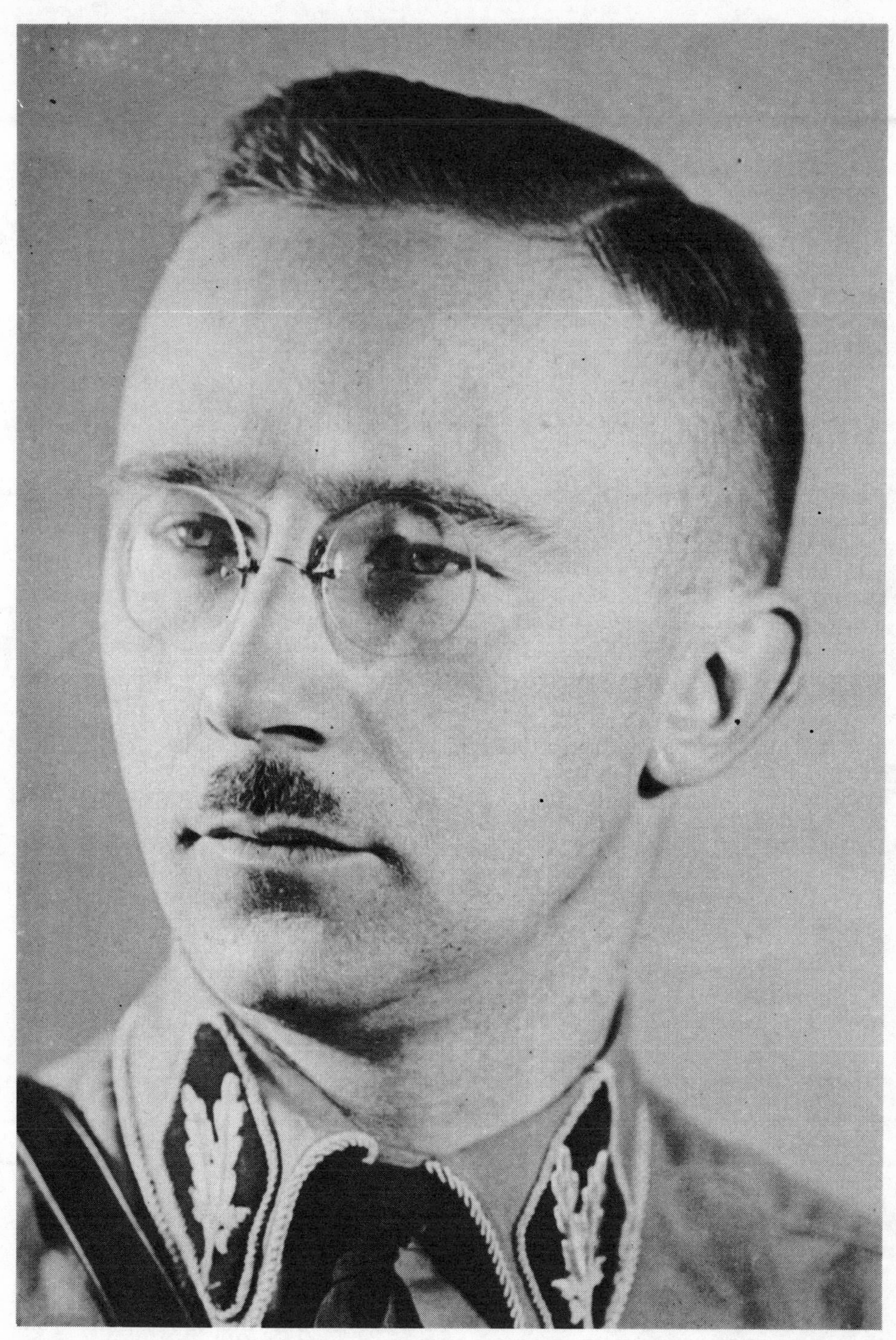

Himmler is appointed *Reichsführer* SS in January 1929

notice; and in 1930 Pfeffer von Salomon complained that the SS was attempting to entice into its own ranks valued SA men. Himmler was a friend and admirer of Röhm, having served under his command in the Munich War Ministry during the beer hall *putsch*. He corresponded with the exile in Bolivia, writing with pride on one occasion that the SS was now nearly 2,000 strong. What Himmler's friendship was worth was soon to be seen.

Towards the end of 1930, Hitler declared the SS independent within the SA, awarding it its own military organisation and notorious black uniforms. Its duties were to watch the Party and act against any backslidings, and protect the precious person of the Führer.

In the same year the conflict between the *Oberste SA Führer* von Salomon and Hitler came to a climax in much the same way and over much the same issues that Hitler had broken with Röhm five years before. Von Salomon and most of his officers resented Hitler's constant interference in SA affairs, and his continual assertion of the Party's supremacy in all things. They also objected to Hitler's policy of 'legality' (a point Röhm was to take up later). For ever since the conspicuous failure of the beer hall *putsch*, Hitler had insisted on sticking to a policy of attempting to 'capture' the state through gaining votes in elections, and by winning over by any means possible the 'citadels of power' within the country, i.e. the army, the police, industry, the federal *Land* governments, etc. Hitler's rejection of armed revolution as a means of gaining power was not due, as may be imagined, to any antipathy to shedding blood.

Hitler's insistence on 'peaceful' attainment of the goal of power by means of gaining the support of sections of the power structure of the state was confirmed by the pitiful collapse of the Munich *putsch* in 1923. Even there he had counted on the police and army being with him; for, as an old soldier himself, he shared none of the romantic illusions of civilian 'armchair' revolutionaries; that is, that armed mobs of devoted fanatics are capable of defeating well-trained regular troops. He knew, as better soldiers than himself (such as Röhm) did not, that the *Reichswehr* was more than a match for all the Brownshirts in Germany, whatever the odds.

Dr Karl Lüger, Burgomaster of Vienna (centre of the three passengers), was taken by Hitler as an object lesson on gaining and keeping power

It was in Imperial Vienna before the war that Hitler had first learned this lesson. He had observed and admired the then burgomaster of Vienna, Dr Karl Lüger, whose oratory and political *savoir faire* had given him complete control over the grand old city. Hitler observed that Lüger 'was quick to make use of all available means for winning the support of long-established institutions so as to be able to derive the greatest possible advantage for his movement from those old sources of power.'

With this brand of *Realpolitik* the SA

was of course very much out of sympathy. If they were not the armed vanguard of revolution, then to what purpose were all their drillings, manoeuvres and secret arms dumps? True, they were still faced with the considerable task of protecting their Party's inalienable right to hold meetings and speeches, and of setting about anyone else who tried to do the same thing, but was that enough? To the old officers from the *Freikorps* who remembered heady days in Silesia and Munich, the whole purpose of their increasingly large and efficient military machine seemed removed. Moreover, what would be the rôle of the SA once the Nazi revolution was accomplished? The answer to this vital question was left open – until a year after the triumph of National Socialism it came to be written in letters of blood.

The result of this apparently unresolvable conflict of views was the resignation, in August 1930, of Pfeffer von Salomon as Chief of the SA. This was followed almost at once by a far more serious threat to Hitler's domination of the Party. Captain Walter Stennes, SA *Gruppenführer* for all of East Germany, thoroughly discontented with what he regarded as the Party's neglect of the SA and with its apparent swing away from the strong proletarian and socialist element in Nazism, sent a firm demand for a greater measure of SA independence from Party control, and for Stormtroopers to be paid on a proper basis. When these demands were rejected, the Berlin SA refused to work for the Party and broke into Goebbels's headquarters, completely wrecking them. Goebbels, the Party *Gauleiter* for Berlin-Brandenburg, had to flee ignominiously. Non-Nazi Germany was delighted at all these upheavals, though in fact this stage of the Stennes revolt soon subsided. Hitler flew to Berlin, and by the exercise of his brilliant personality managed to persuade the rank and file of SA to return to their duties. Stennes, though still

Walter Stennes, SA chief for East Germany, demanded greater autonomy. This was refused and for a time the Berlin SA declined to work for the Party

Röhm returns to Germany and is given the post of *Stabschef*

discontented, was too powerful to remove at this stage and remained in office.

The disadvantages of the existing position of the SA were now thrust upon Hitler's notice. On the one hand he required the organisation to be completely subordinated to the political Party and consequently intervened at every turn with the SA high command, hampering their freedom of movement and independence. On the other hand, a leaderless and disorganised SA could, as the Stennes affair had just shown, result in this important wing of the Party becoming completely out of control. What Hitler needed, he saw clearly, was a strong and capable SA chief who could keep the local units under control, and yet who was bound absolutely by ties of loyalty to the Führer. Where could such a man be found?

There was only one man with these qualities, and he was at that moment on the other side of the world. Before Ernst Röhm had left for Bolivia in 1928, he had become reconciled to Hitler despite the latter's ungrateful treatment of him, and assured him that if ever he had need of him he need only telegraph. Röhm's ability none could doubt, and his loyalty had stood up to tests few others would have submitted to.

If proof of this were required, it appeared in what followed. No sooner did Röhm receive Hitler's urgent plea, than he returned at once across the Atlantic, eager to take up his duties once more. Doubtless he did not miss La Paz overmuch, and he had written letters to friends in Germany lamenting the loneliness of a city 'where they know nothing of this sort of love'. He arrived to find Hitler overjoyed to see his old comrade once more. (So far as he was capable of real affection, Hitler does seem to have felt a real friendship for the battered old warrior.

He and Amann, his publisher, were the only people to whom he used the familiar *du*).

After Pfeffer von Salomon's resignation Hitler had taken the precaution of nominating himself as head of the SA, and demanded a personal oath of loyalty to him from all its members. This of course was intended to prevent any further chance of a rival's presenting himself at the head of the unruly organisation. The effective chief, however, would be Röhm, and he was appointed to his post on 1st January 1931. The office of *Oberste SA Führer* was abolished, and Röhm became instead Chief of Staff, *Stabschef*.

This appointment greatly angered powerful personalities within the Party. Hermann Göring, back in Germany after a period of exile following the beer hall *putsch*, had long coveted the post. As the only other member of the inner Nazi ruling circle with a distinguished war record, he had marked down the SA leadership for himself. (Göring had been an Air Force fighter pilot in Richthofen's immortal 'Circus'; and after the great ace's death became his successor, being awarded the highest German decoration for bravery, the *Pour le mérite*). Goebbels, too, saw in a revivified and efficient SA a threat to his own schemes for gaining control of Berlin. The jealousy and hatred of these two vicious and unprincipled men – Göring in particular – was now to stalk silently behind the new *Stabschef SA*. Their first move was to stir up the unstable and excitable Stennes, now temporarily quiet after his agitation of the previous September.

This was not a difficult task. As had been intended, Röhm set about his new task with brisk efficiency. One of his first acts, whose necessity had already

Dr Goebbels and many others in the Nazi hierarchy saw Röhm's appointment as a threat to their own aims

Above: The offices of *Der Angriff,* Goebbels's newspaper. The printing house was seized again in Stennes's second SA revolt. *Below:* Stennes's replacement, Edmund Heines ; murderer and intimate of Röhm

been evidenced by the unruly behaviour of the Eastern SA, was to purge inefficient or independent-minded officers and replace them with nominees of his own. This in itself was clearly likely to spark off discontent and unrest, but the ill-feeling was greatly aggravated by the fact that many of Röhm's replacements were notorious members of his homosexual 'inner circle'. Stennes, at Göring's prompting, appealed to Hitler against Röhm's action; but Hitler not only ignored the appeal, but had Stennes recalled from Berlin to take up an office post at Party Head-Headquarters in Munich. This was in April 1931. Stennes refused to obey.

Now Stennes came out once again in

open revolt. Every SA unit east of the Elbe telegraphed to Munich protesting at Stennes's transfer. SA men burst into the Party headquarters in Berlin and occupied them, and others also seized the printing house of *Der Angriff*, Dr Goebbels's newspaper. Goebbels himself had to flee once again; ironically, as he had begun to favour Stennes's line. He was not anxious to see Röhm seize a major power situation near the Führer, nor did he wish to see an efficiently centralised SA, as this might well mean that he, as political chief (*Gauleiter*) in Berlin, would have that much less control over the hitherto decentralised local SA.

Once again, however, Hitler acted and showed how little backing within the Party a dissident chieftain could count on. Ordinary members believed Hitler could do no wrong, and blamed backslidings and troubles on subordinate leaders or the Party bureaucracy. An article in the *Vöelkischer Beobachter* by the Führer threatened with expulsion all who supported Stennes. Then, at Hitler's request, the Berlin police moved in and ejected the rebel SA men from the occupied Party buildings. This caused a great deal of irreverent mirth among non-Nazis, for the Party had always affected to despise the ordinary civil police, possessing as it did its own private SA police! Finally, Hitler himself went once again to Berlin and, as before, appealed over the heads of the officers to the rank-and-file SA men. As ever, the appeal was successful and Stennes and his immediate associates found themselves isolated. The revolt collapsed as swiftly as its predecessor in the previous autumn.

Stennes was dismissed from his post and replaced by Edmund Heines, one of Röhm's homosexual aides (he was also a convicted murderer). A purge of the eastern *Gruppe* was then initiated by Röhm, and conducted by the SS under a certain Friedrich-Wilhelm Krüger and Lieutenant Schultz (also previously implicated in a murder). The SS was playing its part as the Party police, a rôle that Stennes had recognised to the extent of taking measures against it.

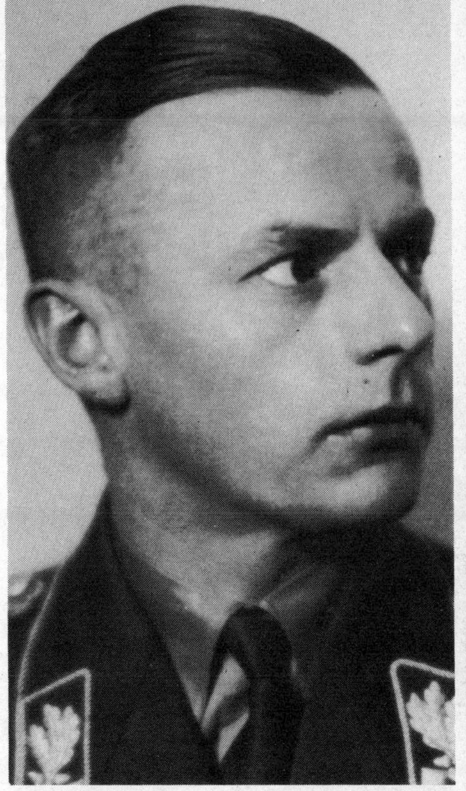

Friedrich-Wilhelm Krüger who with Lieutenant Schultz carried out the purge of the eastern *Gruppe*

Walter Stennes was to have a further brush with the *Schutzstaffeln*. With the Nazi accession to power in 1933, he was locked up by the SS and horribly tortured in one of their terror stations. They had resolved upon his death, but he was rescued at the intervention of the *Reichswehr* (who were interested in his fate as an ex-officer) and smuggled out of the country via Holland by Göring's police. He accepted a commission to reorganise the Chinese police in Shanghai, and ended up commanding Chiang Kai-shek's bodyguard.

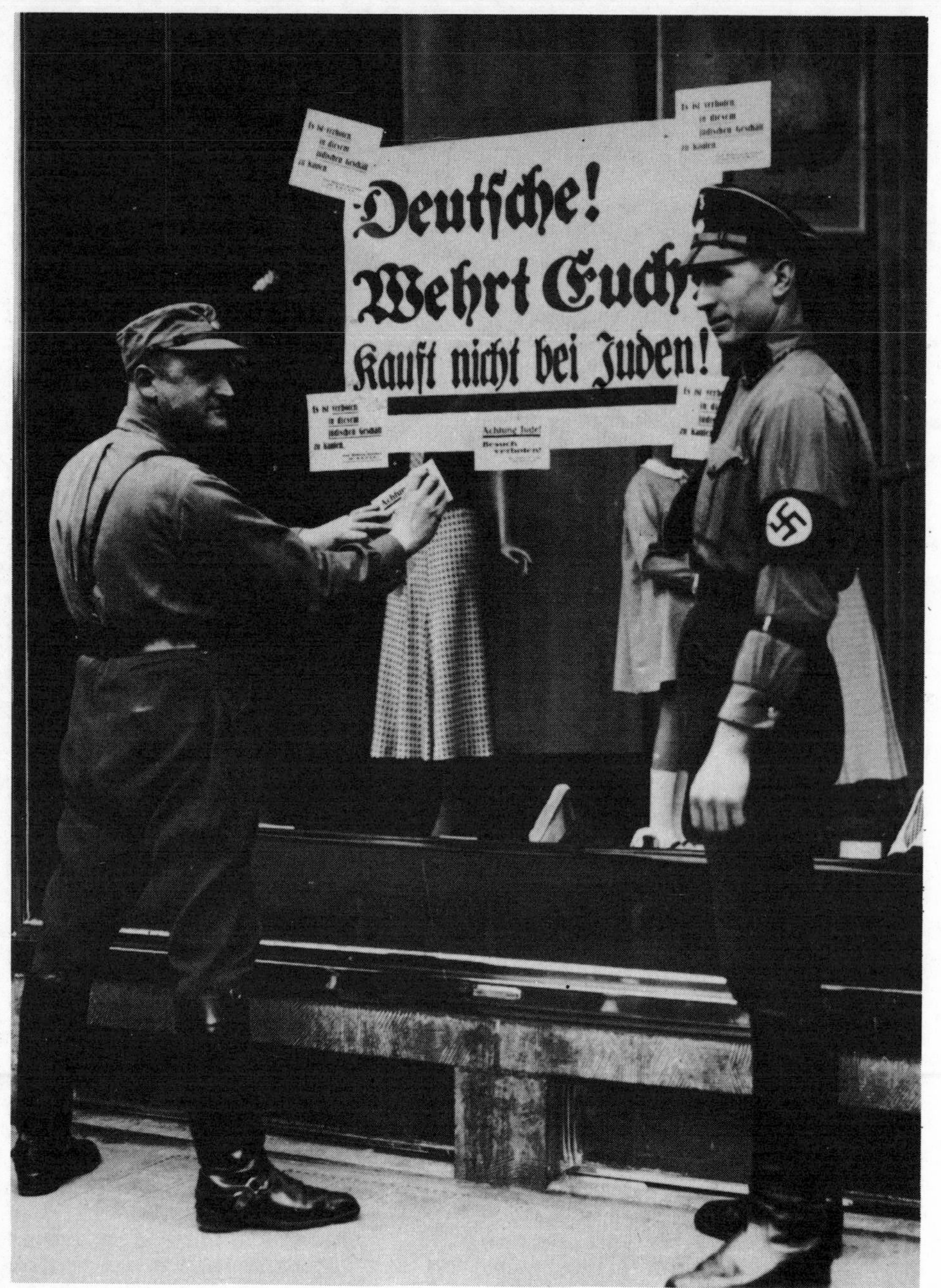

‘Germany awake’

With this awkwardness out of the way, *Stabschef* Ernst Röhm could continue his task of reorganising and reforming the SA. Its headquarters at the notorious Brown House at 45, Briennerstrasse, Munich, began to hum with an activity it had not known even under the bureaucratic Pfeffer von Salomon.

The Brown House was the focal point of Nazi activity in Germany, and its interior was a revelation to those devout Party members who pictured their chiefs' Spartan self-sacrificing life, so contrasted with that of rich Jews or aristocratic generals. Hitler, it is true, was so obsessed with his struggle for power that he seemed to have little time for the sort of ostentatious luxury indulged in by Nazi satraps such as Göring and Ley. The Brown House was a solid-looking three-storied house situated opposite the Papal Nuncio's residence in the most aristocratic avenue in Munich. From outside it looked not unlike the embassy of some great power, until one noticed the huge swastika flag floating above.

On either side of the great doorway two Brownshirts kept menacing guard. Within was a great reception hall with swastikas liberally distributed as decoration on every side. A grand staircase led up to the Führer's offices on the second floor. There, alongside the scarlet-lined Senate Chamber *(Senatorensaal)* was the Party sanctum, Hitler's own office. This was a richly-decorated chamber, whose high windows gazed down on two sides of the lofty Brown House. There Hitler and Röhm paced up and down the thick-piled carpet, planning the moves that would turn the SA into the masters of Germany and the Party into the lords of the Thousand-Years Reich; whilst a painting of Frederick the Great and a bronze bust of Mussolini gazed down on them.

Soon Röhm's burning energy had turned his plans for reform into action. First of all the structure of the SA hierarchy was recreated on an entirely military basis. When the reconstruction was complete, the SA's chain of command was drawn up as follows. At the head of course was Adolf Hitler himself, to whom every SA member, great or small, swore a personal oath of loyalty. Below him was the effective chief, *Stabschef* (Chief of Staff) Ernst Röhm. The SA army was divided at the highest level into Groups *(Gruppe)*, comprising about 100,000 men (each one equivalent numerically to the total complement of the *Reichswehr*) and commanded by a *Gruppenführer*. (Later the largest unit was rearranged into Higher and Lower units, the former being commanded by an *Obergruppenführer*.)

The boycott of Jewish-owned shops

Below the *Gruppe*, which was roughly speaking the equivalent of a Division, came the *Brigade*, commanded naturally by a *Brigadeführer* similar to an army brigade. Within the *Brigade* came the *Standarte*, roughly equivalent to a regiment, and consisting of between 1,000 and 3,000 men. This was commanded by a *Standartenführer* Colonel), and was often, like a line regiment, recruited from a particular locality. The *Standarten* were frequently given the number and regimental banner of a unit of the old Imperial Army.

Each *Standarte* contained several Storm Columns *(Sturmbann)*, led by a *Sturmbannführer* (Major), *Hauptsturmführer* (Captain), and *Obersturmführer* (Lieutenant). These units varied from 250 to 600 men in strength. The smallest unit of all was a Squad of four to twelve men, each one a simple Stormtrooper *(Sturmmann)*, with perhaps a 'Lance Corporal' *(Rottenführer)*, in charge. About three to six Squads made a Troop *(Truppe)*, two or three Troops made up a Storm Detachment *(Sturm)*, and several of the latter formed a Storm Column.

This subdivision at the lowest level was necessary when one considers the special rôle of the SA. The Squad, the smallest section of all, was encouraged to look upon itself as a band of comrades, bound together by common ties of friendship as well as by loyalty to the Führer. Anyone who, from his own initiative, succeeded in raising a Squad from among his friends or workmates, was entitled to have the Squad named after him rather than by a number. Thus, although at ground level the average Squad or Troop was a purely local affair, recruited among a group of young men who had been at school together, a band of wild students from the same university, or a desperate number of unemployed workmen, driven from their factory by the effects of the Slump, they nevertheless formed part of a tightly-knit military hierarchy and could be disposed of in very nearly as efficient a fashion as the regular army.

Thus, a popular figure in a Dresden bar might persuade a number of impressionable cronies to join the local SA. Out of work, and inclined to put some of the blame for this on their former employer, they had all heard Nazi street corner orators expounding on the causes of the nation's ills. With no money and nowhere to go, they had little else to do but trudge the streets, eager for any amusement. No one seemed to care about their fate, yet at the same time surely *something* could be done for them. They were after all able-bodied fellows, keen enough to get down to an honest day's work.

Some of their workmates had joined the Communist Party and were prepared to expound at length how the capitalist classes were exploiting the proletariat, and how this state of affairs must continue until the Revolution placed power firmly in the hands of the workers. But our beer-drinking friend (let us call him Fritz Bauer) is not convinced. Firstly, there is something decidedly alien in Marxism to a 'good German's' way of thinking; the Party's leaders are clearly puppets in the hands of the modern Genghis Khan in the Kremlin. And there are enough White Russian emigrés in Dresden for Fritz to have heard lurid and terrifying accounts of what happened to ordinary workmen like himself in the Red Revolution.

The Nazi speaker he had listened to a few nights ago, on the other hand, was certainly thoroughly German in his sentiments. Indeed, he extolled the mighty spirit of this nation in contrast to its bastardised and greedy neighbours. And what claptrap the Communists talk of the Brotherhood and Unity of Mankind. Who were these brothers? Hostile Poles, Czechs and Frenchmen, armed to the teeth and waiting only for the chance to invade a disarmed Germany once again – as the Poles had done in Silesia, or the French in the Ruhr. As the Nazi said, when one is surrounded by enemies, one has only oneself to look to.

Then again, the Nazis had such clear, confident policies. They did not waver, or disguise their aims with flowery phrases like the old-fashioned politicians of the Centrist or Social Democrat parties. They had a definite programme, something entirely new. The very title of the Party, National Socialist German Workers' Party,

Above: The Brown House, Munich, SA HQ and the Nazi heart of Germany.
Below: Brown House interior, Röhm addressing visitors

seemed to promise something for everyone. And although the street orator, following his master Dr Goebbels, sometimes went off into tirades against corrupt industrialists, monocled barons, and out-of-date generals; nonetheless no Nazi advocated a class war, or cherished a feud against a whole section of society like the Marxists. On the contrary, they showed clearly that the strength of the nation lay in a unity of all classes, working together under a clear-sighted, self-sacrificing Leader.

Of course, some undesirable elements would have to go. For a start there were the Jews. Fritz Bauer felt slightly uncomfortable at times when the 'Jewish question' arose. After all, he knew (not very well, it is true) several Jews, and they seemed harmless and unimportant enough. Indeed, he could feel sorry for them in his good-natured way. Most were refugees from persecution in Russia or Poland, and plied necessary trades industriously and unobtrusively. Many were pathetically poor, and it seemed hard at first to believe that these scattered foreigners could provide a threat to the nation. Nevertheless, here was he, Fritz Bauer, a decent, hardworking German of good peasant stock, out of work while many of these Jews still thrived. And who else could be responsible for the economic disaster that had struck Germany in 1930, leaving her with 6,000,000 unemployed? None of the old school of politicians could answer this question in any way that was intelligible to normal thinking people, so perhaps there was something behind this tale of a Jewish plot. And then there were *The Protocols of the Learned Elders of Zion*. . . .

Fritz Bauer scratched his head: the argument was beginning to get a bit abstruse. Anyway, it was not the ordinary little Jews who would suffer if National Socialism triumphed. They would be safe, German honour would see to that. No, it was a few immensely powerful and secretive financiers who would be prised out and expelled, restoring health to the poisoned body of the German nation. And horrible people they must be; Fritz shuddered as he remembered vivid cartoons of octopuses and spiders in worn copies of *Der Angriff* passed around the ex-serviceman's club to which he belonged.

Then, even as he had grasped the simple truths of the Nazi concept, Fritz Bauer would hear the gripping sounds of a military band, and watch admiringly as a brown-shirted column came tramping shoulder to shoulder up the street. Fresh healthy young men, all in the prime of life, dressed in spick and span uniforms, their eyes shining with patriotic fervour. At their head marched the *Obersturmführer*, a scarred handsome veteran of one of the King of Saxony's crack line regiments. He seemed more like a father to the young heroes marching behind than a stern officer. Surely men like this, with a common purpose and ideal, all selfish interests put behind them, could accomplish all that men can do!

The band crashes out once more, and the column disappears up the next street. But echoing back between the old houses come the rousing notes of the Stormtroopers' chorus:

Drum Brüder auf die Barrikaden!
Der Führer ruft, so folget gleich!
Die Reaktion hat ihn verraten,
Und dennoch kommt das Dritte Reich!
(Onwards, brothers, to the barricades!
The Führer calls, follow him now!
Reaction has betrayed him,
But the Third Reich comes
nevertheless!)

Exalted beyond himself, Fritz Bauer draws himself upright and gazes about him proudly. Once again he feels himself a soldier, but this time fighting not a pointless and destructive war, but a peaceful struggle to create a better Germany. The street is silent once more. Everyone with a job is at work, and the only people on the

The Jewish octopus encircles the globe

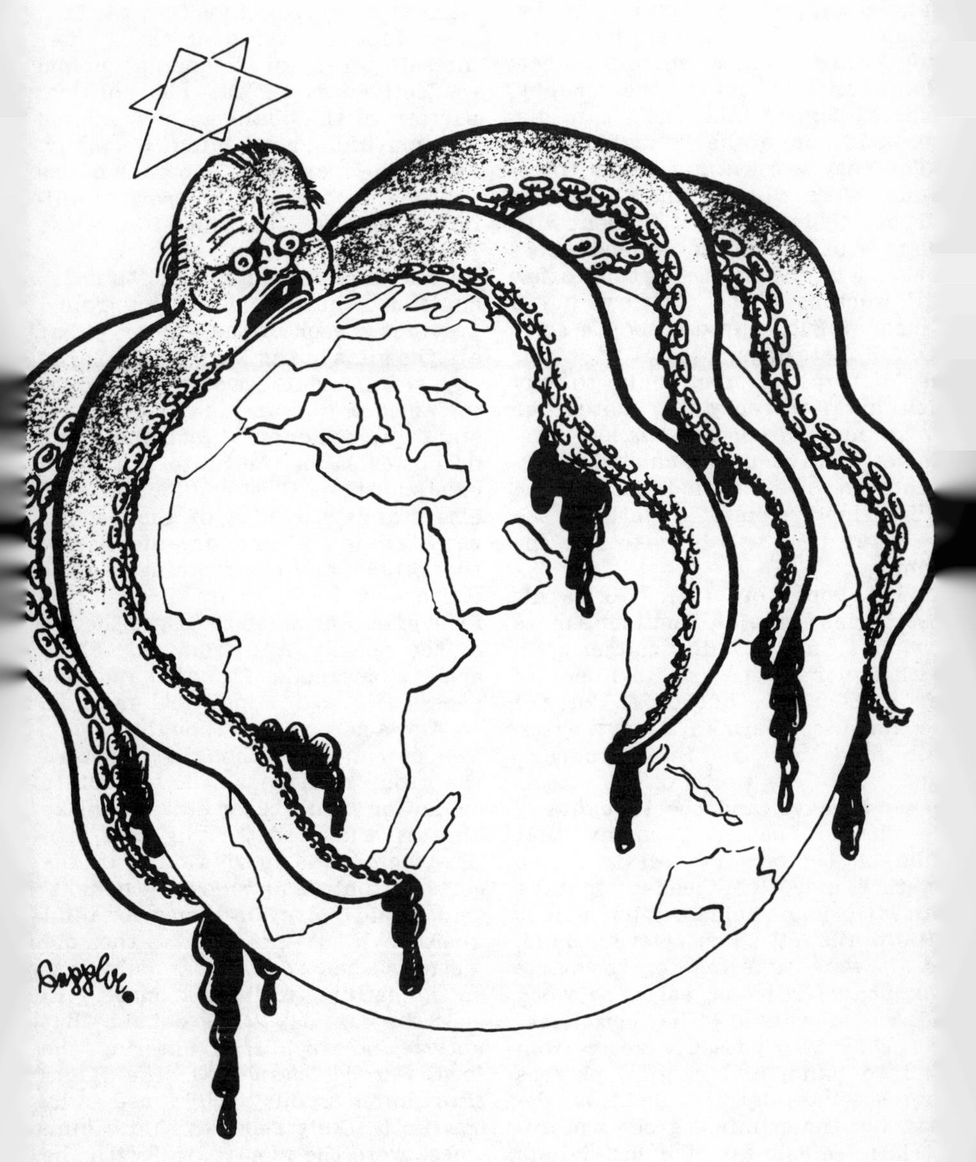

pavements are shabbily-dressed, hungry-eyed unemployed like himself. An older man, probably a Marxist (for this is 'Red Saxony') spits, and a Jewish old-clothes dealer hurries by, glancing apprehensively at the bystanders. But Fritz Bauer gives these people only the most cursory glance: what a contrast between their shabby, defeated figures, and the clean, disciplined vigour of the *Sturmabteilung!*

The very word *Sturm* seems to resound with vigour and relentless purpose. Fritz toys for a moment with the idea of calling on a friend whose husband is one of the fortunate few still working at the factory, but a sterner, loftier purpose soon asserts itself. He sets off purposefully towards the *Bierhaus*, pausing only to buy with his few remaining notes the latest number of *Voelkischer Beobachter* from a brown-shirted newsvendor. In the bar he finds half a dozen of his friends sipping gingerly at the one drink that will have to last the evening.

'What kept you, Fritz?' cries his bosom friend, a laid-off builder's mate now, but once a fellow-soldier with Fritz Bauer in the 1st Regiment of Saxon Grenadiers, of the 12th Corps of the Imperial German Army. Fritz, still fired by the Stormtroopers' music, the fiery words of the street-corner speaker, and the thoughts of the cleaner, better Germany that could be theirs, were all to strive together under the leadership of a man with vision, held forth fluently.

His words fell on receptive ground, for all were suffering for the same inexplicable reasons, eager to work and yet unwanted. The *Voelkischer Beobachter* was passed eagerly from hand to hand, and ringing phrases from speeches by Dr Goebbels, denouncing the criminal greed and unpatriotic selfishness of industrialists and capitalists, were read aloud. They laughed at the rough, good-humoured threats of Captain Göring, when he explained just what he would do with the Marxist poisoners when his hands closed around their necks. An order of the day from *Stabschef* SA Röhm announced that the SA, now nearly half a million strong, would soon provide the task force of a regenerated German army. And then they read the clear incisive words of the Führer himself, telling of the corruption and ineffectiveness of the old political parties, of the challenge now offered by youthful, awakening Germany, and of the inexorable approach of the sublime apotheosis of German fulfilment in the National Socialist Revolution.

'And the question at this time is', continued the article, quoting from a previous speech of the Führer, 'what are the aims of the National Socialist opposition and its leaders? It is a fight for an idea . . . and in the forefront stands a fundamental principle: Men do not exist for the State, the State exists for men. First and far above all else stands the idea of the people: the State is a form of organisation of this people, and the meaning and the purpose of the State are through this form of organisation to assure the life of the people. And from this there arises a new mode of thought and thus necessarily a new political method. We say: a new mode of thought.'

'A new mode of thought', reflected the group of friends . . . 'the State exists for men'. Clear statesmanlike phrases, that had the plight of men like themselves in view. And it was certainly only 'a new mode of thought' that could solve Dresden's dreadful unemployment problem – the old methods had proved an abysmal enough failure, in all conscience!

So the next day saw six shabby but active and keen men entering the local *Sturmabteilung* HQ. The *Haupsturmführer* on duty brightened as he saw such likely recruits before him. These were the men to deal with the Reds! It was not long before the men had been signed on into the *Standarte 100* of the *Gruppe Sachsen*. They swore, with a feeling of sublime elation, an oath to serve the Führer blindly and unquestioningly, whilst the same Leader's eyes gazed down at them from a photograph on the wall, with an expression at once commanding, understanding and reflective. As the man who had recruited his five friends to the SA, our friend Fritz now found himself *Rottenführer* Friedrich Bauer, *Sturm 5 der Standarte 100, Gruppe Sachsen.* So carried away with pride and enthusiasm were the six friends that they barely appreciated the fact that they were now entitled to free meals and uniforms (though no pay).

Deutschland erwache! Germany awoke, and twelve years later what was left of Fritz Bauer after a Russian T-34 tank had passed over his body lay in mud and snow outside Kursk.

The above is of course a fictionalised account of an SA recruit's decision to enlist, though nevertheless reflecting real conditions and attitudes. Here, however, is an eyewitness account of a visit in 1932 to an SA training camp. As Röhm had instituted a remarkable degree of uniformity into the organisation of these institutions, this may serve as a fair example.

'Next I visited the Leaders' School of the "Horst Wessel" Standard ('standard' corresponds to a regiment in the army) which had its quarters in a country inn near Berlin, belonging to an old Party member. Here, as in many other similar schools, SA men were put through a rigorous training, with enough of the Nazi Weltanschauung ['world outlook' – an appropriately vague term] drilled into them to make them political soldiers and unquestioning servants of the Party. In such camps, for a period of fifteen to thirty days, many thousands of Brownshirts lived, ate, slept, and laboured, under strict discipline along military lines. True, they handled no weapons, since their arsenals were secret; but they learned how to use bayonets and hand grenades by means of painted wood imitations. The authorities pretended to believe it was all in sport. For the most part, people of the neighbourhood, hoping that Hitler would some day roll his growing brown juggernaut over the Government which they abhorred, kept the camp commissaries supplied with gifts of food.

'I spent the whole afternoon witnessing their remarkable performance during a final inspection of that particular group, which was under the command of Karl Ernst, who then was still a minor officer, but later became the well known SA leader of Berlin – to be murdered in the Blood Purge of 30th June 1934. The adjutant of the standard had been showing me around. When the inspection was over, I sat with him in the side-car of a motor cycle riding slowly ahead of the men who were returning singing to quarters after their hard day. I asked the adjutant about the financing of the SA, and the really astonishing discipline for a voluntary troop.

"You see," he began, "the driver of this motor cycle owns it. He is a former policeman who was dismissed because he was seen reading the Nazi *Angriff*. This man doesn't get a penny for his vehicle or for the time he gives us. He even buys the petrol whenever he uses it for us. There are thousands like him. This spirit of devotion and sacrifice has made us great. And the discipline is not based on punishment but on an appeal to their honour. The first reproof is made quite privately; if another is needed, it takes place in front of the assembled troops; if that doesn't help, wearing of the uniform is forbidden for a fortnight, and only then, if this also fails, does degradation and expulsion from the ranks follow. But that is very seldom necessary."

'But what about the SA pay? The American Press had reported that every SA man received an average daily pay of four marks.

'The astounded face of this sunburned old soldier who wore the Iron Cross, First Class, was something to see. "What! We – ? Pay? That is fabulous!" He stopped the car and

Various SA groups at their training

Karl Ernst, *SA-Obergruppenführer*

jumped out. "Boys!" he cried. "How much daily pay do you get?"

'For a moment they didn't grasp the question, it was such a novel idea. He had to shout it a second time.

' "What! We – ?" they echoed. "But we don't get any pay!" They bawled it at me, turning out their empty pockets.

'I saw many examples of the admirable sense of duty which at that time seemed a matter of course among the soldiers of the Nazi movement, at least among the rank and file of the SA and the SS. Nobody paid them wages; no military oath bound them legally to their service, like the regular army soldier; no military law hung over their heads, no superior officers had disciplinary power over them. Yet they were the most disciplined, zealous, loyal, and courageous soldiers an army ever possessed. Now they all seemed to take it for granted that Hitler would "make it". And whenever I asked, and I asked many of them, "But what if he doesn't?" there was only one answer: "Then we'll smash the gates in for him!" '

The picture seems too ideal when it is remembered that terrible crimes were committed by these 'loyal' and 'zealous' ruffians. Yet history gains nothing by suppressing the truth, and there is no doubt that great numbers of the young SA men were indeed sincere idealists, who had enlisted with the mistaken idea that they would thereby serve Germany in her hour of need.

Even so, perhaps we should correct the balance by quoting the verdict of one who was certainly in a position to know, since he had been in supreme command of the whole SA just under a decade before the above account took place. Hermann Göring's description of the SA recruits was characteristically terse and to the point: he termed them 'a gang of perverted bandits'.

When Röhm took over the SA in 1931, the recruiting problem was helped immeasurably by the economic disaster under which Germany was suffering more than any other nation. Indeed, though it is easy to exaggerate the economic causes of the rise of Nazism, there is no doubt that the fluctuations in Germany's financial situation paralleled the ups and downs of Nazi fortunes remarkably. It was in 1920 that Hitler left the army and was able to devote all his energies to the Nazi Party. From then until the failure of the beer hall *putsch* at the end of 1923, the Party's fortunes rose and membership increased rapidly. During the same period, as a result largely of the Allied bill for war reparations and the French occupation of the Ruhr (January, 1923), the mark fell from a value of four to the dollar to seventy-five in 1921, 400 in 1922, to 18,000 in January 1923, to 160,000 by July of the same year, to a million by August, and finally, in the same November that Hitler held up von Kahr and Röhm seized the Munich War Ministry, it took four billion marks to buy a dollar.

Then, whilst Hitler was in prison at

A hungry queue at a soup kitchen at the time of the crash of the Mark

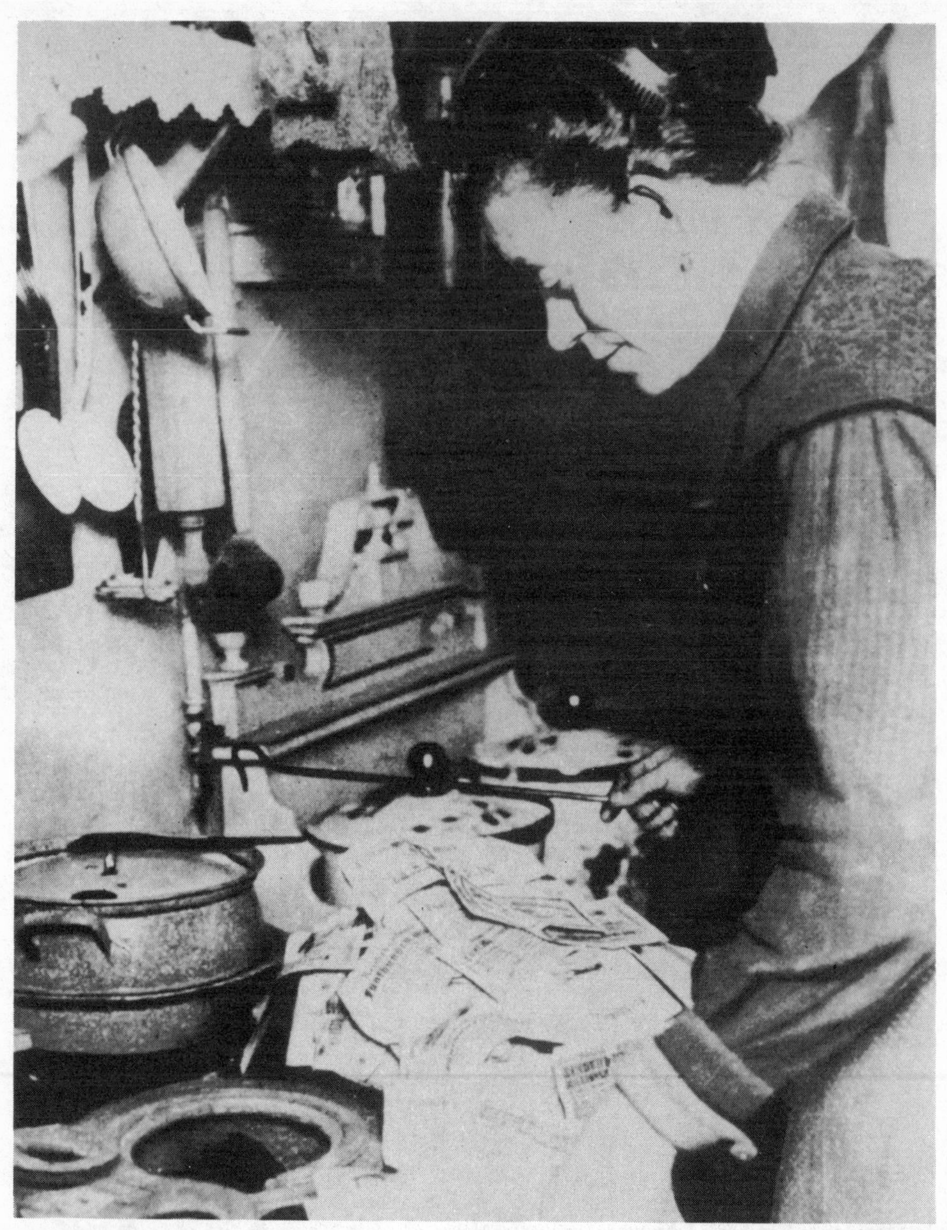

So nearly valueless does the Mark become that currency can be used to light fires

Landsberg in 1924, the economy began falteringly to recover. The French evacuated the Ruhr, reparations were eased by the Dawes Plan, and the brilliant Dr Hjalmar Schacht was achieving considerable success in stabilising the currency. Between 1924 and 1929, a steady recovery took place, so that by 1928 unemployment had fallen to 650,000, the lowest figure since the War. It was during these years that Hitler was slowly rebuild-

The first board meeting of the new Reichsbank. Hjalmar Schacht (centre) was able to give the currency stability

ing the Party after the fiasco of the Munich *putsch*. His unflagging energy and faith undoubtedly had its effect, and Party membership crept up from 27,000 in 1925 to 178,000 in 1929. This was no mean feat in itself, but still left the Nazi Party an insignificant influence in contemporary Germany.

Then, on 24th October 1929, came the Wall Street stock market crash. Largely dependent on American loans, which were in great measure responsible for the four previous years' 'false' prosperity, Germany faced disaster. The loans dried up and repayment of interest on those already received became pressingly due. World trade dwindled, so Germany could not export enough goods to pay for the raw materials and food she depended on. Banks collapsed, plants closed, small businesses folded up. Unemployment soared at a terrifying rate.

It was precisely during these years that Hitler carried the Party to success after success, until in 1933 he himself became Chancellor. The parallel is obvious, but to relate Nazi successes to increasing unemployment wholly would be almost as false as the Marxist theory that Hitler was simply the tool of unscrupulous German capitalists.

Nevertheless, the effect on SA recruiting was direct and unchallengeable, and insofar as the SA helped to pave the way for the Nazi victory of 1933 the effect of the existence of millions of able-bodied unemployed on Germany's future was disastrous. For, though not always paid an actual wage, stormtroopers did receive free meals and uniforms, to say nothing of various other 'perks', such as free transport to rallies, organised sport, club facilities at SA headquarters (those in the Munich Brown House, presided over by the fat jovial chef Arthur Kannenberg, were particularly luxurious), discussion

Above: Just as Germany – largely financed out of American loans – appeared to be near recovery, the Wall Street Crash occurred. Conditions in Germany become ripe for Nazism's final triumph – control of the State. *Below:* Munich unemployed have soup doled out from a 'Goulash cannon'

Above: A typical scene at a Berlin labour exchange. *Below:* Unemployment queue. The SA offered at least food and a uniform, and recruitment showed a significant rise

groups, etc.

Here the garrulous Kurt Lüdecke once again provides a useful insight into just what this involved. When forming his own SA troop in 1923, he and his servant Ludwig 'gathered a few men, taking only well-built and able-bodied fellows who either had served in the war or had some military training. With these as a nucleus, we began regular recruiting. Soon we had a few young students, splendid, strong fellows, among our veterans, and I began to organise a band with four drummers and four fifers. We held drills regularly, and every Wednesday evening we assembled in a hired room at a café in the Schoenfeld Strasse, where I lectured on Nazi principles. Each man took the oath of allegiance on the swastika flag, pledging loyalty to Hitler and the Cause. To have more space for our exclusive use, I leased an apartment which contained, besides living quarters for Ludwig and me, an enormous studio. At once it became a sort of armoury, the meeting-place for the men. Ludwig often had to cook for ten or twenty hungry giants. He was an excellent but very liberal cook, and without batting an eye could use the most appalling quantities of fancy groceries. As most of the men were unemployed, and of course received no pay for serving in the company, Ludwig's bounty was accepted with enthusiasm.' Every Saturday and Sunday the dark sleepy woods outside Munich were roused by the harsh commands and jaunty music of Lüdecke's band out training.

The attractions of such a life to men suffering the deprivations of the times do not need stressing. It gave them the basic essentials of life; and, perhaps more important, it gave them a self-respect they must have sadly needed. They did not want charity: they *did* want to work to build a better Germany. Where better, or indeed where else, could they look for

During the ban on uniforms SA members are searched for weapons

Part of the ceremony at which the *Stahlhelm* (Steel Helmets) are incorporated into the SA

a more suitable opportunity than in the hard, disciplined, self-sacrificing ranks of the SA?

The effect of steeply-rising unemployment on recruitment to the Brownshirts was direct and obvious. Indeed, the Nazis exulted over every fresh disaster and hastened to turn it to their own advantage. Hitler himself wrote in 1931, when over four million were clamouring for employment and joining the bread queues: 'Never in my life have I been so well disposed and inwardly contented as in these days. For hard reality has opened the eyes of millions of Germans to the unprecedented swindles, lies and betrayals of the Marxist deceivers of the people.' Not very much humanity is revealed in these words, but a great deal of awareness of the realities of politics.

Figures again show how unemployment drove thousands each year into the brown-shirted ranks. At the time of Pfeffer von Salomon's resignation in 1930 the *Sturmabteilungen* already boasted 60-75,000 troopers; a great increase on the previous year, largely as a result of the Wall Street crash of 1929. Then, with Röhm's resumption of the leadership in 1931, the number rose steeply to 170,000; this was in part due to Röhm's remarkable drive and organisational powers. But even that cannot account for the enormous accession of no less than nearly 500,000 by the end of 1932. Only the spiralling unemployment figures, quoted above, can explain in full the stupendous success of the Nazi recruiting drive.

Eventually, at the height of its power and prestige, Röhm's private army numbered around 4,000,000 men – that is, forty times the size of the Germany army. But this latter stupendous leap forward was in part due to quite different factors. For, with the Nazi seizure of power in the

making the National Socialist Party eventually the key factor in German politics.

So it was that there existed in Germany what virtually amounted to a state within a state. The country was divided up by the Party into thirty-two districts *(Gaue)* for administrative purposes, each presided over by a *Gauleiter*. Similarly, within each *Gau* was an appropriate section of the SA. Potential officers went to training colleges (set up by *Stabschef* Röhm in June 1931), troops were reviewed regularly by the *Stabschef* or his *Gruppenführers*, drilling, training and exercising were organised on a national and local level, an elaborate series of ranks, uniforms and decorations was established; and so, alongside the Reichwehr regiments and corps were the *Standarten* and *Gruppen* of the National Socialist army. The weekly expenses of this army amounted to no less than 2,500,000 marks a week, raised partly by the highly efficient Party fund-raising machine, and partly from contributions by capitalists such as Fritz Thyssen. That such an organisation should have been tolerated in an advanced Western state must seem strange to an Englishman or an American; but it should be remembered that the nation had already become accustomed to the activities of the *Freikorps* performing duties that any patriotic German would applaud, and to some extent the Brownshirts were able to step into the gap left by the decline from 1925 onwards of the *Freikorps* units, following General von Seeckt's withdrawal of army support. And a very high proportion of SA officers (such as Pfeffer von Salomon) were former *Freikorps* leaders anyway.

Hitler himself, with typically imprecise phraseology, summed up the quasi-legal pretensions of the SA in the following words (in 1930): 'formerly SA stood for '*Saalschutzabteilung*' (the corps for protecting the halls where National Socialist meetings

beginning of 1933, the SA absorbed thousands of new recruits, anxious as is usual to support the victorious faction. A very high proportion of these were ex-Communists, who found the difference between Red Guards and Brownshirts not so very great. Indeed, Röhm himself welcomed them, as having a radical outlook similar to his own men, and christened them 'beefsteaks' (brown outside but red within). In addition, a cunning Nazi manoeuvre amalgamated the Nationalist's private army, the *Stahlhelm* ('steel helmet') into the SA wholesale.

It would be a grave and dangerous mistake to attribute Hitler's success entirely to the wretched economic situation of the years between 1929 and 1932, but there is no doubt that the effectiveness of his private army owed a great deal to this factor. And in turn it is undeniable that the mixture of bullying, terror, and threatening display of armed might employed by the Brownshirts during these years played a major part in

were held); later it had stood for *Sport-Abteilung*, and lastly for *Sturm-Abteilung* (storm-division). But these meanings of the letters SA were really irrelevant, for SA is a special conception and stands for itself: it has grown out of and beyond the original significations attached to the words.'

Though the SA was never tested in open battle (unlike its rival and successor the SS), and never attempted to engage in armed revolution against the state, nevertheless despite its ruffianly activities it acquired a lively *esprit de corps*. Badges, ranks, units, uniforms: all served to give the Stormtroopers a strong sense of military brotherhood and purpose. This sentiment found its most lasting evocation in the sombre, doom-laden melody of the march lament composed in memory of a Berlin *Sturmführer*, Horst Wessel, mortally wounded in a brawl with local Reds in February 1930. This stirring tune became the SA and Party anthem, and reached its apotheosis in July 1933 when bands of the *Reichswehr* itself were graciously

Above: **Hans von Seekt. He withdrew army support from the *Freikorps* units, and from 1925 they declined. *Below:* Horst Wessel stands by trucks loaded with his men. Killed in a fracas, he became a symbol worshipped by the Nazis and inspired the SA and Party anthem 'The Horst Wessel Song'**

permitted to play it on parade.

Die Fahne hoch! Die Reihen dicht geschlossen!
SA marschiert mit ruhig festem Schritt,
Kam'raden, die Rotfront und Reaktion erschossen,
Marschiern im Geist in unsern Reihen mit.

The young hero

(Banners high! Ranks closed!
The Storm Troopers march with firm, calm stride,
Comrades, whom the Red Front and Reaction have shot,
March in spirit among our ranks)

A formidable combination

Röhm had proved a good friend and servant to Hitler. In the two years 1931 and 1932 he had raised the SA to a peak of strength and efficiency unimaginable in the days when the ragged ex-*Freikorps* levies had attempted to take over the Bavarian government. Though unwaveringly opposed to the idea of armed revolution on grounds of political strategy, Hitler knew that the effectiveness of NSDAP propaganda depended very largely on the mailed fist of the SA; which had, by savaging Party opponents and protecting its own speakers, made the never-ending thunder of that propaganda possible. Nor is it likely that anyone besides Röhm could have accomplished the task with anything like the same efficiency and success.

Firstly, he possessed an astonishing capacity for hard work, organisation and efficiency, and the ability to instil these qualities into his subordinates. Secondly, he possessed contacts vital to the emergent Nazi Party; contacts they could not do without, despite their vaunted independence. He was increasingly closely in touch with General Kurt von Schleicher, in charge of the Ministry Bureau (*Ministeramt*) at the War Ministry. Schleicher, through persistent intrigues and dabbling in politics, was a considerable power in the officer corps as well as in certain political circles. He was also an old regimental comrade and friend of Colonel Oskar von Hindenburg, the trusted son of the eighty-four year old President (Schleicher and the young Hindenburg had served together in the 3rd Foot Guards, President Hindenburg's old regiment), and of Otto von Meissner, the President's State Secretary. As the aged President fell more under the influence and control of his son and Meissner, so did Schleicher's power rise in that vital quarter. So that though President Hindenburg himself loathed the upstart homosexual Captain Röhm, the avenue remained open. Finally, Röhm was unswervingly loyal to Hitler personally, even though his opinion differed on matters of policy and at times resented the hold his weakness had given Hitler over him.

'Enough of this ! Vote Hitler'

The years 1931 to 1932, ultimately so successful for the Nazi cause, did not at the time seem always so propitious. Indeed, as far as the SA was concerned, it was for a time threatened with permanent dissolution. The Weimar Republic was of course tottering to its close, and though there is no space here to describe at length the fortunes of the successive governments that feebly tried to stave off the threatened disaster, it will perhaps make the situation clearer if we summarise in the barest outline the succession of ministries in power before 1933.

For the whole of the decade up to March 1930, Hermann Müller, a Social Democrat, was Chancellor. He was succeeded by Heinrich Brüning of the Catholic Centre Party, who was to a large extent, though honest and painstaking himself, the unwitting nominee of Schleicher and the army. His Chancellorship ended on 30th May 1932, largely through manoeuvres of General Schleicher. Brüning was succeeded by Franz von Papen, a wily but not over-wise ex-cavalry officer, placed in power once again by the machiavellian Schleicher.

On 2nd December 1932 Schleicher ousted Papen and, coming at last into the open, became Chancellor himself. But he in turn found he could not gain the necessary support in the Reichstag, and was forced to resign on 28th January 1933.

It is important to remember that the multiplicity of parties, and the failure of any one of them to gain an overall majority, resulted in constantly shifting coalition alliances and compromise Chancellors. For the same reason the Chancellor was often forced to rule by Presidential decree, by-passing the Reichstag. This had the ill effect of accustoming the nation to authoritarian rule, and also meant that

Above: **President Hindenburg's son Colonel Oskar von Hindenburg, with Hitler. The colonel was another of Röhm's valuable friends.** ***Below:*** **Hermann Müller, Chancellor for the decade preceding 1930**

behind-the-scenes cabals and intrigues were virtually unavoidable.

Thus the Chancellors. For the Presidents: after the death of Friedrich Ebert in February 1925, Field-Marshal Paul von Hindenburg, the illustrious and respected former Commander-in-Chief of the Imperial Army, was elected the second German President, In the spring of 1932 he stood for re-election, and though opposed by Hitler was re-elected (10th April.) His second term of office lasted until his death on 2nd August 1934.

A fantastic web of intrigue permeated government and party circles under the Chancellorships of Brüning, Papen and Schleicher, and it can be imagined that Hitler was not backward in pressing the claims of the hugely strengthened National Socialist Party. However, as he never gained an overall majority while out of office, he too was obliged to negotiate with his rivals of the Nationalist and Centrist parties. But any alliance with them was of course regarded only as a stepping-stone to an exclusive Nazi seizure of power.

The highly efficient and numerically vast Brownshirt army, whose organisation under Röhm we surveyed in the previous chapter, played its usual rôle in browbeating rival groups and terrorising the population generally. But there was a brief period when it seemed that Germany might be freed altogether from its gang of licensed bullies.

During the Presidential elections of March 1932, the Nazis had been so anxious to see Hitler in office that they had made tentative plans for a *putsch*. Röhm, always the one for armed revolution (despite his many failings, he was a man of reckless bravery), alerted the SA Stormtroopers and set up a cordon around Berlin. At a word from Hitler he would have unleashed his 400,000-strong army on the Government and *Reichswehr* and placed Hitler in iron control of Germany's destiny. But Hitler remained as obdurate as ever in refusing to risk the use of

General Kurt von Schleicher. Röhm's association with the War Ministry Bureau chief was one reason the Nazi party still needed Röhm's cooperation

General von Papen, placed in power by Schleicher in 1932. Like his predecessor in the Chancellorship, Heinrich Brüning, he was deposed; his place was taken by Schleicher himself

Above: Hindenburg at the elections which returned him as President, even though he stood against Hitler. *Below:* In April 1932 the SA, SS and Hitler Youth were banned. 'The Brown House' is cordoned off

Röhm visiting an SA contingent during the ban on uniforms

force so long as there was any real hope of achieving his goal through success at the ballot-box and party manipulations. On the other hand, he thoroughly approved the *threat* of force. So he held his hand, and the Brownshirts and Blackshirts (SS) remained chafing in their barracks, even when it was found that Hindenburg had been re-elected with nearly 6,000,000 more votes than Hitler.

But all was not over. The Reich and State police had amassed considerable evidence of Röhm's plans, and after a raid on Nazi headquarters in Berlin possessed damning proof that a *coup* had been planned. As a result the Reich government at last acted, and General Groener, Brüning's Minister of the Interior, on 13th April 1932 issued an order totally banning the SA, the SS and the Hitler Youth as 'private armies', intolerable in a properly ordered state.

The Nazis were aghast, and only Hitler's absolute insistence on compliance prevented the long-contemplated revolt from breaking out at once. Röhm was furious; but there can be little doubt that from his point of view Hitler was right. For, apart from the very open question as to whether such a revolt could ever have succeeded, the claim that the National Socialist accession to power had been entirely peaceful and constitutional was undoubtedly to pay dividends later.

Unhappily for Germany the ban was not imposed for long. At the end of May the eternal conspirator, Schleicher, engineered the downfall of Brüning, and set up in his place von Papen and the 'Barons' Cabinet', which consisted largely of inept (as events were to prove) aristocrats.

Among the complicated intrigues that resulted in this ephemeral ministry was a pact between Schleicher and Hitler (to gain the latter's support for the overthrow of Brüning), one of whose main conditions was the lifting of the ban on the SA and SS. This agreement had been largely engineered by Röhm, who acted as go-between for Hitler and Schleicher. Hitler would support, or rather tolerate, the Papen government in exchange for a rescinding of the ban. Papen himself alleged that Schleicher had lured Brüning and Groener into imposing the ban in the first place deliberately in order to bring about their downfall. So devious was Schleicher's character (the very name means 'creeper' in German) that there may well be truth in this assertion.

A month later Papen attempted to undo some of the harm he had done his country by prohibiting political demonstrations, but the Pandora's box was open once again. After the greatly increased Nazi vote in the Reichstag elections of July, Hitler began to bargain from a position of strength with Schleicher for the Chancellorship. Once again the militant SA found their patience severely limited, and the daily terror and riot that had induced Papen to impose his temporary ban before the election broke out again with redoubled viciousness. 'Daily workouts in the form of pitched battles with Sozis (Social Democrats) and Communists kept the men of the SA at the top of their form', wrote the fatuous Lüdecke – much as if he were describing the training programme of an exuberant public school athletics team. Murders, bombings and raids took place daily. *Stabschef* Röhm began once again the preparations cancelled after the Presidential elections in March. 60,000 SA men formed a ring of steel around Berlin, trucks and arms were ready. If Schleicher and Hindenburg could not be persuaded by reasoning to appoint Hitler as Chancellor, then they would see what the gun could do. The army and police would very probably welcome them, as the alternative was Bolshevism.

So thought Röhm, when Hitler was summoned into the presence of the aged President. Röhm accompanied him, but only Göring was actually present with Hitler at the interview. Ten minutes later a shaken Hitler re-emerged: not only had the Field-Marshal peremptorily rejected his demand, but he had gone on to dress down the 'Bohemian corporal' in stern lanugage. If he wished to be considered for this high office, he must show himself and his party in a considerably more responsible light. The vicious behaviour of his SA hoodlums must be checked, motiveless persecution of Jews and political rivals must cease, and Hitler himself must show himself rather more of a statesman and be prepared in particular to co-operate with the other parties of the Right and Centre. Until this happened, he might be considered for office in a coalition, but it would be inconsistent with his Presidential oath and responsibilities to the German nation as a whole to appoint a party leader whose aims were so equivocal, and whose methods so unchivalrous.

With that, the old President having remained standing and leaning on his cane throughout the whole interview, the would-be Chancellor was curtly dismissed. Later, Hindenburg was to assure Schleicher: 'I give you my word of honour as a Prussian general that I will never make this Bohemian corporal Chancellor of Germany.' Within three months he had reluctantly to eat those words, but the detestation felt by the proud old soldier, once the servant of the Emperor-King, for the 'gutter revolutionary' was never wholly extinguished.

When Röhm heard the news his indignation knew no bounds. Once again the landowning Junkers were blocking the path of the National Socialist revolution. Well, the time for bargaining was over. 60,000 Brownshirts were spoiling for a fight; within an hour they would be in Berlin and every count, baron and general in the city behind bars. As for the Old Gentleman . . .

Above: SA members arrested in Berlin, 1932. *Below:* Hindenburg swore never to let the 'gutter revolutionary' Hitler have the Chancellorship. Soon after he had to eat his words

But once again, and his success reveals the utter dependence of the movement on his will alone, Hitler decreed that no action was to be taken. Legality, despite this unexpected and humiliating rebuff, was the only guaranteed path to success. A *putsch* was a gamble; its failure would mean more than nine months' retirement in Landsberg this time. Röhm was dismissed and given the thankless task of telling the SA they were to go home quietly. So anxious for bloodshed were many of the Stormtroopers that a number of their officers declared they could no longer restrain them. It says much, therefore, for the discipline of Röhm's organisation that in fact nothing did happen, and all dispersed peaceably.

But he was far from satisfied. What was the purpose of this superb force of fighting men, if not to seize power? Then, and only then, could Germany be transformed into the colossal fighting machine he desired; a machine, moreover, that would not be hamstrung this time at the top by aristocratic noodles. Some months later he gave open expression to this theme.

'Of course I expected a showdown after the thirteenth of August . . . But my hands are tied – now I'm only a soldier who obeys. I must confess Hitler didn't find it hard to persuade me to his course, though I had a hard time keeping my men in check . . . Nothing but words, and yet millions of hearts beat for him – fantastically enough, he's still my only hope. Never did a man have a better material to work with! Look at the Nazi Youth, the SA, the SS – splendid stuff, ready to fight, to die, to conquer! And now he asks them to fight with the ballot again! Instead of giving us the order to march, Hitler makes us wade into the morass of parliamentarianism. He's taken so much out of Mussolini's book – why can't he imitate his March on Rome? And they praise his 'legality' as a ruse, as clever strategy! . . . Oh, but what's the use of talking!

There's nobody to replace Hitler, even less now than in 1924. We can't do without him, but something ought to be done. If I could see a way out, I wouldn't hesitate.'

However, despite Hitler's implacable aversion to the use of force as a means of gaining political power, there can be no doubt that he had the highest regard for the Stormtrooper method of expressing political differences with their opponents. Only three days before President Hindenburg's exhortation to Hitler 'to conduct the opposition on the part of the NS Party in a chivalrous manner', an exemplary instance of National Socialist methods and ethics had occurred at Potempa in Upper Silesia.

On the night of 9th August, five SA men had broken into the home of a Communist miner named Pietrzuch, dragged him from his bed and kicked him to death in front of his mother and brother. On 22nd August a special court at Beuthen condemned all five to death, taking in mind particularly the cold-blooded nature of the crime. At once an extraordinary howl of indignation arose from the Nazi leaders. Hitler himself sent the five culprits the following notorious telegram: 'My comrades! In the face of this most monstrous of blood-judgements, I feel myself linked to you in unbounded loyalty. From this moment on your freedom is a matter of our honour, the battle against a government under which this was possible, our duty.' Göring gave each murderer's family 1,000 marks, and Goebbels made the amazing discovery that 'the Jews are to blame'. As for Röhm, their commander, he visited the martyrs in jail to assure them of his support. At first Papen stood firm against these outbursts, but eventually he weakened and commuted the sentence to life imprisonment. Within six months, however, the murderers were freed by a Nazi amnesty, Hitler having gained power in the interval. A more illuminating example of SA heroism and National Socialist ethics

Above: **The guard before the Beuthen prison gates. The five SA members within were condemned to death for brutally murdering a Communist miner; they were released with the aid of the Nazi Party after serving six months.**
Below: **Gregor Strasser. He refused to join Schleicher's cabinet**

could hardly be found.

This continual holding in check harmed the *élan* of the Brownshirt movement, and Hitler's unwavering adherence to 'Legality' appeared to many within and without the movement to remove much of the purpose of its existence. In November 1932 Thyssen, the industrialist, warned that he could no longer maintain his large contributions to Party funds. Thousands of SA men roamed the streets with collection boxes; local Brown Houses, arms and uniform stores, and publishing houses ran into debt: it seemed as if the SA must strike and gain its well-earned rewards, or slowly collapse. Nonetheless, light lay just around the corner.

The wily Schleicher, the last Chancellor of the Weimar Republic, had been out-manoeuvred in the very game he had so long and successfully practised. Unable eventually to obtain even the support his predecessor von Papen had enjoyed, he made a desperate effort to split the Nazis and gain a section of the Party in support of his government. He made an unsuccessful bid to lure one of Hitler's right-hand men, Gregor Strasser, to come into the Cabinet. But, despite Strasser's initial interest (he had long objected to Hitler's 'all or nothing' policy, particularly after Hindenburg's snub in August), the attempt failed and, faced by a secret pact of Hitler, Papen, Hugenberg (the Nationalists' leader) and the entourage of President Hindenburg, Schleicher resigned.

Two days of desperate intrigue followed; and then, on 30th January 1933, Adolf Hitler, the former railway porter and carpet beater, was summoned before the President to head the new coalition government. The Thousand-Year Reich had begun.

That evening a colossal torchlight parade of SA, SS and *Stahlhelm* (Hugenberg's Nationalist private

Parade of the victors after Hitler's acceptance of the Chancellorship on 30th January 1933

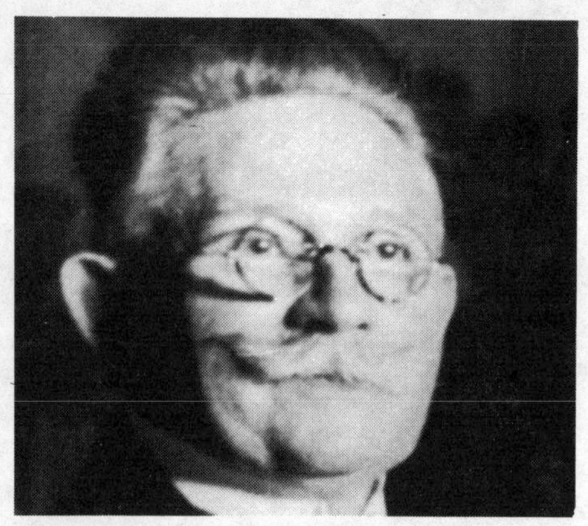

Hugenberg, who, in league with Hitler, von Papen and Hindenburg's entourage, forced Schleicher's resignation

army) surged through Berlin. For hour after hour some 25,000 men tramped under the Brandenburg Gate and along the Wilhelmstrasse. Under the Presidential Palace they passed, brass bands blaring out the Horst Wessel song, eager exultant faces below the yellow flaring of the torches, thousands of iron-shod heels crashing on the street as if impelled by a single machine.

Wir sind das Heer vom Hakenkreuz,
Hebt hoch die roten Fahner!
Der deutschen Arbeit wollen wir
Den Weg zur Freiheit bahnen.
(We are the army of the swastika,
Raise high the red banners!
We want to build German labour's
Road to freedom)

The aged President, now verging on senility, tapped his cane approvingly to music whose words, with very slight alteration, might have been played by the band of the Red Army before Comrade Stalin. A respectful cheer came from the brown ranks passing, perhaps from rough comrades of the Potempa murderers, or slim girlish-looking protegés of Röhm or Heines. Hindenburg nodded in acknowledgment – the same nod he had given sixty years before when the glittering 4th Foot Guards paraded before their officers to the tune of *Preussens Gloria*. Times had changed in Germany.

A dutiful cheer was raised for the old President. But when the SA columns came beneath the balcony of the Reich Chancellery, a ferocious triumphant cry of '*Heil, Heil, Sieg Heil!*' burst out as they saw above them the ecstatic, laughing, crying figure of Germany's new master. Hitler twitched, jerked and bowed happily to his loyal Stormtroopers. As a German writer put it: 'He had never looked so happy in public since 8th November, 1923, at the Bürgerbräu Keller in Munich. His bearing was one laugh of triumph; the upper part of his body jerked backwards and forwards as he bowed.'

Beside the Führer strutted the bloated figure of another hero of the beer hall *putsch* of ten years before. Hermann Göring was there still; nearby too stood Frick, and Papen hovered discreetly in the rear. But what of the man to whom Hitler had cried in that other, fleeting, hour of triumph, 'This is the happiest and most wonderful day of my life!'? The man to whom he owed more than Göring or Frick, and who had stood by him when Goebbels had called the Führer a betrayer of the workers?

Chief of Staff Röhm it was who had been for eleven long years Hitler's ablest and most faithful companion. And above all it was he who had created this endless brown army marching below the exultant Nazi chiefs. Yet it was not to this brown army that Hitler owed his rise to power – if anything it was to General von Blomberg, who had kept the *Reichswehr* from intervening to save the Republic. And what was the *Sturmabteilung* to do now that the goal was reached? Over half a million armed and desperate men, embittered against authority, were very useful helpmates in forging a revolution. But what was to be done with them now that the Revolution itself was in power? This was the question many interested parties, within and without the Party, were beginning to ask.

The new Chancellor acknowledges the plaudits of his trusting countrymen

Out on a limb

One person at least had a very clear conception of the SA's future rôle in Germany, and that was Ernst Röhm himself. Already in the previous year private discussions had taken place between him and Schleicher on this subject. Both wished for a similar end in one respect, but their opinions differed on the vital question of its framework. Röhm wished for the SA (the SS should be understood as included, since it formed part of the SA) to be amalgamated with the army, and for the *Reichswehr*, numerically vastly inferior, to form part of a new reformed National Army based on SA principles. Schleicher, too, saw from the army's standpoint the advantages of drawing into the *Reichswehr* influence the vast pool of active and semi-trained recruits that the SA represented. But, in common with every other German general, he had no intention of placing the leadership of the expanded new army in any hands but those of the High Command. So these tentative negotiations came to nothing, more particularly as Röhm believed that when the National Revolution came he would be able to dictate terms to the generals.

But now the National Revolution, so often on the point of achievement and so often snatched away, had arrived and no immediate programme was proposed for the SA or its faithful leader. Backed by the increasing disillusionment of his Brownshirt followers, Röhm began to press publicly and privately for their contribution to the Nazi victory to be recognised and rewarded. On 5th November 1933 he addressed 15,000 SA officers, admitting rather plaintively, 'One often hears . . . that the SA had lost any reason for existence.' Behind the injured protests lay a barely-concealed threat: if the new masters of Germany had forgotten who had placed them in their present lofty position, then there were nearly two million Stormtroopers who could remind them.

Röhm, determined to obtain full military status for himself and his stormtroopers

Whilst Röhm in private pressed the cabinet and the army to accept the military rôle of the SA in the new Germany, in public he advocated in uncompromising terms what soon came to be known as 'the second revolution'. Along with Gregor Strasser and Goebbels, Röhm had always been a convinced member of the radical wing of the Party, one who believed in the 'Socialist' aspect of National Socialism. In 1928 Röhm had written in his memoirs: 'We are not going to be saved by going back to the old, to the *Reaktion*, to the generals and excellencies, but by the men of action, the youth and the front soldiers.'

Apart from that large proportion of the veteran SA that was in any case inclined to radical solutions of national problems, as already noted the post-Weimar SA was hugely swollen by recruits anxious to jump on the successful bandwagon. And vast numbers of these were not only not true Nazis, but recent ex-Communists. Röhm had no objection: 'some of my best men are former Communists . . . I like them radical . . . most of the ones who join us become Nazi revolutionaries, and that's what we want . . . No, Hitler doesn't mind the swelling of the SA .On the contrary, he wants to use us at will, as pressure on the *Reichswehr* and on big business here and abroad. But if he thinks he can squeeze me for his own ends for ever, and some fine day throw me on the ash-heap, he's wrong. The SA can also be an instrument for checking Hitler himself.'

So threatened Röhm in private, though all along he seems to have believed, like so many other Nazis, that Hitler could be lured or pushed into coming over to his camp. In addition there was always the unspoken threat of the use that could be made of Röhm's private life. 'It's also true, and I admit it to my shame, that the vulnerability you mentioned has

Above: SA and SS marching together. *Right:* Some of the 2,000,000 stormtroopers ready to demand their say in the new regime. *Below:* Hitler tolerated the power of the SA until the faithful Himmler's SS was strong enough to take over

Röhm, misunderstanding his relationship with Hitler (like others he thought he could manipulate the Führer), was perhaps his own executioner

delivered me into his hands. It's a terrible thing . . . I've lost my independence for always.' This was not to say that Hitler was actually blackmailing him – Röhm's tendencies were already too notorious for that danger to be relevant. But Hitler could, as he finally did, affect to 'discover' this scandalous business and repudiate his SA Chief of Staff. As Hitler had frequently declared that his followers' private lives were their own, to take exception now would be consummate hypocrisy. When complaints about Röhm reached his ears, he was wont to dismiss the matter with a: 'Why should I concern myself with the private lives of my followers! My concern is their service to the cause. In time of crisis one can't make changes in important posts for such reasons. Ridiculous! I love Richard Wagner's music – must I close my ears to it because he was a pederast? The whole thing's absurd . . . And quite apart from Röhm's great achievements, I know I can absolutely depend on him.' It is not difficult to recognise the sting in the tail of that speech.

Within two years Hitler was to address the Reichstag in a famous harangue on the same subject, this time in terms of injured and high-flown morality. 'The life which the Chief of Staff and with him a certain circle began to lead was from any National Socialist point of view intolerable. It was not only terrible that he himself and the circle of those who were devoted to him should violate all laws of decency and modest behaviour, it was still worse that now this poison began to spread in ever wider circles.' Had Röhm been alive to hear this speech it would not have surprised him.

To understand Röhm's aims and conduct in the years 1933 to 1934, the nature of Hitler's charismatic appeal and personal leadership must be appreciated. Quarrels among his leading followers he positively encouraged, that none might grow too powerful and challenge his leadership. And, just as he had deceived the public, from extreme Right to Left, into seeing their views as his, so each Nazi leader, whether Göring, Frick, Ley, Goebbels or Röhm, hoped to 'capture' Hitler and persuade him to adopt their particular policies. So Röhm urged, we must push him soon, lest the others push him first'. This belief was excessively naïve, and was to lead Röhm to his downfall.

Hitler, whilst speaking out significantly against the concept of the 'second revolution' ('The revolution is not a permanent state of affairs, and it must not be allowed to develop into such a state'), nevertheless maintained a studied neutrality with regard to Röhm's aims for the SA, and in general terms maintained the warmest regard for his old comrade.

Above: **Defence Minister Blomberg's pro-Nazi aide, Major-General von Reichenau.** ***Below:*** **General Werner von Blomberg (arms folded) witnesses manoeuvres with Hitler**

On 30th June 1933 Röhm, without attaining ministerial office, was empowered to attend Cabinet meetings. And on 11th December of the same year he was made Reich Minister without Portfolio; but did not get the job he wanted – the Ministry of Defence. This was held by General Werner von Blomberg who, backed by his pro-Nazi aide Major-General von Reichenau, became more and more determined not to let Röhm and his hoodlum army swallow up the proud German army and its officer corps.

On New Year's Day 1934 Hitler wrote (the letter was published in the next day's *Voelkischer Beobachter*) a letter couched in exceptionally warm and grateful tones.

'My dear Chief of Staff,

The fight of the National Socialist Movement and the National Socialist Revolution were rendered possible for me by the consistent suppression of the Red Terror by the SA. If the army has to guarantee the protection of the nation against the world beyond our frontiers, the task of the SA is to secure the victory of the National Socialist Revolution and the existence of the National Socialist State and the community of our people in the domestic sphere. When I summoned you to your present position, my dear Chief of Staff, the SA was passing through a serious crisis. It is primarily due to your services if after a few years this political instrument could develop that force which enabled me to force the final struggle for power and to succeed in laying low the Marxist opponent.

'At the close of the year of the National Socialist Revolution, therefore, I feel compelled to thank you, my dear Ernst Röhm, for the imperishable services which you have rendered to the National Socialist Movement and the German people, and to assure you how very grateful I am to Fate that I am able to call such men as you my friends and fellow-combatants.

In true friendship and grateful regard, Your Adolf Hitler.'

Reassured by indications like this of his Führer's regard, Röhm continued to press as avidly as ever for an amalgamation of the *Reichswehr* and the SA – clearly with the latter as the predominating party. In the autumn of the previous year, Reichenau for the army proposed an arrangement whereby the SA should supervise all military training outside the 100,000-strong *Reichswehr*, and assist in guarding the eastern frontier. In addition he proposed that the Nationalists' equivalent of the SA, the *Stahlhelm*, should be amalgamated into the SA. Whether this was intended simply as a sop to placate the powerful and vociferous Röhm (it did not after all basically alter the status of the *Reichswehr* in the nation), or whether it was in addition a trap is not certain. For it has been suggested that the idea was for the 314,000-strong *Stahlhelm* to swamp the SA, while regular army officers were deputed to command the sections on the Polish frontier. In this way the SA would come effectively under *Reichswehr* control.

Röhm, however was far too much of a realist to be taken in by a scheme like this. He arranged for the *Stahlhelm* contingent to be distributed in such a way that it was overshadowed by the original SA *Standarten* and *Gruppen*. And he countered the attempt to place army officers in charge by demanding that he choose the officers; on top of which the SA must control many of the eastern arms depôts. These negotiations, which revealed the total incompatibility of Röhm's aims with those of the High Command, were broken off in December 1933.

So the new year, the fateful 1934, saw an impasse between Röhm and the army, that could only be resolved by one side giving a great deal of ground. Aware of this, and anxious to put an end to the embarassing difficulty, Hitler called on 28th February a meeting of *Reichswehr* and SA leaders in the *Reichswehr* ministry. There he gave them an impassioned lecture in which he urged unity upon them, and proposed that the SA should take over all responsibility for pre-service training. Röhm was obliged temporarily to put a good face on this proposal, though of course it fell far short of the least of his aims.

Afterwards all adjourned for lunch to Röhm's headquarters. The expression on the SA chief's battered features was stormy, and the moment the officers of the army had left, Röhm burst out in drunken rage: 'What that ridiculous Corporal says means nothing to us . . . I have not the slightest intention of keeping this agreement. Hitler is a traitor and at the very least must go on leave . . . If we can't get there with him, we'll get there without him.' Certainly no one could accuse Röhm of lack of courage, and such a speech from any of the other Party leaders would have been inconceivable.

SA chief for Hanover Viktor Lutze. He reported Röhm's unwise statements about Hitler and his policies to, among others, the Führer

Amongst the SA chiefs to whom this challenge was addressed was the fussy, inconsequential *Obergruppenführer* of Hanover, one Viktor Lutze. Deeply shocked by his superior's treasonable utterances, he left hurriedly and reported the terrible words in turn to Hess, Hitler and Reichenau. Disappointingly, they appeared little impressed. But the straw showed the way the wind was starting to blow.

It may be imagined that this threat to their right to be the exclusive arms-bearers of Germany did not leave the army generals indifferent. They had not allowed Hitler's accession in January 1933 in order that they might be swallowed up in the huge horde of armed louts led by an ex-Captain, whose moral code was an affront to Prussian honour. Röhm's persistent claims began thoroughly to alarm the military chiefs, and in the same month that Hitler unavailingly tried to patch up the difference, Röhm had pressed on the Cabinet a scheme whereby the army, SA, and SS should be grouped under a single Defence Ministry, over which, it was strongly implied, he himself would preside. The generals rejected this outrageous scheme with indignation; in the words of General von Brauchitsch, 'rearmament was too serious and difficult a business to permit the participation of speculators, drunkards and homosexuals.'

President Hindenburg, too, would have no truck with any such plan, and Hitler began to wonder whether he might not reluctantly have to act in some way. It was much against his practice to intervene amongst the warring factions within the movement, if there were any chance of their settling matters amongst themselves. And the mere existence of Röhm and his army of greedy 'have-nots' acted as a counterpoise and veiled warning to the 'haves', – the leaders of big business and the army. Wary and cunning as ever, Hitler watched and waited, Röhm and he appearing still the best of friends even if not at one on military policy. Despite this, the reckless Chief of Staff of the SA was moving more and more into the wilderness. As in a Greek tragedy, hostile fates began to threaten from every side. In order to see just how

SA and SS at a Party rally

Hitler in conversation with Christian Weber

unenviable was Röhm's position in the spring and early summer of 1934, it would be as well to move aside for the moment from the strict chronological order of events and separate the various factions and circumstances rallying against the powerful, blundering Brownshirt chieftain.

Firstly there was, as we have seen, the army. To recapitulate: the generals objected to the whole notion of the proud Prussian officer corps, with its glorious traditions, being subjected in any way to the self-made amateur military body of 'thugs' headed by Röhm. They objected to the despicable private life, now all too public, of its chiefs. They objected, too, to their truculent arrogance when dealing with real soldiers. Plans, such as the incorporation of 500 Brownshirt officers and 2,000 NCOs into the *Reichswehr*, were anathema; what could these men know of the traditions of the Prussian army? As for honour, that and the SA ethic were two things apart. As the *Reichswehr* Commander-in-Chief, von Hammerstein, said in April 1933: 'Any village bully can rule, like the Nazis, by terror'.

And it was not just the threat of an SA takeover that affronted the army leaders. The mere existence of this grotesquely swollen armed force created a permanent drain on the best sources of army recruiting. The army, after all, was concerned solely with one aim: to regain as soon as was practical its old position of parity or superiority with neighbouring nations, particularly France. To do this would require an abrogation of the Versailles Treaty clause, whereby the German army was restricted to a mere 100,000 men. This was one of the many wholly unrealistic clauses of that inept Treaty; even at the time the British General Staff had proposed a total of four times the amount. It was likely therefore that in time the Entente powers could be induced to accept a more realistic figure. This was scarcely likely to happen, though, while France and Britain could point to the existence within Germany of an armed force several millions strong. In the generals' opinion, on the one hand the SA was militarily valueless; on the other its existence might well be preventing the building up of a real army.

Secondly, the Entente powers were extremely suspicious of the potential threat offered by the Brownshirt legions. Their colossal increase in size after January 1933, coupled with the fact that their leader was now German Chancellor, made them a factor in any military assessment. In December 1933 the French Ambassador noted his country's disquiet over the million-strong SA. (It should here be noted that the figures given by different authorities for the total strength of the SA vary (a) according to the guesses involved in the estimate, (b) according to whether the *Stahlhelm* is included, and (c) whether the great increase in the first year of Nazi rule is allowed for. In June 1933 Röhm himself estimated the figure at nearly 2,000,000.)

On 1st January 1934 Germany received a French note expressing strong concern at the threatened expansion of the German army, and more particularly 'the para-military organisations, which for many years have been ceaselessly expanding'. The same question must have taxed foreign statesman as puzzled native Germans: what was the purpose of the SA now that the National Revolution was achieved? Two months later, when Anthony Eden arrived in Berlin to discuss the disarmament question, Hitler proffered in return for concessions for increasing the *Reichswehr* to

Anthony Eden, in Berlin to discuss the disarmament question. Hitler offered to disband two-thirds of the SA and clamp down on the remainder in return for agreement to allow expansion of the *Reichswehr*

Barthou, French Foreign Minister, refused point blank to countenance any increase in Germany's armed forces

Hjalmar Schacht through the cartoonist's eyes

demobilise two-thirds of the SA and to allow a system of inspection to check the activities of the remainder. How this was to be done in the face of Röhm's views was not explained. In fact, these remarks reached Röhm, whose indignation was thereby increased. And when the new French Foreign Minister, Barthou, abruptly rejected any prospect of an increased German army, the generals of that army were not slow to lay much of the blame on the existence of the SA.

Hitler himself of course was not wont to pay much heed to the demands or threats of foreign statesmen. All the same, another stone was added to the cairn, and the army's opposition was greatly increased.

Thirdly, conservative circles largely centred around President Hindenburg and Vice-Chancellor von Papen became more and more concerned with the 'uncivilised behaviour' and revolutionary nature of the Brownshirt mobs. It was Hindenburg in the spring of 1934 who rejected outright the suggested incorporation of SA officers and NCOs into the *Reichswehr*. The President had reluctantly accepted Hitler as Chancellor only on the understood condition that, influenced by Papen and his conservative colleagues, he would 'civilise' himself and his Party. But to accept the blackguard Röhm as head of all of Germany's armed forces was very much more than the old gentleman would tolerate.

Papen, though an arch-intriguer and often misguided in his actions, was nevertheless a strong conservative at heart. He warned Hitler repeatedly of the Brownshirt danger, and when Hitler appeared unresponsive, was goaded into delivering the famous Marburg speech, of which more later. Though the opinions of the *Reaktion* must have been familiar enough to Hitler, nevertheless it was the Marburg speech that finally brought about the succession of events that roused Hitler to action.

Closely connected with the circles

Nazi anti-Semitic sarcasm: 'Pity you're not Kosher!'

of the old governing class were the rulers of big business, industrialists and bankers. In his old revolutionary days, Hitler had frequently inveighed against these 'allies of Jewish capital'. But Hitler in power was a very different person from Hitler in opposition. Now he needed the powerful institutions of the State to consolidate and confirm his rule.

On 20th February 1933 a meeting was held at Göring's Reichstag President's Palace (Göring led the 'Right' faction of the Nazis, just as Röhm and Strasser led the 'Left'. Goebbels belonged to the Left by conviction, but cared more for backing the winner). Dr Hjalmar Schacht, the financial wizard who had come over to the Nazis, acted as host while Hitler explained that very soon democracy would be abolished and an iron order imposed on the German social system. Krupp, Thyssen and the other business pashas present were so delighted at the prospect that 3,000,000 marks were donated to the Party at that meeting alone. Henceforth big business backed Hitler to the hilt.

But business exists for profits, and these to a great extent depend on a country's internal stability. Party members and Stormtroopers continued to talk of the Second Revolution, and the latter kept up their natural pastimes of beating up and murdering political and personal rivals, terrorising Jewish-owned businesses, and interfering in the course of work and justice. Nazi radicals marched into offices and factories, escorted by brown-shirted bravos, demanding to take over and administer the amazing economic theories of their apostles Feder and Darré.

In July Hitler took strong measures against these self-appointed managers and their like, and made it very clear that, whatever might have been said in the old rough-and-tumble days, the National Socialist German Work-

ers' Party and big business were working together for the same aims now.

For a cloud loomed on the economic horizon. By June 1934 Dr Schacht, Director of the Reichsbank, was preparing to declare a moratorium on transfers. All was not well with the financial situation of the Third Reich. At Hitler's accession to the Chancellorship, Germany's gold reserves stood at 920,000,000 marks. Now, nearly a year and a half later, they had fallen to 150,000,000 marks. The backing for banknotes in circulation was down by five per cent. As Hitler's great platform in opposition had been the evil of inflation, he could not view the prospect of a repetition occurring with equanimity.

And to tide over the awkward period ahead, Hitler was shrewd enough to know he would be utterly dependent on the skills of the old governing class to see him through. Von Neurath at the Foreign Office, Karl Schmitt at the Economics Ministry, Seldte, the Minister of Labour, von Blomberg, Minister of Defence; all these, as Göring reminded the omniscient Führer, were men who knew their jobs. And skill at this moment was more necessary than ideals.

Hitler could not afford to offend the old order yet. And as their demands for the SA to be brought under control became more shrill, so he was forced to face up to the problem he had shelved for so long. For a time the SA had been useful as a stick with which to threaten big business; those days were over.

On 28th June 1934 Hitler toured some arms factories in company with their owner, Herr Krupp von Bohlen. Krupp took the opportunity of complaining of the frequent absences of those

Von Neurath in London for the World Economic Conference of June 1933. Hitler knew he would have to rely on the experience and skill of members of the governing class such as Neurath

workmen who were members of the SA. On the slightest pretext they would down tools and set off for drill or instruction. Hitler paused, his pale blue eyes reflective, his jaw set.

'The SA is going on leave', he muttered tightly, 'and there will be no more parades or meetings of its members.'

Franz Seldte was not only Minister of Labour, but also head of the ex-servicemen's association, the *Stahlhelm* ('Steel Helmet'). This was a conservative, less militant, version of the SA, numbering about 314,000. Because of its association with Hugenberg and the Nationalists, Röhm looked upon the *Stahlhelm* as 'the private army of the *Reaktion*', and was determined to liquidate it. In the end he had to be content with the compro-

Above: **Herr Krupp von Bohlen, armaments magnate. His complaints of absenteeism among his employees who were also SA members did nothing to moderate Hitler's intentions towards the stormtroopers. *Below:* Franz Seldte and the ex-Crown Prince review the Stahlhelm corps in May 1933. Soon, however, 'there will be no more parades . . .'**

mise described above, whereby the organisation was amalgamated with the SA. At the same time Seldte was paid the empty compliment of being made an SA *Obergruppenführer*. Despite this, relations between the two para-military bodies became increasingly strained, until in June 1934 a series of ugly incidents erupted, including the temporary arrest of Seldte himself at Magdeburg (11th June) and the killing of an SA *Standartenführer* at Quitzingen (24th June). In certain districts Party chiefs suppressed on their own initiative the local *Stahlhelm*, and Seldte countered with an angry protest (28th June). So that by the fatal 30th June, the *Stahlhelm*, influential by its numbers and its Nationalist representation in

Rudolf Hess, deputy Party leader, publicly spelled out the fate of those who thought themselves above the Party

the coalition government, was bitterly inflamed against the SA. At the mass level, the *Stahlhelm* ex-servicemen despised the Stormtroopers, veterans only of uncouth civil disturbances.

Not only had Röhm raised up powerful enemies against himself in influential conservative circles, but within the Party itself he had found himself increasingly out on a limb. With the Nazi accession to power, a ferocious struggle between the Party bosses developed, each seeking to carve out his own private domain within the Reich. These plottings and quarrels were if anything encouraged by Hitler, as they made his position as the ultimate arbiter the more assured. His practice was not to intervene directly unless Party policy or unity was in danger of being wrecked.

In one respect Röhm of course had an important card to play, in the shape of his enormous Brownshirt army. Unlike Ley, Ribbentrop, Rosenberg, Hess and the rest, he was not a man whose position owed all to Hitler's favour, and who could be as easily cast down as raised up. But it was his misfortune to desire the one post the accession to which was opposed by the only entrenched institution Hitler dared not offend. The army would never tolerate as Minister of Defence the man who wished to swamp the *Reichswehr* with his private army.

Röhm's relative independence, power and frustrated ambition aroused the jealousy and dislike of many of his colleagues. Furthermore, his absorption in the affairs of the SA, relative straightforwardness in his dealings and ill-concealed contempt for the other Party leaders, coupled with his homosexuality all helped to set him aside from the jostling henchmen of the Führer.

In the 22nd January 1934 issue of the *Voelkischer Beobachter* Rudolf Hess, the deputy Party leader, declared in measured terms that neither the SA nor any similar body could ever pursue a course independent of the Party

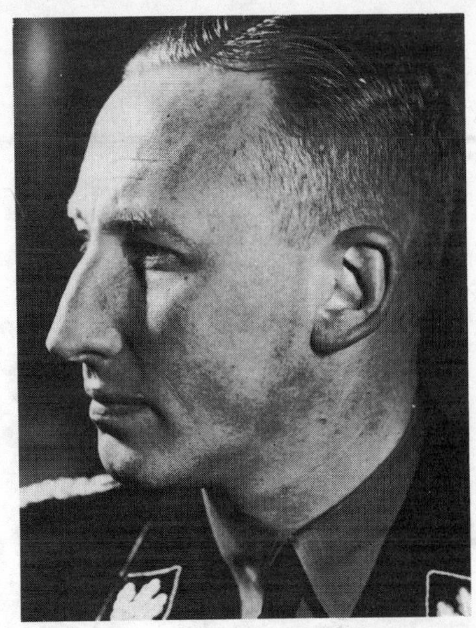

Himmler's aide Heydrich, visited by Hess after the latter's warning broadcast

proper. The hint was unmistakable; and on 25th June of the same year he made a nationwide broadcast, in which, after extolling the Führer as the only man capable of planning the Reich's future, he ended on a threatening note: 'Woe to him who breaks faith, and thinks to serve the Revolution through rebellion! Woe to him who clumsily tramples the Führer's strategic plans in the hope of quicker results!' On the very next day – a sinister touch – Hess paid a call on Himmler's dreadful aide, Heydrich. The full significance of this we shall see shortly.

A far more dangerous foe of the largely unsuspecting Röhm was the bulky Hermann Göring, now Prime Minister of Prussia. The former air force pilot had hated the SA chief since the time of the beer hall *putsch* in 1923. With his military background and grotesque love of grandiose ranks, uniforms and decorations, he had from the beginning cherished ambitions of becoming head of the Nazi strongarm

Göring and Röhm at a Party Day assembly; deadly rivals for power in the Third Reich

The SS, Himmler's challengers to Röhm's SA, its parent body

forces and in the event of a Nazi government coming to power, high in the hierarchy of the nation's armed forces.

In 1930, when Pfeffer von Salomon resigned as head of the SA, Göring had hoped to succeed him. His jealousy had greatly increased when instead Hitler chose the undeniably more efficient and hardworking Röhm as *Stabschef*. In the following year Göring conspired with the unprincipled Goebbels to release to the anti-Nazi press a series of compromising letters written by Röhm to friends from his exile in Bolivia. These revealed all too plainly his homosexuality, and were given wide publicity by the Party's enemies. Despite this, Hitler stood by Röhm, as usual asserting that the private life of loyal Party members could not affect their position.

Once the Nazis were in power at the beginning of 1933, Göring became involved in a series of complicated intrigues. His aim, however, was consistent: he must grab as much as he could for his private empire. In particular, he was aiming at the Ministry of Defence and the control of the Reich's greatly-expanded armed forces. As in 1930, Röhm stood in his way. Throughout 1933 and the early part of 1934 the position of the two Nazi chiefs appeared roughly balanced. If Röhm possessed his colossal Brownshirt army, Göring controlled the government and police of two-thirds of Germany. A secret and desperate struggle for power began.

Apart from his personal vendetta against Röhm, Göring had a political motive for working against him. For Göring, from his personal background and social contacts, represented the 'Right wing' of the Party: that which favoured working with the army, industry and landed gentry. Röhm, as we know, held pronounced socialistic views of an individual kind.

Very soon Göring acquired an invaluable ally within the movement. One of the most fanatically devoted of all the Führer's motley followers was an insignificant-looking ex-poultry breeder, Heinrich Himmler. Ever since he had clutched a banner in the 1923 beer hall fiasco, he had devoted his strange, narrow existence to serving the divine Führer. For long the leader of the SS (still a section of the SA) he seemed to be alone amongst Nazi chiefs in not acquiring the plums of office in 1933. True, he was made President of Police in Munich, but this was of little consolation to the man whose ambition was to control the police of the whole Reich. During 1933 he gradually gained control over the police of several other German states beside Bavaria. But the limits to his accession of power appeared to be severely circumscribed.

Göring, Minster-President of Prussia, was only too aware that it was his control over the Prussian police far more than his premiership that gave him his power. Any move by Himmler to extend his activities into Prussia was abruptly checked. When Himmler sent his far more able and unscrupulous aide Heydrich to Berlin, the latter found himself humiliatingly rebuffed by Göring's police. His every effort and intrigue checked by Göring, it looked as if Himmler was reduced to a permanently subordinate rôle: his SS dwarfed within the enormous SA, and his police ambitions confined without the bounds of Prussia. Above him loomed the bloated figures of Röhm and Göring.

But Himmler was patient and persistent, and, guided by the cold, merciless Heydrich, he began to profit by the split between the two leaders. For Göring's dislike of Röhm had been increased immeasurably by the latter's accession to ministerial rank in December 1933. It seemed more than ever likely that Röhm would gain his ambition and become Germany's first Nazi commander-in-chief. Symbolically, in August 1933 Göring had, on being made an army general, exchanged his Brownshirt uniform for the far more glamorous field-grey of the *Reichswehr*. From now on he

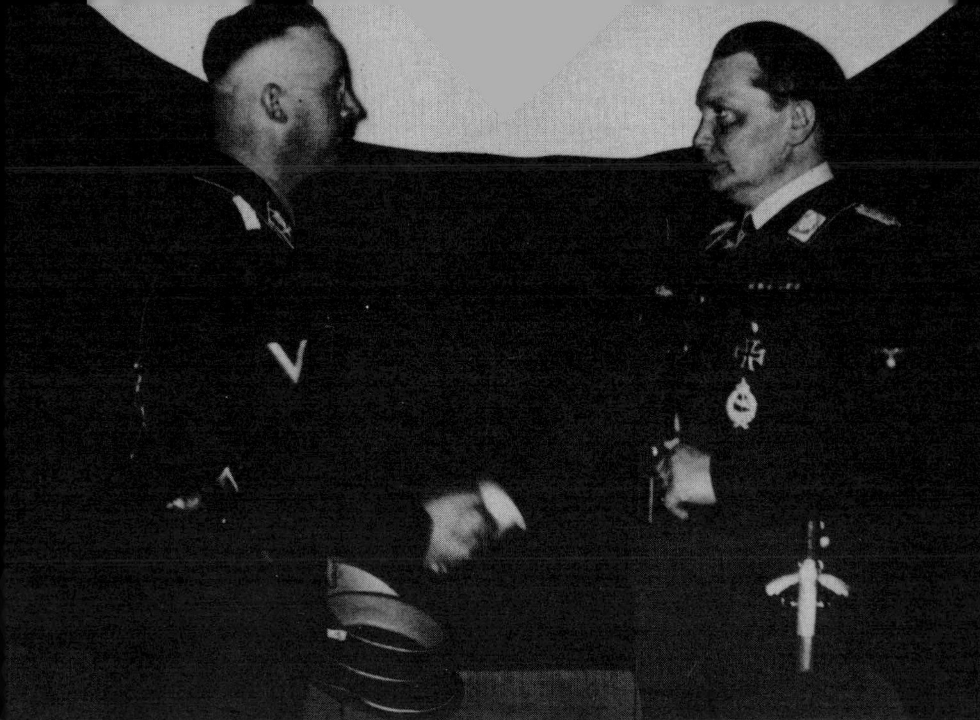

was working with the army for the destruction of Röhm. At the same time he created his own private police force, the *Landespolizeigruppe General Göring*, whose headquarters was at the Lichterfelde barracks outside Berlin.

Unnecessary fuel was added to the flames in spring 1934. Then Röhm visited Yugoslavia, where he was fêted by the authorities at Ragusa. Shortly afterwards arrived the Minister-President Hermann Göring; but the thrifty Yugoslavs decided they had done enough to honour the representatives of the new Germany, and treated the vain, bemedalled general as a private visitor. The normally good-humoured Göring seethed with rage. Röhm would have to go!

Now Göring saw the need for an alliance with Himmler and his élite SS, who had been kept increasingly aloof of the SA. Considerable pressure had been exercised for Himmler to be accepted as head of the Prussian police, as even Hitler himself saw the

Göring recognises the wisdom of allying with the SS, and appoints Himmler head of the *Geheime Staatspolizei* – Gestapo

advantages of a single unified police force throughout the country. Göring suddenly acceded with a good grace, and appointed Himmler as head of the Prussian police (*Gestapo*) on 20th April 1934. The former head, Rudolf Diels (who had largely favoured Röhm), was transferred to a safe post at Cologne.

Göring and Himmler, backed by Heydrich, now began to plan the destruction of Röhm. Göring of course had always loathed him, but Himmler's part in the plot was a typically Nazi *volte-face*. For he, on the other hand, had been a loyal follower of Röhm since they had first met in 1922 at the Arzberger Keller in Munich. He had served under Röhm in the beer hall *putsch* the following year, and his SS had been and still was a subdivision of Röhm's SA. Only the previous year

Himmler – 'most loyal to you' – and Röhm

(1933) Röhm and he had been godfathers to Heydrich's son; and on Röhm's birthday that winter (28th November) he had written effusively to the SA Chief of Staff: 'I wish you, as a soldier and friend, everything that one can promise in faithful service. It has been and is our greatest pride always to be numbered among those who are most loyal to you.' Now, within a few months of these birthday greetings, he was preparing the murder of this 'friend'.

Himmler was thus finally persuaded to ally himself with Göring for the destruction of Röhm, but it was his ruthless *alter ego*, Heydrich, who finally prodded him into action. In April Heydrich on his own account set his spies to work in an effort to uncover incriminating evidence against the Chief of Staff of the SA. In full accord with this was the pro-Nazi General Reichenau, who had conducted abortive negotiations with Röhm to try and arrange a *modus vivendi* between the army and the SA. After the failure of that attempt and the recognition that Röhm's ambitions aimed at nothing short of control of the whole armed forces, Reichenau (later with the connivance of the Minister of Defence, von Blomberg) began increasingly to work hand-in-glove with the murderous Heydrich.

Meanwhile, army complaints about Röhm's ambitions were beginning to have an effect upon Hitler, but for reasons largely extraneous to their own grievances. It must be remembered that Hitler, with his obsessional belief in his own rightness and historical mission, was by no means easily subjected to the influence of pressure-groups, particularly where old and valued colleagues were concerned. One has only to remember his

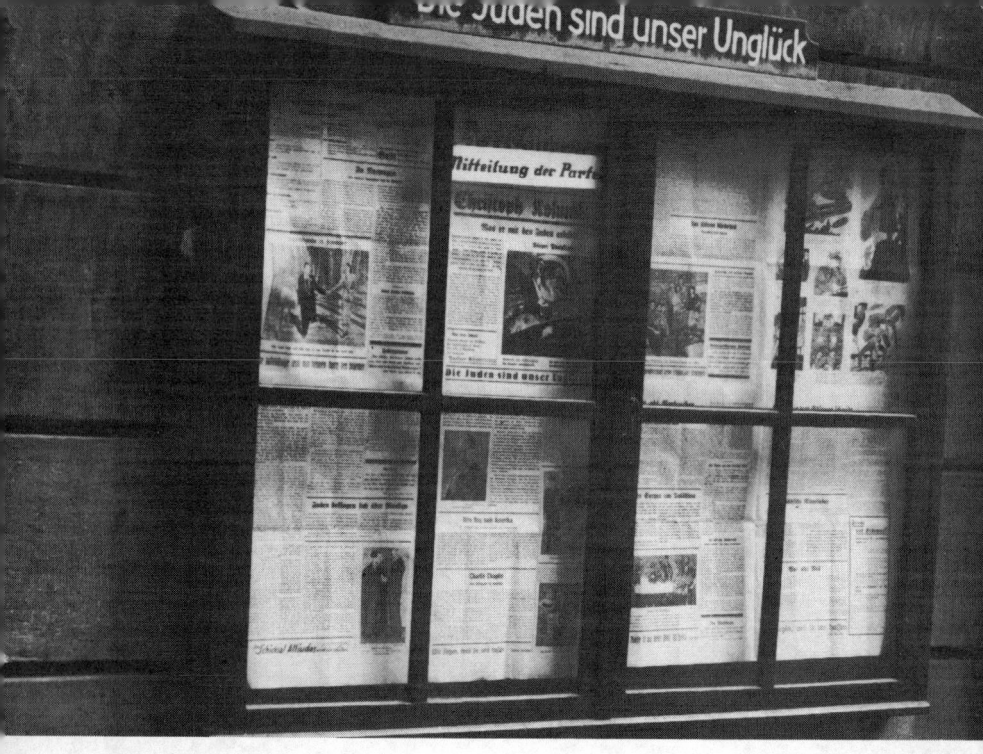

Julius Streicher postures for the camera. Hitler's cronies from the early days could usually rely on his protection

***Der Stürmer,* the anti-Semitic weekly newspaper edited by Streicher**

protection extended over the monstrous Gauleiter of Nuremberg, Julius Streicher. This criminal sadist, who edited a pornographic anti-Jewish weekly, *Der Stürmer*, revolted even loyal Party members, who made unceasing appeals to have him expelled – without avail.

But now Hitler was looking forward to an event that in the nature of things could not be long deferred. This was the death of the aged and fast-failing President Hindenburg. Hitler's whole strategy was now directed towards ensuring his own succession to the Presidency once the illustrious Field-Marshal was gone. It was widely suspected (probably with good reason) that Hindenburg might nominate as his successor a Prince of the House of Hohenzollern. Such a wish would naturally have no legal effect, but the President enjoyed immense respect throughout the country. In addition the restoration of the monarchy was favoured by many senior army officers and other pillars of the *Reaktion* – including the two ex-Chancellors, Brüning and von Papen. And, apart from Hitler's determination to seize the office for himself, the restoration of the hereditary dynasty in any form would for numerous obvious reasons be a far greater threat to Hitler's proposed dictatorship than the election of some unobtrusive politician.

To guarantee his own succession, Hitler had to ensure that he had the support of the *Reichswehr*. Already many officers and men were Nazi sympathisers, and Blomberg and Reichenau worked openly in his cause. However, unless he were backed by von Fritsch and the senior generals, Hitler could not feel secure. On 11th April 1934 Hitler embarked on the cruiser *Deutschland* for the Baltic. There, accompanied by his unprincipled Minister of Defence, he conferred with the commanders-in-chief of the army and navy, General von

Fritsch and Admiral Raeder, on this delicate question. He proposed bluntly that the armed forces should support his succession to the Presidency. In return he offered a greatly increased army and navy – that went without saying – and the drastic reduction of the SA and curbing of Röhm's military ambitions. (It should be noted, however, that some historians query whether any such pact took place on the *Deutschland*. It may well be that the pact came later.)

Raeder agreed at once, but the far more vital von Fritsch stated that he

Hitler with Blomberg aboard the *Deutschland* during the Führer's highly successful Baltic cruise

would have to consult his fellow-generals. This he did at Bad Nauheim on 16th May, and there the foolish generals dishonourably accepted Hitler's bait. In return for the ending of Röhm's pretensions, they would endorse Hitler's succession to Hindenburg. Hitler began at once to consider what measures would be necessary to curb Röhm.

Hitler with Raeder. The Admiral readily agreed to support Hitler's bid for the Presidency in return for an expanded navy and the clipping of Röhm's wings

The closing net

Throughout the spring and early summer of 1934, Röhm's demands for the 'Second Revolution' and an early recognition of the SA's rôle in the coming Nazi state became increasingly vociferous. They were accompanied by mass parades, para-military manoeuvres, and other measures likely to drive home the moral to the forgetful Führer. These were the tactics that had brought Hitler to power, and Röhm blindly imagined that similar methods could now be used to 'guide' the Nazi Revolution onto correct lines. The immense power of the SA, now equipped with its own laws, police, education, press and civil rights (to say nothing of its military structure) represented surely the most formidable pressure group in the country.

But for the character of Röhm and his brutal organisation, one might almost feel sorry for his pathetic gullibility. Largely unaware of the tidal wave now darkening his political horizon, he recognised that opposing elements obstructed his plans, but believed that the temporarily misguided Führer could be 'redirected' along sounder lines. The only tactic the simple Röhm could envisage towards his enemies was the use of force; and towards recalcitrant friends, the threat of force.

'We must push him soon', he declared, 'lest the others push him first . . . If Hitler is reasonable I shall settle the matter quietly; if he isn't I must be prepared to use force – not for my sake but for the sake of our revolution.' Röhm persuaded himself that Hitler could not do without the SA. Were they not, as Hitler himself was to declare a few years later, 'a stout fist against him who ventured with violence to hinder our campaign of the spirit and of reason'? True enough, the threat of SA violence had done much to make Hitler Chancellor; but having scaled the heights Hitler no longer needed the ladder.

Röhm, unconscious of his peril, smiles while surrounded by SS officers

Almost as if desperately trying to convince himself, Röhm fondly argued that the Brownshirt battalions were as necessary now as ever. 'No', he explained to a friend, 'Hitler doesn't mind the swelling of the SA. On the contrary. He wants to use us at will, as pressure on the *Reichswehr* and on big business here and abroad. But if he thinks he can squeeze me for his own ends for ever, and some fine day throw me on the ash-heap, he's wrong. The SA can also be an instrument for checking Hitler himself.'

What Hitler's own plans were during May and early June will probably never be known. Most likely he hoped that the problem would somehow solve itself, for he was an inveterate procrastinator when faced with problems as apparently insoluble as this. However, others were not so nice in their scruples, and began increasingly active preparations for the final reckoning with the wayward SA Chief of Staff.

Already in the spring, Gestapo Chief Heydrich had warned Hitler that Röhm was planning to introduce a machine gun company into every *Gruppe* and *Obergruppe* of the SA. Similarly, every move of the SA *Stabschef* and his principal aides that could possibly bear a sinister interpretation was laid before the Führer. The brutish SS leader, Sepp Dietrich, showed the *Reichswehr* ministry a 'death-list' of generals, 'compiled by the SA' – it included the names of von Fritsch and Beck. Equally imaginary threatening orders supposedly emanating from the SA were 'leaked' to the army command. When SA *Gruppenführer* Karl Ernst tried to protest his organisation's innocence, he was prevented by Göring's Gestapo chief, Kurt Daluege. Within the army itself, Reichenau encouraged and furthered these and other largely groundless fears and suspicions.

So passed the month of May 1934, with Göring, certain army leaders and the SS preparing the downfall of

13177

Left: SA quasi-military manoeuvres and parades take place; their purpose, to remind Hitler of where his gratitude should lie. *Above:* Sepp Dietrich, SS commander, played his part in blackening Röhm and the SA to Hitler. *Below:* Generals von Fritsch and Beck, both down on the invented 'death list' of the SA

Kurt Daluege, Gestapo chief, in conversation with Dietrich

Röhm. At the same time Hitler was decided at last that *something* would have to be done, but what? According to Papen, neither Himmler nor Goebbels knew at this time what the Führer's decision would be.

On 4th June Hitler met Röhm and (according to his own account) warned him that those elements in the SA that were advocating a second revolution were heading for disaster. He urged Röhm to keep the organisation under control, and promised to come to a satisfactory arrangement within a few weeks. Meanwhile the SA were to go on leave for the whole of July, and were strictly prohibited from engaging in any military activities during that time. What Hitler intended as the outcome of this move it is now impossible to say. It may be that he wished temporarily to remove the overt threat, whilst he hit on some scheme with which to present the SA on its return to duty as a *fait accompli*.

Röhm apparently took this in good faith, and possibly felt relieved that at last something was going to be done. At any rate, on 8th June the *Voelkischer Beobachter* published a message from SA Headquarters, announcing that Chief of Staff Röhm, suffering from an old wound, was going on a week's iodine course at the resort of Bad Wiessee. The notice concluded, however, on a minatory note; directed doubtless against Göring, Papen, Blomberg and the other 'reactionaries':

'I expect then on 1st August the SA, fully rested and strengthened, will stand ready to serve the honourable tasks which People and Fatherland may expect from them. If the foes of the SA are nursing the hope that SA will not return from their leave or that a part only will return we are ready to let them enjoy this hope for a short time. At the hour and in the form which appears to be necessary they shall receive the fitting answer.'

Before leaving Berlin, Röhm invited Hitler to come to Bad Wiessee on the day before the SA leave was due to begin, 30th June, and confer with him and other SA leaders. Hitler readily agreed; and the appointment was indeed to be kept. Perhaps Röhm would have done well to consider one of his Führer's favourite maxims: 'Never antagonise potential enemies. Attack them only when you can destroy them.'

At any rate, it was about this time that elaborate and careful preparations – of a kind not tending to the advantage of the SA leaders – began to be put into effect. Two days after Hitler's meeting with Röhm, the security service of the SS was created the Party's sole Intelligence agency. This was the SD (*Sicherheitsdienst*), whose head, Heydrich, had placed spies everywhere in the Reich. Heydrich kept secret files on all public figures (including, it is said, on Hitler himself); but since April his men had been directed to find out anything that could compromise Röhm and his supporters in the SA. It was not of course the scandal of their private lives that concerned him: that had long been public knowledge. What Heydrich was determined to produce was proof that the SA high command was plotting against Hitler.

It must soon have been apparent that nothing of the sort was contemplated. Despite their grievances and grumbles, the Brownshirt leaders held a naïve faith in Hitler and believed he would before long reward them suitably for their past services. In particular, the promise of a meeting with the Führer at the end of the month filled most of them with hope that the settlement would not be long deferred.

But the same move that began to

The hotel in Bad Wiessee to which Röhm invited Hitler and where Hitler ordered him arrested

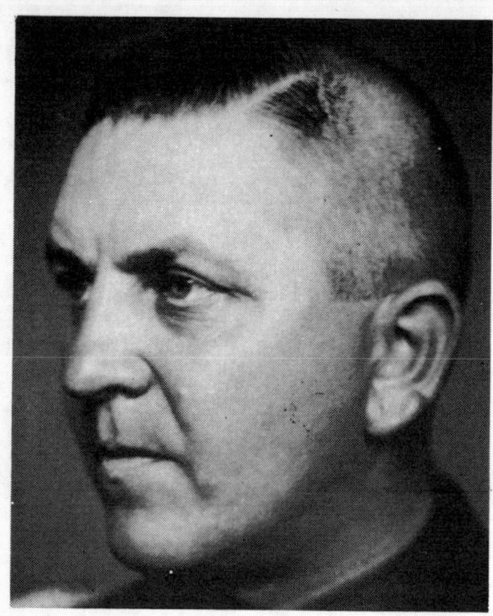

Theodor Eicke, *SS-Obergruppenführer*

raise the SA leaders' hopes appalled the scheming Heydrich. For, if Hitler were to meet Röhm and the others at Bad Wiessee on 30th June, was there not a chance after all of a reconciliation? And with the SA going on leave the following day, how could the idea of a proposed SA *putsch* be made credible? The threat of an SA revolution removed would also lessen the army's interest in seeing the destruction or muzzling of the SA. Heydrich set frantically to work, backed now (after initial reluctance) by his official master Himmler.

In early June the SS *Oberführer* Theodor Eicke organised the local SS in practise manoeuvres against an enemy imagined to be operating from Munich-Lechfeld and Bad Wiessee. In Munich itself SS *Untersturmführer* Max Müller of SS Motor Sturm No 3 was placed on alert and given a prearranged code signal on which to act; whilst the HQ of the SD at 10, Leopoldstrasse kept a wary eye on the unwitting invalid at Bad Wiessee. All over Germany similar preparations were going on.

The SS was ready with its murder squads, the SD was assiduously feeding the story of the SA 'plot' to the appropriate sources, Göring's police was preparing, and Reichenau assured Heydrich that the army was there to see the SA did not strike back. The trap was ready and its victim totally unaware of the danger threatening him. All that was needed was one word from the Führer – and Ernst Röhm would suffer the savage death he had meted out to so many others.

But the Führer was very reluctant to utter that word. For though a concatenation of events had conspired to make Röhm's removal almost a necessity, he still felt unwilling to act. For, with the faithful *Stabschef* gone, might not a dangerous vacuum be created? If Himmler or Göring stepped into the gap so made, might not either or both of them become perilously over-mighty subjects? Then again, a strongly independent and powerful SA made a useful counterweight to the army, which might on their removal feel less obliged to come to terms with Hitler. Brute force was what counted in the world, and Hitler's share of it rested largely on the serried ranks of the brown battalions.

These problems revolving in his fertile mind, Hitler set off on 14th June to Venice, where he met for the first time his fellow-dictator, Mussolini. All did not go well at this meeting, for the touchy Führer in his shabby mackintosh found himself hopelessly outshone by the more experienced Duce, who strutted at the head of his well-drilled Blackshirt hordes in a resplendently gorgeous Fascist uniform. Moodily, Hitler complained to the Italian dictator of the apparently insoluble problem exercising his mind. Shrewdly, Mussolini observed that it takes one set of men to make a revolution, but another sort to maintain the new order. 'It rests with you to put your house in order', remarked

Mussolini and Hitler at their June meeting in Venice. Il Duce offers Hitler veiled advice on his SA problem

Röhm with von Papen. The latter's call for an end to brutal measures and lawlessness meets with warm approval from the public

the Duce significantly. Later, however he was to condemn Hitler's resulting moves as clumsy and ill-executed.

Hitler returned disgruntled but still undecided, just as a storm broke unexpectedly from quite a different quarter of the political spectrum. Vice-Chancellor Franz von Papen, a staunch conservative and traditionalist at heart, even if he lacked too frequently the courage to stand by his principles, had been asked to address a large and influential audience at the university of Marburg on 17th June. The speech had been largely prepared by von Papen's aides, who felt even more strongly than the Vice-Chancellor that the time had come to halt the reign of terror overtaking Germany. Terror camps had been established by various Nazi organisations, opposition parties were suppressed or terrorised, freedom of speech and publication had virtually vanished, and SA bullies commited crimes unchecked.

Von Papen called for an end to terror, brutality, and the ubiquitous control of the Party machine: 'the suppression of individual thought indicates confusion between vitality and brutality, and reveals a respect for naked force which is a danger to the nation. No nation can live in a continuous state of revolution, if it

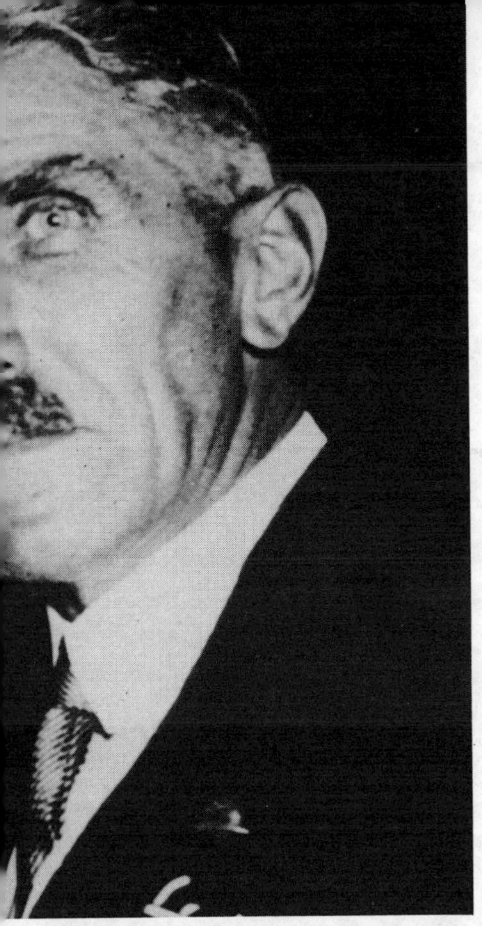

wishes to justify itself before history. Permanent dynamism permits no solid foundations to be laid. Germany cannot live in a continuous state of unrest, to which no one sees an end.'

The roar of applause from the assembled professors and students present was echoed throughout a tired and frightened Germany. At last someone in an official position had spoken out uncompromisingly against the Nazi abuse of power and the threat posed by the colossal revolutionary bands of Brownshirts. A few days later, at the Hamburg Races, von Papen was lionised by thousands of cheering racegoers. Goebbels, who was also present, was largely ignored.

Naturally, however, the Nazi leaders were outraged at this drastic challenge to their rule and methods. Goebbels, who had himself on numerous occasions advocated the very 'second revolution' now being condemned, used his powers as Propaganda Minister to suppress every reference to the speech on radio and in the press. Hitler, infuriated that the man he had looked on as a cypher should interfere with his plans in this way, denounced 'the pygmy who imagines he can stop, with a few phrases, the gigantic renewal of a people's life'.

But Papen, isolated as he was in the government, still held a trump card – the ace as it happened. He went straight to Hitler, furious at Goebbels's action: 'The Vice-Chancellor of the Reich Government could not tolerate a ban by a junior minister on the publication of an official speech. I had spoken as a trustee for the President . . . I told him that Goebbels' action left me no alternative but to submit my resignation from the Government. I would advise Hindenburg of this immediately, unless the Goebbels ban was lifted and Hitler declared himself prepared to adopt the policy I had outlined.'

Hitler was shaken. For von Papen was undoubtedly a protegé of the President and, for aught the Führer knew, might have been encouraged from influential quarters to issue the Marburg speech. And Hindenburg was the one man in Germany Hitler dared not offend at this time. Not only was the aged warlord's influence immense with the Reichswehr, but there was also the question of the Presidential succession. For Hitler, as we have seen, was determined to be the next President himself, and for that he needed the backing of the army and the blessing of Hindenburg.

Hastily placating von Papen (a man all too easily mollified) – he laid the blame for all the troubles on the SA, and threatened to deal with them shortly – Hitler flew on the next day (21st June) to the President's estate at Neudeck in East Prussia. He was determined to find out the truth about

Hitler visits Hindenburg to get the President's views

Hindenburg's views, and anticipate any protests made by von Papen. The interview that followed confirmed the Nazi Chancellor's worst fears. Both the President himself and the hitherto pliant Defence Minister, von Blomberg, told Hitler brusquely that unless order was restored throughout the Reich very swiftly, martial law would be declared and the government of the country handed over to the army.

Hitler left Neudeck humiliated, fearful, and angry. Total control of Germany's destiny was in his grasp – only to be in danger of being snatched away by the treachery and indiscipline of Röhm and his homosexual cronies. Well, the *Stabschef* and his immediate associates must go. But how, and in precisely what manner? Hitler's old doubts and irresolution arose again; but now they were ready to be allayed by the incriminating 'revelations' of Himmler and Heydrich. Hitler gave the chiefs of his Praetorian Guard, the SS, permission to prepare measures against the SA leadership. But even at that late hour he does not seem entirely to have made up his mind as to exactly what those measures should constitute.

Meanwhile, the grim apparatus of the SS death-squads got under way. On 24th June Himmler and Heydrich held a conference of the SS in Berlin, and the following day the SD was placed on permanent duty. At the same time lists of potential victims were drawn up by the principal conspirators. Intoxicated by the sudden realisation that potential or real rivals could be so easily eliminated, the list began to extend far beyond the original conception of a simple liquidation of Röhm and a handful of his right-hand men. The SS, Göring, the Gestapo and Wagner (the Gauleiter of Bavaria) all added their own suggestions. Occasionally a name proposed by Himmler would be struck out by Göring, who extended his protection to men like Diels, his former Chief of Police. But in general it was a question of adding more and more names from an ever-widening circle of prominent figures who had at one time or another offended the plotters. The original list was kept by SS *Oberstürmführer* Ilges of the SD, who was heard to say in exultant tones: 'Do you know the meaning of the word bloodlust? I feel as if I was going to wade in blood.'

At the same time the army was placed on alert by the Commander-in-Chief, von Fritsch. It was alleged that the long-expected SA *coup* now threatened, and that troops must be ready to repel it. Barracks, transport and weapons were to be placed at the disposal of the SS where required – the army wished to keep its own hands 'clean', While the majority of officers was only too pleased that action was at last to be taken against their ruffianly rivals, few actually believed in Heydrich's 'plot'. Indeed, General von Kleist, commander in Silesia, asked the local SA chief, Heines, point-blank about the rumours. On obtaining an indignant denial, von Kleist felt obliged to report the matter to von Fritsch. Von Fritsch, accompanied by the pro-Nazi Reichenau, listened moodily and then broke in: 'That may be, but it's too late now'. Reichenau, in order to absolve the army conscience, had Röhm expelled from the Officers' Association. The army, whilst avoiding involvement in any unprovoked bloodshed, was heavily implicated in the bloodthirsty conspiracy.

The jaws of the trap were closing round the SA Chief of Staff, who took the waters as unsuspectingly as ever at Bad Wiessee. But in what form would the trap be sprung? That still no one knew, when Hitler flew on Thursday, 28th June, to attend the wedding of Gauleiter Josef Terboven (six years later appointed Reich Commissar for Norway) at Essen. Yet something had to be decided, for it was only two days to go before Hitler's appointment with Röhm, agreed on at the beginning of the month.

Wagner with Hitler and Röhm. The Gauleiter of Bavaria, Himmler and his SS Chiefs, together with Göring and the Gestapo, were responsible for drawing up the list of 'eliminations'

Bloodlust

British cartoonist Low's view of Hitler and Göring taming the SA after the massacre. 'Now they salute with both hands'

Hitler's immediate moves on his arrival at the Kaiserhof Hotel in Essen, and indeed the whole purpose of his visit, seem to indicate that even at this late hour he continued to vacillate. That evening, as if trying to work himself up into a rage, he telephoned Röhm to complain that SA men had insulted a foreign diplomat in the Rhineland. He warned the SA Chief of Staff that this would not do, and that it and similar outrages would be thrashed out at the meeting now fixed for 11am on the 30th. Röhm acquiesced, but showed no signs of undue perturbation. A settlement of differences was, after all, what he sincerely desired.

Yet on the very same day Hitler assured an SA *Gruppenführer*, Ritter von Krausser, that the whole purpose of the meeting at Bad Wiessee was to promote a reconciliation between all parties concerned. This scarcely tallied with his previous pledge to General von Blomberg that Röhm would be arrested and dealt with summarily, nor even his words to Lutze, whom he told Röhm would be dismissed.

The following day Hitler fulfilled public duties in Westphalia, returning in the evening to an hotel at Godesberg, overlooking the Rhine. With the Wiessee rendezvous due for the next morning, Hitler decided to take a firm step. The army must be placated, and President Hindenburg induced to nominate him as his successor. Hitler summoned to his presence the ineffectual SA *Obergruppenführer* of Hanover, Viktor Lutze, and informed him abruptly he was appointed SA *Stabschef* in lieu of Röhm. The astonished Lutze stammered out his thanks, but was vouchsafed no explanations.

Almost immediately before Lutze's arrival, another car had drawn up in front of the Tilleuls Hotel. A thin waspish figure came limping up the steps – a flustered and nervous Goebbels. Aware from his spies that something was going on that might bode ill for those not favoured by the Führer,

Ritter von Krausser, assured by Hitler that the Bad Wiessee meeting was only for the purpose of reconciliation

the Minister of Propaganda had flown to be by his Leader's side; there at least he should be safe. Still not altogether clear as to which faction was being threatened (he had recently been intriguing with his companion on the Nazi 'Left', Röhm), he determined to probe the Leader's mind and make sure he threw in his lot in time with the right party. It was soon clear how the land lay, and Goebbels lost no time in informing Hitler darkly that the SA chief at Berlin, Karl Ernst, was alerting the Stormtroopers – doubtless for some ill purpose.

Confirmation of Ernst's plotting seemed to come from his supposed presence in Berlin. Why had he not gone to Bad Wiessee for the morrow's meeting? Clearly he had remained to direct the planned rising. As Hitler explained afterwards in his speech to the Reichstag: 'Gruppenführer Ernst with this end in view had not after all gone to Wiessee but had remained behind in Berlin to undertake the conduct of operations there.' Yet, whatever Hitler had believed on 29th June, by the time of the Reichstag speech (13th July) he knew this crucial statement to be a lie. For Ernst, like many of his colleagues, was setting off to enjoy the leave the SA had been awarded for all of July. At the time he was alleged to be mobilising the Berlin SA, he was in fact on the road to Bremen, newly-married, and about to take ship with his bride for a honeymoon in Maderia.

At one o'clock in the morning of 30th June Hitler received urgent messages from Göring and Himmler, confirming in stringent tones that an SA rising was being synchronised in Berlin and Munich for the following day. These men, the real plotters of 30th June, must have been able to communicate a conviction born of desperation. For if nothing happened within the next few hours, Hitler would meet his old comrade Röhm. The following day the SA would be on leave, as all Germany knew; and who would then believe the tale of a massive SA plot?

However, Hitler was now roused to a drastic decision. Röhm, the ungrateful plotter, must go. He ordered Göring to take action against the Party's enemies the next day. He himself determined to deal with Röhm. Dr Wagner, Minister of the Interior for Bavaria, was ordered to take action at once in Munich, and be prepared for the Führer's immediate arrival. Already the same evening Hitler had ordered the murderous head of his bodyguard, Sepp Dietrich, to proceed to Munich and await orders. Arriving at the Brown House, Dietrich found himself instructed to move to Kaufering (near Landsberg am Lech) and take over two companies of SS *Leibstandarte* newly arrived from Berlin. Thence the black-uniformed band drove through the warm night to Bad Wiessee.

Meanwhile Hitler himself, accompanied by Lutze and Goebbels, the latter of whom realised that the one safe place in all this turmoil was at Hitler's side, drove to Hangelar aerodrome near Bonn. Soon after two

Goebbels reasoned that the safest place to be was beside his leader

o'clock a great grey aeroplane was droning southwards across Germany, whilst below the Reich slept. At four o'clock the plane touched down at Munich, and the hollow-eyed Nazi leaders emerged, to find a messenger from Dr Wagner awaiting them. The Minister had not been idle. On his instructions, the army had sent detachments to occupy the railway station and other key points. At the same time trusted sections of the SS had been assembled under Hitler's thuggish former bodyguard, *Standartenführer* Emil Maurice. These had arrested, on Hitler's instructions, SA *Obergruppenführer* Schneidhuber and *Gruppenführer* Schmidt, the chiefs of the Bavarian SA. Ironically, these two had been in Wagner's office conferring about the Bad Wiessee conference when Hitler had telephoned.

Röhm and Göring attend Ernst's marriage in Berlin. At the time that Ernst was supposedly directing an SA rising in Berlin he was in fact off on his honeymoon

Sepp Dietrich (left, front row), placed in charge of two picked companies of SS *Liebstandarte* which descended on Bad Wiessee

On receiving this intelligence, Hitler and his entourage at once drove to Dr Wagner's Ministry. There they found the Minister, together with Emil Maurice's SS detachment and the two prisoners. All appeared, in the grey light of approaching dawn, bemused and quite uncertain of what the crisis portended. The tension was soon broken, however.

As Hitler burst into the room, Schneidhuber and Schmidt rose from their chairs and saluted. The Chancellor, to their fear and surprise, appeared to be beside himself with hysterical rage. He rushed up to the two unfortunate SA leaders and, tearing their insignia of rank from their shoulders, screamed a tirade of abuse at them. One of them made a gesture of surprise or self-defence.

Count von Spreti (right) and friends. *Below:* Hess shakes hands with Heines who was later shot dead while in bed with his chauffeur at the hotel on 30th June

Hitler sprang back, reaching for his revolver. But before he could act, there was a flash and report beside him as *Standartenführer* Maurice shot Schmidt at point-blank range. Schneidhuber had just time to cry in amazement, 'You are mad!' when he too fell before the blazing SS guns. 'These were not the most guilty!' shrieked the Führer, kicking one of the corpses vindictively. Then he swung on his heel and raced downstairs.

Gathering together his followers and SS guards, he set off at the head of a cavalcade of cars and taxis to Bad Wiessee. With two of Röhm's most trusted colleagues dead, the Chief of Staff could not be left at large a moment longer. Arrived at Bad Wiessee, the band burst into Röhm's hotel. While Hitler raced towards Röhm's own room, a detachment of SS kicked open the door of SA leader Count von Spreti. He and his fellow-*Standartenführer* Uhl were unceremoniously bound hand and foot and made prisoner. In another room *Obergruppenführer* Heines was found in bed with his young chauffeur. Both were shot dead on the spot and their naked bodies, dripping with blood, dragged from the building. Meanwhile, Hitler banged furiously on Röhm's door. 'Open up! Open up!' he screamed frantically. 'Who is there?' came Röhm's sleepy voice from within.

'It's me, Hitler!'

'Oh', replied the drowsy *Stabschef*, getting out of bed to unbolt the door, 'already? I didn't expect you until mid-day tomorrow.'

The next moment he was staring dumbfounded at the open doorway, crowded with Hitler and his SS assassins.

'Arrest him!' shrieked the Führer.

Röhm and the other prisoners, together with the corpses of Heines and his chauffeur, were bundled into the waiting cars. As the cavalcade roared out of the gates, Hitler was saluted by the amazed bodyguard troops of Röhm, who had just driven up unawares at that moment.

Now came one of many ironic touches. On the road back to Munich, Hitler's column met a stream of cars conveying SA leaders, who had spent the night in Munich and were now heading for the appointed conference at Bad Wiessee. An eyewitness, afterwards Nazi ambassador in the Protectorate of Slovakia, gave this account:

'I, together with a quantity of other senior SA leaders, was seized on the open road by the Führer's column coming towards us. We were utterly dumbfounded when we learned what had happened. We had to form up in a single rank, and the Führer went from man to man, giving each one a look which now for the first time seemed to me as I had so often heard it described – magical. Hitler said not a word. Only when he reached me did he pronounce the single word, 'Ludin', without any particular emphasis, sunk in his thoughts – and I did not know whether with this word he had condemned me to die or to live. I was the most senior of the SA leaders there. I was condemned to live.'

Back in Munich, Wagner, Lutze and the newly-arrived Deputy Führer, Hess, had turned the Brown House into a mousetrap. SA men arriving were welcomed in, but on no account permitted to leave by the SS cordon. Quite unaware of events going forward, the Brownshirt leaders chatted about that morning's meeting, and drank healths to Hitler (approaching along the Wiessee road), Röhm (a prisoner) and Schneidhuber (dead). While at the railway station SS guards (backed in case of necessity by units of the *Reichswehr*) rounded up all SA arrivals and took them to the Stadelheim Prison.

Soon Hitler arrived at the prison, his bloodlust far from satisfied. Four veteran SA leaders, Heydebreck, Hayn, Krausser and Spreti were at once ordered to be shot. Hitler's blazing eyes rested on the sullen and defiant Röhm. This was a bad moment for Goebbels, also watching. Would

COLUMBUSHA
USKUNFTS- u. WERBEZENTRAL
„DEUTSCHLAND"
Ausstellung
Deutsche
See.
Eintritt frei.
GEÖFFNET
WERKTAGS
10-18 UHR
BUND
DEUTSCHER
VERKEHRS-
VERBÄNDE
u. BÄDER
Palast

Röhm denounce him and reveal to the maddened Führer their secret pact of eight days before? But Hitler could not meet Röhm's gaze; they were after all in the very city where Röhm, eleven years before, had stood so valiantly beside the embryo Führer, and in the very prison where he had been interned immediately afterwards. Hitler moved on, to relieve his pent-up feelings by adding *Standartenführer* Uhl and other lesser fry to the number hauled off to the SS firing-squad.

But as he left Stadelheim, Hitler revealed suddenly within himself the sadist who seeks to avert injury and pain to himself by inflicting it on others. 'Shoot his chauffeur Max', he snapped viciously, 'tell him when it has happened, lock him in his cell – and then await my orders'.

It was two days later that Ernst Röhm died. Hitler had ordered a revolver to be left in his cell so that he might – very conveniently – take the 'honourable' way out. Röhm refused to oblige, and awaited his fate with the same fierce courage he had shown throughout his career. Then, on 2nd July, two SS guards acting on Sepp Dietrich's orders entered Röhm's cell. Stripped to the waist, he rose as if to say something; but his words were silenced by a noise familiar to him all his life – the crack of pistol shots. An expression of gross contempt on his face, he slumped dead to the ground.

The shots that rattled out in Munich were not the only ones to make 30th June 1934 a night of blood. In Berlin, as soon as they had received the go-ahead from Hitler, Göring and Himmler set to work. All day long, the French Ambassador recorded, came the noise of firing squads at work in the Lichterfelde Barracks, the headquarters of Göring's special police. About 150 SA leaders suspected of loyalty to Röhm were rounded up and

Left and above: **Göring's special police in Berlin. From their barracks came all day the noise of the firing squads**

shot. *Gruppenführer* Karl Ernst, the supposed organiser of the SA 'plot' in Berlin, was attacked and seized by SS men near Bremen, and flown back to Berlin to be slaughtered too.

The Vice-Chancellor of the Reich, von Papen, was summoned to Göring's headquarters at the Air Ministry in no very dignified fashion. There he was told of the current suppression of Röhm's *putsch* in Munich. When he demanded that the President be told and martial law declared, he was taken to his home and kept a prisoner in all but name for the next three days, surrounded by SS guards. Göring explained blandly that they were for the Vice-Chancellor's protection.

While von Papen was being hustled off, protesting weakly, SS men broke into the Vice-Chancellery, gunned down von Papen's principal secretary at his desk, and took away several of his other aides to concentration camps. His collaborator on the Marburg speech was murdered in jail.

For it was no longer a question of merely eliminating Röhm and his clique. Goebbels, Himmler, Heydrich, Göring and others less celebrated all had their lists of victims. Private reckonings of the most sordid and lowly sort took place alongside elaborately conceived state assassinations.

Back in Munich, Emil Maurice and Sepp Dietrich's blackshirted murder squads moved from house to house, settling many old scores. The two Bavarian leaders who had suppressed the beer hall *Putsch* as recounted at the beginning of this history, von Kahr and von Lossow, were savagely butchered. The monarchist, von Kahr, now seventy-two and retired from politics, was hacked to pieces with axes and his body thrown into a swamp near Dachau. Hitler's memory was long.

On a lowlier but equally tragic

Von Papen and his wife, kept under SS guard for some days after the 30th June, are allowed at last to leave their home

level was the disappearance of the owner and two waiters from a small restaurant, the *String of Sausages*. They were the only known witnesses of Goebbels's private meeting with Röhm a week before the massacre.

The former Chancellor, von Papen, had escaped a similar fate only at the intervention of Göring, who perhaps feared the wrath of Hindenburg. About ten days previously another ex-Chancellor, Brüning, had wisely escaped from Germany, perhaps warned too by Göring. But the only other remaining ex-Chancellor in the Reich was not so fortunate.

General von Schleicher, the unprincipled intriguer who had done so much to allow Hitler to gain the Chancellery, had been living in retirement since January 1933. Of late, however, he had appeared more often in public. It was said that he was attempting again to meddle in politics, and from his character this seems probable enough. He had, for example, attended the Bad Nauheim meeting at which the generals had endorsed Hitler's succession to the Presidency. Nevertheless, it is scarcely likely that he was involved in a conspiracy with Röhm (as Hitler alleged on 13th July), seeing that only a month before Röhm had warned the *Reichswehr* that Schleicher was plotting against the regime. And Schleicher himself always spoke of Röhm with disgust, or so reported the French Ambassador.

But Schleicher's reputation as an intriguer, his lack of political principle and his widespread contacts among those elements antipathetic to the present Nazi order, were to prove his undoing. On the same morning that Hitler flew to Munich, a detachment of SS disguised in civilian clothes drew up in a car outside Schleicher's villa at Neu-Babelsberg, just outside Berlin. Six bulky-looking men emerged and rang at the doorbell. A servant opened the door – to be thrust to one side as the newcomers raced to the dining room.

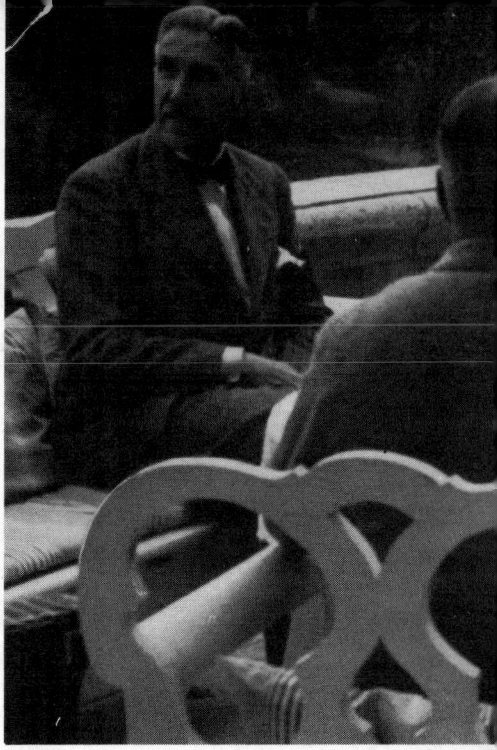

There they found a domestic scene: the General was having breakfast with his wife and fourteen-year-old stepdaughter.

'Are you General von Schleicher?' rapped out a harsh voice.

'Yes, but what . . .'

Schleicher began to rise to his feet, when the six SS men pulled out their revolvers and fired point-blank into his body. His wife started up, half in terror, half protectively – to be gunned down beside her husband. The killers turned on the young girl and warned her she would suffer the same fate if she told what she had seen. They drove off, leaving the horror-struck girl alone with the bodies of her dead stepfather and dying mother.

It was Göring who had ordered the former Chancellor's murder. Jealous of his military rank and position, and fearful of his capacity to organise and perhaps unite the different elements hostile to Nazism, he had placed the General's name high on the death-list. At four o'clock that evening Göring held a press conference at the Chancellery. There he announced the dismissal of Röhm and measures taken against certain SA leaders.

'What of Schleicher?' asked a journalist.

'General von Schleicher was plotting against the government. I was obliged accordingly to order his arrest.'

Göring rose to leave the hall, but at the doorway he paused and turned round, a ferocious grin on his face as he added:

'As they went to arrest him, he attempted to resist.'

It was with these ambiguous words that the lie was launched, that Schleicher had died resisting arrest and his wife with him.

An associate of Schleicher's, General Kurt von Bredow, was arrested that afternoon and shot two days later. According to Hitler he had been a 'political agent in foreign affairs for General von Schleicher', responsible for plotting on the General's behalf with certain unspecified foreign

Above: **Schleicher (right) with Hindenburg.** ***Below:*** **Kurt von Bredow suffered death for his association with Schleicher**

powers. But it is far more probable that he was marked down for his personal devotion to the former Chancellor. Indeed, a foreign diplomat had offered him the chance of spending the fatal evening at his embassy, but von Bredow firmly declined the opportunity.

'They have murdered Schleicher, my chief, the only man who could have saved Germany. What do I count?'

According to Hitler's later account, the great plot directed against him was organised by Röhm, Schleicher – and the retired Nazi leader Gregor Strasser. Through von Bredow contact was maintained by the conspirators with foreign powers, England and France being clearly implied. The full cunning of Hitler's version will be appreciated when it is realised that, had there been any serious move to oust the Dictator or alter the structure of his regime, then undoubtedly these three men were precisely those on whom such a movement would have focussed. Röhm, discontented and powerful, could supply the men and arms; Schleicher had the contacts with the army and the 'old' politicians; whilst Gregor Strasser was the one leading Nazi with a reputation for honesty, independence, and the power to influence the Nazi masses.

It will be remembered that Strasser had been the leader Schleicher, when Chancellor, had hoped to prise away from the Nazi Party, so at the same moment strengthening his own position in the Reichstag and weakening the Nazis. But Hitler had got wind of the intrigue and forced Strasser's resignation from the Party. Since then the former radical National Socialist had retired officially from politics, taking up a directorship at a chemical works. This did not prevent him, however, from meddling in politics like everyone else.

A fierce enemy of Goebbels and none too respectful of the Führer himself, he probably maintained contact with Schleicher. The more practical Röhm, however, had little time for him, recognising his political impotence. A further disadvantage for Strasser was the fact that his brother Otto had broken with Hitler about the time of the Stennes revolt in 1930 over the interpretation of Nazi doctrine. Otto Strasser had gone into exile in Czechoslovakia, whence he conducted a largely ineffective opposition to Hitler, the Black Front. Later he was to publish, with the help of some of the fugitives, an account of the Blood Purge. Though Gregor had completely broken with his brother over this, the inescapable connexion kept him a marked man in the Nazi hierarchy.

Doubtless with Hitler's strong approval, Göring's police seized Gregor Strasser in his Berlin home and conveyed him to the Prinz Albrechtstrasse Gestapo jail. In the same dread building was imprisoned Baron von Tschirschky, one of Chancellor von Papen's private secretaries. According to his testimony, he heard the fatal shot and from his cell saw an SS man emerge with a smoking revolver, shouting, 'We have finished off this swine Strasser'. The SS man was not quite accurate, however. Gregor Strasser lay weltering in his blood, but did not die for another two days.

Thus it was merely enough to be suspected of conducting a policy adverse to Hitler's interests to appear on the 30th June death-list. Röhm, Schleicher and Strasser had all at different times and for different purposes put out 'feelers' towards each other; but the atmosphere of intrigue prevalent in the Third Reich made such contacts and alignments virtually unavoidable. We have seen that Dr Goebbels was deeply implicated on this score.

One historian, it should be noted, has urged that Hitler did *not* intend to have Strasser murdered, and that he died as a result of the enmity of Goebbels, or merely on the initiative of individual SS killers. Again, so secret and obscure were the intrigues behind the Blood Purge, we certainly cannot rule out this alternative.

Many people died that day with whom Hitler had little concern, and it was not the sort of affair that could be subjected to any official enquiry.

An illustration of the confusion that obscured measures necessarily so secret is provided by what must be the most macabre incident in the whole massacre.

On the evening of 30th June, a highly-respected and entirely non-political music critic in Munich, Dr Willi Schmid, was playing his cello in his study, while his wife and three little children were preparing for the evening meal. The fatal doorbell rang, four SS men entered, and Dr Schmid was taken away. A few days later a coffin was delivered to Frau Schmid, accompanied by Gestapo orders that it was on no account to be opened. The SS had confused Dr Schmid with a condemned SA leader, Willi Schmidt. Awkardly, Dr Schmid was too well-known a personality merely to vanish unobserved, as so many did that week-end. Indeed, the 'cultured' General Göring had often expressed admiration for his work. Hess himself visited the victim's widow to apologise (it would be interesting to know how such an apology would be phrased), and a benign government consoled her with a pension.

It is doubtful if it was this sort of incident that Hitler had in mind when he promised (15th February 1933) that: 'We want . . . to restore to the German intelligentsia the freedom of which it has been robbed by the system which has hitherto ruled.'

Hitler and his myrmidons had struck at the SA and Party dissidents, at Schleicher the supposed 'middleman', and at the anti-Nazi entourage of Vice-Chancellor von Papen. Personal and Party rivals were liquidated. The Socialist and Communist threat having been removed in the first months of Nazi rule (by the simple expedient of imprisoning virtually all their Reichstag deputies, and terrorising the rank-and-file), there remained the opposition of the Right, the Centre and that within the Party itself. It was against these three latter elements that the Purge was largely directed.

Erich Klausener, head of Catholic Action in Berlin, shot by two young SS men in his office

The Catholic Centre Party, the only remaining party in the Reichstag holding views independent of (and frequently in opposition to) the Nazis, was viciously bludgeoned into acceptance of the new order.

Erich Klausener, head of Catholic Action in Berlin, was shot by two young SS men in his office. The latter kept guard for over an hour outside the door as he lay dying, in order to prevent his having the consolation of a priest's services, for whom he had managed to telephone. Later that evening a van arrived, the corpse was carried off and cremated, without any consultation with his relatives.

The Catholic editor Fritz Gerlich, kept in prison without trial since March of the previous year, was murdered in his cell on 1st July. Another victim was Adalbert Probst, head of a Catholic youth group in Munich, and formerly a deputy in the Bavarian Landtag. The body of Father Bernhard Stempfle, a former associate

of Hitler's, was discovered in a forest outside Munich with his neck broken and three bullets in his heart. It is said he knew too much of the strange suicide of Hitler's niece, Geli Raubal, with whom the Führer had had an incestuous love affair.

More fortunate was the former minister, Treviranus, a Nationalist who had served under Brüning and Schleicher. When the SS came to his house, he was playing tennis at a club at Wannsee. They followed him there, and found the ex-minister in the middle of a game. Before the assassins could identify him, however, Treviranus had noticed them talking to club servants at the entrance. Entirely calm, he apologised to his partners and made his escape through a neighbouring property and so into the woods around the lake. He travelled for some miles under cover of the trees until he reached a friend's house. There he borrowed a change of clothes and managed by the end of a week to escape to England, whence he helped to lead the exiled German opposition.

So perished or vanished the enemies of Hitler, Göring, Himmler, Heydrich, and Goebbels. So perished also victims who had incurred the humbler but no less deadly dislike of individual SS ruffians such as Sepp Dietrich or Emil Maurice. And in Franconia, where the influence of the paranoiac sadist Julius Streicher held reign, a number of Jews were massacred; as were a few of their fellow-countrymen by the SS at Hirschberg, Glogan and Gunzenhausen. What part they could have played in a plot supposedly organised by the almost equally antisemetic Röhm, it was not thought necessary to explain. This may seem strange, as it would surely not have taxed Dr Goebbels's ingenuity very far to have put the whole blame onto them, not only for the 'plot' but also for the subsequent purge.

But then the Nazi outlook was not very concerned with reason, logic and practical assessments of realities; their cloudy doctrines owed far more to idealism, enthusiasm, and a romantic fervour for ill-defined goals. All of which are admirable qualities in gifted individuals, but dangerous in the extreme when inspiring semi-educated demagogues and their dupes.

But chief and most necessary to Hitler's immediate aims was the destruction of the potential opposition within the SA. Röhm was dead in Stadelheim Prison. *Obergruppenführer* Ernst, a former café waiter, had been seized when about to embark on honeymoon at Bremen with his bride, roped up like a parcel and flown back to Berlin. There, at Göring's Lichterfelde barracks, he was shot by firing squad. His last words were: 'Heil Hitler!' Like many other Brownshirt victims he thought himself the victim of an army and right-wing coup against the SA. No less than twelve Reichstag deputies had disappeared over the week-end, every one of whom was an SA leader: *Stabschef* Ernst Röhm; *Obergruppenführers* Karl Ernst, Hayn, Heines, von Heydebreck, Schneidhuber, von Krauser; *Brigadenführers* Kasche and Schragmuller; *Standartenführer* Schmidt; SA political chief von Detten; and SA police chief Ramshorn.

How many people perished throughout the Reich on 30th June 1934 and the days following is not and cannot be known precisely. The evening papers of 30th June simply announced the replacement of Röhm as Chief of Staff SA by Lutze; and the morning papers of 1st July announced that the Führer had been obliged to execute summarily eight SA leaders (including six out of the total of ten *Obergruppenführer*'s): von Krauser, Ernst, Heines, Schneidhuber, Hayn, von Heydebreck, Schmidt and Spreti. General von Schleicher was announced to have died while resisting his arrest.

No mention was made of the deaths of Klausener, Gregor Strasser, or Frau von Schleicher, nor of the con-

Geli Raubal, Hitler's niece, with whom he had an affair

Einzelnummer 10 Pfg.

Extra-Blatt

Oberbayer. Gebirgsbote, Holzkirchen • Miesbacher Anz., Miesbach • Tegernseer Ztg., Tegernsee
Aiblinger Ztg., Bad Aibling • Rosenheimer Tagbl., Rosenheim • Kolbermoorer Volksblatt, Kolbermoor • Chiemgau-Ztg., Prien • Tölzer Ztg., Bad Tölz • Wolfratshauser Tagbl., Wolfratshausen
Wasserburger Anzeiger, Wasserburg a. I. • Grafinger Zeitung, Grafing.

Samstag, 30. Juni 34

Röhm verhaftet und abgesetzt

Röhm aus Partei und S.A. ausgeschlossen

München, 30. Juni

Die Reichspressestelle der N.S.D.A.P. teilt folgende Verfügung des Führers mit:

Ich habe mit dem heutigen Tage den Stabschef Röhm seiner Stellung enthoben und aus Partei und S.A. ausgestoßen. Ich ernenne zum Chef des Stabes Obergruppenführer Lutze.

S.A.-Führer und S.A.-Männer, die seinen Befehlen nicht nachkommen oder zuwiderhandeln, werden aus S.A. und Partei entfernt bzw. verhaftet und abgeurteilt.

gez. **Adolf Hitler**
Oberster Partei- und S.A.-Führer

Der Führer an den neuen Stabschef

München, 30. Juni

Der Führer hat folgendes Schreiben an den Obergruppenführer der S.A. Lutze gerichtet:

An Obergruppenführer Lutze.

Mein lieber S.A.-Führer Lutze!

Schwerste Verfehlungen meines bisherigen Stabschefs zwangen mich, ihn seiner Stellung zu entheben. Sie, mein lieber Obergruppenführer Lutze, sind seit vielen Jahren **in guten und schlechten Tagen ein immer gleich treuer und vorbildlicher S.A.-Führer gewesen.** Wenn ich Sie mit dem heutigen Tage zum Chef des Stabes ernenne, dann geschieht dies in der festen Ueberzeugung, daß es Ihrer treuen und gehorsamen Arbeit gelingen wird, **aus meiner S.A. das Instrument zu schaffen, das die Nation braucht und ich mir vorstelle.**

Es ist mein Wunsch, daß die S.A. **zu einem treuen und starken Glied der Nationalsozialistischen Bewegung** ausgestaltet wird. Erfüllt von **Gehorsam** und **blinder Disziplin,** muß sie mithelfen, den neuen deutschen Menschen zu bilden und zu formen.

gez. **Adolf Hitler**

Aufruf des neuen Stabschefs

Der Führer hat mich an seine Seite als Chef des Stabes berufen. Das mir dadurch bewiesene Vertrauen muß und werde ich rechtfertigen durch unverbrüchliche Treue zum Führer und restlosen Einsatz für den Nationalsozialismus und dadurch für unser Volk.

Als ich vor etwa 12 Jahren zum erstenmal Führer einer kleinen S.A. war, habe ich drei Tugenden an die Spitze meines Handelns gestellt und sie von der S.A. gefordert. Diese drei Tugenden haben die S.A. groß gemacht und heute, wo ich in schicksalsschwerer Stunde meinem Führer an hervorragender Stelle dienen darf, sollen sie erst recht Richtschnur für die ganze S.A. sein:

Unbedingte Treue!

Schärfste Disziplin!

Hingebender Opfermut!

So wollen wir, die wir Nationalsozialisten sind, gemeinsam marschieren.

Ich bin überzeugt, dann kann es nur ein Marsch zur Freiheit werden.

Es lebe der Führer! Es lebe unser Volk!

Der Chef des Stabes:
gez. Lutze.

Befehl des Obersten S.A.-Führers Adolf Hitler

Adolf Hitler hat an den Chef des Stabes, Lutze, folgenden Befehl gegeben:

Wenn ich Sie heute zum Chef des Stabes der S.A. ernenne, dann erwarte ich, daß Sie sich hier eine Reihe von Aufgaben angelegen sein lassen, die ich Ihnen hiermit stelle:

1. Ich verlange vom S.A.-Führer genau so wie er vom S.A.-Mann blinden Gehorsam und unbedingte Disziplin.

2. Ich verlange, daß jeder S.A.-Führer wie jeder politische Führer sich dessen bewußt ist, daß sein Benehmen und seine Aufführung vorbildlich zu sein haben für seinen Verband, ja für unsere gesamte Gefolgschaft.

3. Ich verlange, daß S.A.-Führer — genau so wie politische Leiter —, die sich in ihrem Benehmen in der Öffentlichkeit etwas zuschulden kommen lassen, unnachsichtlich aus der Partei und der S.A. entfernt werden.

4. Ich verlange insbesondere vom S.A.-Führer, daß er ein Vorbild in der Einfachheit und nicht im Aufwand ist. Ich wünsche nicht, daß der S.A.-Führer kostbare Diners gibt oder an solchen teilnimmt. Man hat uns früher hierzu nicht eingeladen, wir haben auch jetzt dort nichts zu suchen. Millionen unserer Volksgenossen fehlt auch heute noch das Notwendigste zum Leben, sie sind nicht neidig dem, den das Glück mehr gesegnet hat, aber es ist eines Nationalsozialisten unwürdig, den Abstand, der zwischen Not und Glück ohnehin ungeheuer groß ist, noch besonders zu vergrößern. Ich verbiete insbesondere, daß Mittel der Partei, der S.A. oder überhaupt der Öffentlichkeit für Festgelage und dergleichen Verwendung finden. Es ist unverantwortlich, von Geldern, die zum Teil sich aus den Groschen unserer ärmsten Mitbürger ergeben, Schlemmereien abzuhalten. Das luxuriöse Stabs-Quartier in Berlin, in dem, wie nunmehr festgestellt wurde, monatlich bis zu 30 000 Mark für Festessen usw. ausgegeben wurden, ist sofort aufzulösen.

Ich untersage daher für alle Parteiinstanzen die Veranstaltung sogenannter Festessen und Diners aus irgendwelchen öffentlichen Mitteln. Und ich verbiete allen Partei- und S.A.-Führern die Teilnahme an solchen. Ausgenommen davon ist nur die Erfüllung der von Staats we-

Folgende sieben Verräter wurden bereits erschossen:

Im Zusammenhang mit dem aufgedeckten Komplott wurden folgende Meuterer erschossen:

Obergruppenführer A. Schneidhuber;
Obergruppenführer Edmund Heines;
Gruppenführer Ernst, Berlin;
Gruppenführer Schmidt, München;
Gruppenführer Hans Heym;
Gruppenführer Heydebreck;
Standartenführer Graf Spretti, München.

Druck: Münchner Buchgewerbehaus M. Müller & Sohn, G. m. b. H., München. Verantwortlich: Hauptschriftleiter W. Rettich.

Left: **'Röhm arrested and removed'.**
Above: **Lutze, Röhm's replacement**

finement of Vice-Chancellor von Papen, nor of the numerous lesser victims immolated that day. No other official list was ever issued, apart from the figures given by Hitler himself in his speech to the Reichstag on 13th July, nor was any direct attempt made to bring it up to date, to allow for those 'executed' on 1st July and the days following. All one can say with safety is that several hundred people lay dead after Hitler's *Reichsmordwoche*, Blood Purge. Of the high proportion of SA victims, it may be confidently asserted that the majority were guilty of many evil crimes. It may be asserted with equal truth that no one who died during those bloody days was guilty of the crimes imputed to him by Hitler and his black-uniformed henchmen.

Supreme Justician

The *Reichsmordwoche* was over, and an uneasy Germany began to digest the stunning news. Of direct information, there was of course very little at all. On 1st July, it was announced, as we have seen, that eight SA chiefs had been executed. Then came the news of Schleicher's 'accidental' death, followed on 2nd July by the announcement that 'the traitor Röhm, having refused to take the consequences of his deed, has been executed'. On 5th July a foreign press conference was told that about ten other people had suffered the death sentence. Finally, on 13th July came Hitler's speech to the Reichstag in which he announced a total of seventy-seven deaths in connexion with the Purge.

But no further names or details of the circumstances of these deaths and arrests were given, and foreign and native observers were reduced to curious exigencies; such as observing which names were omitted from the new official Reich directories, or that the urn presented by the Gestapo to the widow of a murdered Berlin *Oberführer*, containing her late husband's ashes, bore the significant and sinister number 262. In this way a dossier, more or less accurate as regards the principal victims, was built up and published abroad.

In Germany itself, people were stunned and bemused by the totally unexpected and largely inexplicable events of the Blood Purge. Rumours ran rife, and it was with the greatest avidity that the public awaited Hitler's own account, which was finally delivered at considerable length in a speech to the Reichstag on 13th July, and published in the national press immediately afterwards.

It must be allowed that the speech was a masterpiece. Not only of misrepresentation and falsification of the facts, but also in the way that the maximum of truth consistent with Hitler's version of events was included in his account. In this way even people influential and well-informed in political circles were widely taken in. After all, the principal witnesses were all dead, and the story as told by Hitler was so near to what might well have happened that it was impossible, unless one had an exceptionally intimate knowledge of the facts, to be able positively to contradict it.

Hitler's explanation may be summarised as follows. After the usual introductory reminder of the incompetence and treachery of National Socialism's predecessors in office, coupled with a recapitulation of the Party's achievements past and future, he moved on to list the threat posed by four dissident elements still active in the country. Firstly came the Reds, backed of course by Jews, who would very soon be rooted out altogether. Secondly came the political leaders of the old parties, who resented their exclusion from power. Thirdly (and here the allusion to Röhm and his associates is plain), came a band of revolutionaries who, though prepared to assist the Party in opposition, were temperamentally incapable of assisting it when in power with the vital work of reconstruction.

'They became revolutionaries who favoured revolution for its own sake and desired to see revolution established as a permanent condition.'

The fourth group listed (its characteristics and activities are described in brilliantly satirical vein) was that of self-appointed critics and rumour-mongers. Worthless in themselves, they 'are, however, dangerous because they are veritable bacillus-carriers of unrest and uncertainty, of rumours, assertions, lies and suspicions, of slanders and fears, and thus they contribute to produce gradually a state of nervousness which spreads amongst the people so that in the end it is hard to find or recognise where its influence stops.' A fair description of a group existent in all societies at all times – indeed, not a bad summary of Hitler's own activities when in opposition.

Hitler at the 13th July Reichstag assembly where he gave his account of the Night of the Long Knives

Röhm with aides

According to Hitler, he began some months previously to hear rumours of a plot against the new order. At first he assumed it was the work of his obvious enemies, groups one, two and four delineated above; but soon 'certain departments of the Party administration' detected dangerous trends amongst the leaders of the SA. These were its greatly increased size (true), the tendency to promote men on grounds of ability rather than long and faithful service (true, but Hitler's words are clearly aimed at fanning the envy of SA officers so neglected), a tendency of the SA to increasing autonomy alongside the Party (true), and the widespread knowledge of the disgraceful lives led by many of the top SA chiefs (true).

Following these 'revelations', in April and May Hitler came to be warned of a definite SA plot for a new revolution ('true' only in that it was at this time that Göring and Himmler had begun the real pressure to have Röhm removed). Now came the most brilliantly ingenious justification of Hitler's lawless actions. Having step by step led up to a slanted but in many ways accurate picture of the differences between the SA leadership and the Party, he hypocritically denounced the 'bad behaviour, drunken excesses, the molestation of peaceful decent folk' so notoriously characteristic of the Brownshirts, as 'unworthy of a leader, they are not National Socialist, and they are in the highest degree detestable'.

Sentiments to which every decent German must have uttered a heartfelt cry of assent; which being so, how could one contradict the words with which the Führer continued? 'I have for this reason always insisted that in their conduct and behaviour higher demands should be made of National Socialist leaders than of the rest of

The SA chief feigns absorption in a picture of himself when younger

The Führer and a 'poor victim' of the prefabricated SA plot

the people. He who desires to receive higher respect than others must meet this demand by a higher achievement. The most elementary demand that can be made of him is that in his life he should not give a shameful example to those about him. I do not desire therefore that National Socialists guilty of such offences should be judged and punished more leniently than are other fellow-countrymen of theirs; rather, I expect that a leader who forgets himself in this way should be punished with greater rigour than an unknown man would be in a like case.'

The implication was clear: Hitler's ruthless actions, so far from being illegal and barbaric, in reality belonged to a higher justice altogether, a justice far above mere written forms. But before coming to his logical conclusion, Hitler switched back cunningly to the supposed plot. The loathesome private lives of the SA chieftains was dwelt upon with sanctimonious horror (here again, Hitler's own undeniably puritanical mode of life seemed to point a healthy contrast), and he moved on to detail the nature of the plotters' aims.

Once again, his adroit manipulation of the facts was superlative. Tempting though it might have been, he did not represent Röhm as a born plotter, intent on his Führer's downfall. Instead, he pictured him as encouraged by Schleicher to envisage himself as becoming Minister of War in a reformed Cabinet. Hitler himself was to be placed in protective custody whilst the Second Revolution was taking place, afterwards to be presented with a *fait accompli*. In the meantime the SA was to wreak a bloody vengeance on its opponents within the *Reaktion* and the Party; ' "The Night of the Long Knives" was their ghastly name for it' – so Hitler, with supreme irony, assigned to Röhm's imaginary plot the title which ever since has been attributed to Hitler's own savage purge: *Die Nacht der langer Messer*. Rather lamely, and as if by an after thought, Hitler added without elaboration: 'Gregor Strasser was brought in'. Then in dramatic outline he gave an account of his flight to Munich and the drastic measures taken.

The reader will see that virtually the whole of Hitler's account tallies with what did in fact occur. Not only this, but Röhm's own views and hopes are reproduced with fair accuracy. Even the flagrant flouting of the law that the Purge involved seemed justified, considering the desperate state of the emergency. All closely paralleled the truth; except for the one factor that the whole case hinged upon: the existence of the plot itself. For the coming absence on leave of the SA, the relaxed unpreparedness of Röhm at Wiessee, the absence from Berlin of Ernst, all indicate beyond any doubt that there was no plot.

Then came – what the world would have liked to have known a great deal more about – a list of the victims, precise in numbers but in nothing else. 'The penalty for these crimes was hard and severe. Nineteen higher SA leaders, thirty-one leaders and members of the SA, were shot, and further, for complicity in the plot, three leaders of the SS, while thirteen SA leaders and civilians who attempted to resist arrest lost their lives. Three more committed suicide. Five who did not belong to the SA, but were members of the Party, were shot for taking part in the plot. Finally there were also shot three members of the SS who had been guilty of scandalous ill-treatment of those who had been taken into protective custody.' There were no mention at all of those victims unconnected with the

The hooks from which were hung Field-Marshal von Witzleben, General Hoepner and General Hase, implicated in the July Plot

Funeral of Hindenburg

SA or the Party.

The real intended effect of both massacre and speech came in a deadly threat towards any who dared oppose Hitler's dictatorship: 'If anyone reproaches me and asks why I did not resort to the regular courts of justice for conviction of the offenders, then all I can say to him is this: in this hour I was responsible for the fate of the German people, and thereby I became the supreme Justiciar of the German people . . . The nation must know that its existence – and that is guaranteed through its internal order and security – can be threatened by no one with impunity! And everyone must know for all future time that if he raises his hand to strike the State, then certain death is his lot.'

Hitler and SA mascot

Like a cobra poised and ready to strike in any direction, Hitler was clearly ready with his SS to stamp out opposition from any quarter. Understandably, on every side representatives of different institutions and parties hastened to assure the Führer of their undying loyalty. The fact that men had been assassinated, not for plotting or rebellion, but merely for representing sectors of society outside the Nazi movement, left no one safe. As von Papen admitted, the threat of assassination hung daily over their heads, and his own over-obsequious attitude from

'The big and little Chancellors' – Hitler and Dollfuss in an adaptation of the previous photograph. The Austrian Chancellor was the next sacrifice on the altar of Nazism

thenceforth was also adopted by many less notable functionaries.

An extraordinary law was framed by Frick and passed through the Reichstag, under the terms of which all Hitler's actions in the Purge were declared legal and statesman-like. This totally unprecedented act, which legalised retrospectively and without examination a whole series of mysterious murders, was not only passed by the puppet deputies in the Reichstag, but was accepted without adverse comment (even in some cases with fulsome praise) by virtually all of Germany's judges and legal associations.

The one body in Germany that could have set its heel on the poisonous monster that Nazism now revealed itself to be was the *Reichswehr*. But it could only act constitutionally on orders proceeding from Hindenburg as President, or von Blomberg as Minister of War. Hindenburg was nearing his end (he died a month later) and it is quite likely that his shifty *chef de cabinet*, Meissner, deliberately prevented von Papen's emissary Ketteler from laying the facts before the President. Whether Hindenburg believed Hitler's version of events, or whether Meissner simply concocted it on his own account is not now known; but the Chancellor's position was immeasurably strengthened by a telegram from Neudeck congratulating him on his firm action, which had 'saved the German people from a grave danger.'

As for Blomberg, his prime concern had in any case been to get rid of Röhm – a view that was widely held in the army. The murder of von Schleicher stuck rather harder in the generals' gullets; but there had been no love lost between him and Blomberg, who had in any case been tricked out of the supreme command of the army by Schleicher in 1930. Von Fritsch, the existing Commander-in-

Hitler his triumphant motorcade through Vienna after the Anschluss

Chief, was depressed by events, but felt it was too late to do anything now. Eventually a feeble compromise was arranged to save the easily-placated honour of the Reichswehr, and on 3rd January 1935 Hitler privately announced the deaths of Schleicher and Bredow to have been a mistake.

In this way the once-proud German army abjectly handed over control of its destiny to the arbitrary rule of the one-time corporal. In fact the wheel was to turn full circle. Ten years later, in the July Bomb Plot, a number of senior officers tried belatedly to retrieve the army's besmirched honour by removing the dictator. While Hitler was at work bloodily suppressing the conspiracy, someone reminded him of the Röhm 'plot'. Screaming and foaming at the mouth, Hitler shrieked that what he had done to Röhm and his followers was nothing to what he would now do to the army plotters. He was as good as his word.

The real victors of the Night of the Long Knives were Himmler and the SS.

On 20th July the SS became independent of the SA and its leaders received due promotion from a grateful Führer. As the SS rose in power, numbers and influence, so the SA, under its bumbling new Chief of Staff Viktor Lutze, sank gradually to a relatively unimportant rôle in organising gymnastic and pre-military training. On the outbreak of war, even these activities were largely taken over by the Wehrmacht.

Hitler himself was overjoyed at the unimaginable success achieved by his bloodthirsty methods. Indeed so intoxicated was he by the apparent ease with which his adversaries could be removed, that within a month he attempted to repeat the same tactic; this time, however, outside the frontiers of Germany. On 25th July 1934 a band of SS men burst into the Austrian Federal Chancellery in Vienna and shot Chancellor Dollfuss in the throat A morbid characteristic of SS killings occurred here too, and for three hours the Chancellor lay dying, refused the aid of doctor or priest. Dollfuss died; but nonetheless the attempt was an embarassing failure, for the Austrian government quickly suppressed the *Putsch*, whilst Mussolini rushed troops to the Brenner Pass to warn Hitler against any precipitate action.

Hitler hastily backed down and publicly expressed his sorrow and regret at the tragic event. He had to bide his time for nearly four years before he entered Vienna in triumph, and was able to honour publicly the murderers of Dollfuss. One minor failure of this sort did not mean the abandonment of a whole system.

Far to the East, another dictator, fully as ruthless and cunning as Hitler himself, had followed with keen interest the events of 30th June and 1st July 1934 in Germany. Joseph Stalin learned much and said nothing; but in three years' time he was to apply to the Red Army the same merciless judgment that Hitler had inflicted on the Brownshirts.

Bibliography

Prelude to Calamity: The Nazi Revolution 1933-35 by Eliot B. Wheaton (London, 1969)
Charisma and Factionalism in the Nazi Party by Joseph Nyomarkay (Minneapolis, 1967)
The Speeches of Adolf Hitler edited by Norman H Baynes (Oxford, 1942)
Memoirs by Franz von Papen (London, 1952)
The Order of the Death's Head by Heinz Hohne (London, 1969)
I Knew Hitler by Kurt G W Ludecke (London, 1938)
A History of National Socialism by Konrad Heiden (London, 1934)
Heydrich: Hitler's Most Evil Henchman by Charles Wighton (London, 1962)